STRANGE CUSTOMS, MANNERS
AND BELIEFS

1. SOMALI HAIR STYLE (*p. 43*)
2. NEW BRITAIN DEVIL DANCER (*p. 169*)
3. NEW GUINEA HEADDRESS (*p. 17*)
4. SOUTH AMERICAN INDIAN CHEEK DECORATION (*p. 38*)
5. BOTOCUDO INDIAN, STRETCHED LIP AND EAR LOBES (*p. 30*)

STRANGE CUSTOMS, MANNERS AND BELIEFS

A remarkable account of curious beliefs and odd superstitions, strange ways of living, and amazing customs and manners of many peoples and tribes around the earth

BY

ALPHEUS HYATT VERRILL

ILLUSTRATED BY THE AUTHOR

Essay Index Reprint Series

 BOOKS FOR LIBRARIES PRESS
FREEPORT, NEW YORK

Copyright © 1946 by L. C. Page & Company
(Incorporated)

Reprinted 1969 by arrangement with
Farrar, Straus & Giroux, Inc.

STANDARD BOOK NUMBER:
8369-1199-7

LIBRARY OF CONGRESS CATALOG CARD NUMBER:
75-86791

PRINTED IN THE UNITED STATES OF AMERICA

LIBRARY
FLORIDA STATE UNIVERSITY
TALLAHASSEE, FLORIDA

INTRODUCTION

SOLDIERS and sailors of the Second World War, writing about and returning from distant corners of the globe, have related wonderful tales of things unfamiliar to them which they have seen and heard in those faraway places. Strange sights and sounds, odd foods and drinks, amazing customs and weird costumes have furnished their share in awakening the interest and enlarging the knowledge of these much-traveled men in uniform.

Undoubtedly some of the tales grow better in the telling, especially when related to persons who have seldom traveled far from home firesides. But many of the seemingly incredible facts are true, and most of them have been known to explorers and scientists for a very long time. From the widely scattered sea islands of the South Pacific; from the broad stretches of Australia, New Guinea, India, Siam, and China; from North, Central, Southern, Eastern, and Western Africa; and from countless other places little visited by many white men before, stories of strange customs, manners and beliefs will be told in civilized homes for years to come.

This experience of fighting men in visiting other peoples in the world and of studying their habits of living, so different from their own, cannot help but have broadened the viewpoint of these visitors and made them more tolerant of all races, conditions, and habits of living. It is to be hoped that the effect upon the distant tribes of prolonged visits from Americans and other so-called civilized persons also has proved more beneficial than harmful.

To some primitive tribes the soldiers and sailors must have appeared very strange and addicted to extremely curious habits and beliefs. Whether the distant tribesmen and World War servicemen have succeeded in talking each other out of some of their respective taboos, or whether their close association has caused them to adopt freely of each other's superstitions to add to their own, is a matter which only time will reveal.

At any rate we can be sure of two things. There will be an added interest throughout the civilized world in the curious or "different" customs, manners, and beliefs everywhere; and there will be a continuance of that interest for many years to come, as distances upon the earth's surface become shorter and shorter with the expansion of fast travel routes. It will take a very long period of time and an immense amount of readjustment on the part of many human beings to bring the peoples of the earth to such a state of similarity in customs and beliefs that at last no race or tribe will seem peculiar to any other.

It all simmers down to the fact that what is strange and what is not is mainly a question of familiarity. As soon as a belief, a custom, or a costume becomes an everyday matter, it is no longer strange. It is really remarkable how quickly one becomes accustomed to unusual things. When one visits for the first time some remote,

INTRODUCTION

little known race of primitive people, or some distant land where old-time native customs and costumes still prevail, everything seems wonderfully strange. But in a short time weird costumes or even lack of costume, amazing ceremonies, and bizarre customs seem perfectly natural everyday matters.

The disappointing thing about visiting strange places and peoples is the fact that once one has visited them, they no longer seem strange.

For that matter, motion pictures, travel-book photographs, and popular tours have played havoc with the allure of strangeness. But there are still many odd customs of faraway people that have not become as familiar to the modern public as have, for example, the temple dances of Siam and the rhumba dance of Cuba.

It is the less familiar customs that are mentioned in this volume, and if by chance some customs are described which are well known to some readers, there are many more which I feel sure will prove both new and interesting.

Naturally I have not attempted to describe all or even a small proportion of the peculiar customs of all the earth's people. To do so would require many volumes, for every race on earth has innumerable customs and beliefs which are peculiar to persons of other races. A civilized man or woman in conventional garments appears just as strange to the members of a jungle tribe as the feather-and-tooth-bedecked savages appear to the white visitors.

For example, merely to touch upon all of the weird religious ceremonies or the various dances of all the Indian tribes of the United States or of South America would require a voluminous book. In the following pages I have mentioned only those which have outstandingly odd features, and I have followed the plan of generalizing and grouping various strange customs which are more or less similar in widely dispersed quarters of the globe.

A. HYATT VERRILL

TABLE OF CONTENTS

	INTRODUCTION	v
CHAPTER		PAGE
I.	STRANGE HEADDRESS	3
II.	BEAUTY IS SKIN DEEP	21
III.	TATTOOS AND TABOOS	50
IV.	STRANGE SUBSTITUTES	72
V.	CHARMS FOR LUCK	85
VI.	LEOPARD MEN AND BLOOD AVENGERS	97
VII.	MEDICINE MEN	106
VIII.	DEADLY SAVAGE WEAPONS	115
IX.	GRUESOME SOUVENIRS	139
X.	PRIMITIVE MONEY	149
XI.	PRIMITIVE MAN AT PLAY	158
XII.	STRANGE MARRIAGE CUSTOMS	181
XIII.	STRANGE FOODS	204
XIV.	TALKING DRUMS AND MUSIC	226
XV.	STRANGE SAILING CRAFT	248
XVI.	OTHER STRANGE CUSTOMS	267
	INDEX	287

LIST OF ILLUSTRATIONS

FRONTISPIECE   PAGE

1. SOMALI HAIR STYLE *(p. 43)*
2. NEW BRITAIN DEVIL DANCER *(p. 169)*
3. NEW GUINEA HEADDRESS *(p. 17)*
4. SOUTH AMERICAN INDIAN CHEEK DECORATION *(p. 38)*
5. BOTOCUDO INDIAN, STRETCHED LIP AND EAR LOBES *(p. 30)*

Plate I.   1
    6. *Sloping skull, Flathead Indian, p. 48.* 7. *New Guinea devil dancer, p. 167.* 8. *Panamanian Indian animal mask, p. 164.* 9. *Wire adornments in Burma, p. 29.* 10. *Lip stretching, Ubangi women, p. 32.*

Plate II. CHAPTER I   7
    11. *Coup bonnet with guide plume (A).* 12. *Gift bonnet given to author.* 13. *Chief's otterskin hat.* 14. *Bear-clan medicine bonnet.* 15. *Tehuana headdress.* 16. *and* 17. *Feather head adornments.*

Text Cuts. CHAPTER I
    18. *Indian wooden crown, p. 10.* 19. *Indian headdress and mask, p. 11.* 20. *Aymara Indian plumed headdress, p. 12.* 21. *Aymara Indian headdress and jaguar-skin cape, p. 13.* 22. *Dyak cape, p. 14.*

Plate III. CHAPTER I   15
    23. *Kavirondo headdress.* 24. *Zulu headdress.* 25. *South African headdress.* 26. *Samoan headdress.* 27. *Mindaya hat.*

Text Cuts. CHAPTER I
    28. *Japanese beggar's hat, p. 18.* 29. *Siamese hat, p. 19.* 30. *Druse bridal headdress, p. 20.* 31. *Maltese faldetta, p. 20.*

Text Cuts. CHAPTER II
    32. *Aural pockets, p. 26.* 33. *Stretched ear lobes, Masai woman, p. 28.* 34. *Mobira woman of Africa with lip disc, p. 31.* 35. *Panamanian earring and nose ring, p. 34.* 36. *Mapuche ear pendants, p. 35.* 37. *New Guinea nose and ear plugs, p. 36.* 38. *Dyak hoop ornaments, p. 37.* 39. *Sharpened teeth, Central America, p. 39.*

Plate IV. CHAPTER II   41
    40. *Hair wad, southeastern Uganda.* 41. *Mangebetou umbrella-like coiffure.* 42. *Fanti hairdress.* 43. *Fulah hair arrangement.* 44. *Hair style of Nusu women of China.*

xi

xii   LIST OF ILLUSTRATIONS

Text Cuts. CHAPTER II

45. Braided hair, Bulgaria, p. 45. 46. Cap of sago-palm leaves, Solomon Islands, p. 46. 47. Wasp waist, African tribes, p. 47. 48. Deformed head, Peruvian Indian, p. 49. 49. Deformed head, Nigerian tribes, p. 49.

Text Cuts. CHAPTER III

50. Head and neck cicatrization, p. 52. 51. Maori tattooing, p. 57. 52. Tattoo stamping cylinder, p. 59. 53. Guaymi stamp painting, p. 60. 54. Paiwari drink-charm tattooing, p. 62. 55. Florida Indian body tattooing, p. 63. 56. Carib Indian moustache tattoo design, p. 66.

Plate V. CHAPTER IV 75

57. Pre-Incan symbolic image. 58. Image of Inti, the Incan sun god. 58A. Peruvian amulet for insuring good crops. 59. Kuna effigy. 59A. Guaymi wooden image. 60. Fanti village fetish.

Text Cut. CHAPTER VII

61. Curing by means of needles, China, p. 109.

Plate VI. CHAPTER VIII 121

62. Congo sword. 63. Shark's-teeth weapon. 64. Aztec maquahuitl. 65. Paddle-like weapon of jungle tribes. 66. Square club. 67. Skull-cracker club. 68. Stone-headed club. 69. Stone-bladed club. 70. Club of gunstock form. 71. Boomerangs. 72. Spear-throwing stick. 73. Aztec atlatl. 74. Incan throwing stick.

Text Cuts. CHAPTER VIII

75. Aztec atlatl in throwing position, p. 129. 76. Indian quiver for poisoned darts, p. 135.

Text Cut. CHAPTER X

77. Woven feather money, p. 153.

Text Cuts. CHAPTER XI

78. Hockey stick, Sioux Indians, p. 160. 79. Rawhide-covered hockey club, Mapuche Indians, p. 160. 80. Guaymi Indian dressed for the stick game, p. 162. 81. Painted masks, Bolivian Indians, p. 165. 82. Carved wooden masks, Iroquois Indians, p. 166. 83. Mask of New Ireland devil dancer, p. 168. 84. African palm-leaf and feather costume, p. 169. 85. South African Kaffir symbolic dancer, p. 170. 86. Parasaran palm-leaf costume, p. 172. 87. Carib mechanical top, p. 178. 88. Carib and African flower-bud canoe, p. 179.

Text Cuts. CHAPTER XIII

89. Chinese bird and nest, for bird's-nest soup, p. 210. 90. Sea cucumber, or beche-de-mer, p. 219.

LIST OF ILLUSTRATIONS xiii

Plate VII. CHAPTER XIV 237
91. *Decorated drum.* 92. *Voodoo tamboola.* 93. *Water drum.*
94. *Snakeskin drum.* 95. *Drum of hollowed-out wood.* 96. *Voodoo drum.* 97. *Drum with closed end.* 98. *Drum with skin heads.* 99. *Square drum.* 100. *Thin drum.* 101. *Nose flute.* 102. *Indian love flute.* 103. *Ocarina.*

Plate VIII. CHAPTER XIV 243
104. *Tortoise-shell rattle.* 105. *Horn rattle.* 106. *Round and oval rattles.* 107. *Hollow-ring rattle.* 108. *Rawhide rattle.*

Text Cuts. CHAPTER XIV
109. *Indian birchbark and rawhide rattle, p. 245.* 110. *Primitive Panpipes, p. 246.*

Text Cuts. CHAPTER XV
111. *Indian birchbark canoe, p. 252.* 112. *Primitive dugout canoe, p. 252.* 113. *Carib dugout with plank seats, p. 252.* 114. *Polynesian catamaran, p. 253.* 115. *Mesopotamian wickerwork gufa, p. 254.* 116. *North American Indian bullboat, p. 255.* 117. *Briton coracle, p. 256.* 118. *Peruvian sea-lion raft, p. 257.* 119. *Balsa, Lake Titicaca, p. 259.* 120. *Eyes painted on bows of Chinese junks, p. 263.* 121. *High bow stems of Venetian gondolas, p. 264.* 122. *Ram's-horn design on ship's bow, p. 265.*

Text Cuts. CHAPTER XVI
123. *Grass-spur razors, p. 270.* 124. *Chinese fingernail socket, p. 272.* 125. *Anatolian felt cape, p. 276.* 126. *Oriental yashmak, p. 278.* 127. *Shepherd of Landes district, France, on stilts, p. 280.*

PLATE I

6 sloping skull, Flathead Indian 7 New Guinea devil dancer 8 Indian animal mask 9 wire adornments in Burma 10 lip stretching, Ubangi woman

Chapter I

STRANGE HEADDRESS

A CURIOUS sight during the latter phase of the Second World War in Europe soon became a common one to the resident Europeans who remained in the bombed areas. It was that of American frontline soldiers walking along the broken streets wearing high black silk hats atop their otherwise regulation army uniforms. It seems that GI Joe could not resist the startling incongruity of an opera hat, presumably denoting superelegance, in close juxtaposition to that most lowly of costumes consisting of his own muddy, khaki uniform, heavy-soled shoes, gun, and cartridge belt.

There was other spectacular clothing he might have selected from the shops or ruined houses; but it was this particular topper that he invariably chose. To him it was a means of "dressing up" and of attracting attention the most forcefully without any undue interference with the freedom of his bodily movements.

The human animal has always been particularly fond of unique headgear. Does a man or woman desire to appear important, powerful, commanding, rich? Then there must be a head decoration to impress that wish upon others. Even if the desire is merely to appear beautifully decorated or of being coy and inviting, it is head decoration that most quickly catches the eyes that are intended to be attracted.

Nothing, however, that modern man and woman has worn in stunning headgear can surpass the varying beauty, startling effect, natural artistry, or even the ugliness of the various head decorations of primitive man.

Everyone is familiar with the ornate and striking feather headdress known as the "war bonnet," which is worn by some of the North American Indians. Comparatively few persons, however, realize the significance of that headdress.

In the first place, this Indian headdress is not really a war bonnet. No Indian with an atom of common sense would ever go to battle wearing one of these gorgeous but cumbersome things. It would make him more than conspicuous, which is usually the last thing an Indian warrior desires. It would encumber him, too, and make it difficult for him to use his weapons. In fact, he dresses up in a showy, feathered bonnet only for special dances and other tribal ceremonies.

It would be far more accurate to call these headdresses "peace bonnets," but there is decidedly a connection between the bonnets and the idea of warfare. Every feather on a bonnet and each tuft of horsehair at the tips of the feathers is a badge signifying some brave or noteworthy deed, or coup, on the part of the wearer. The word "coup" in this case signifies a sign or a stratagem which either brings victory over the enemy or is in itself a symbol of victory.

When an Indian wears a bonnet with one hundred or

STRANGE HEADDRESS

more feathers extending in a double tail down his back to his heels, you may be sure he is a famed and brave man (Plate II, Fig. 11). That is, if he is wearing a genuine coup bonnet and not a show bonnet or cheap imitation affair, such as are made by the dozen for sale to tourists, boy scouts, and other curio collectors.

Only one who is a student of Indian customs and craftsmanship can distinguish between a commercial bonnet and a genuine coup bonnet. But you always may be sure that a bonnet is nothing more than a decoration, if it is worn by any Indian other than a member of one of the North American Plains tribes. Many of our Eastern Indians, as well as some of the Seminoles of Florida, the Pueblos of the Southwest, and others, wear these so-called war bonnets when dressed up, but they do so merely for modern show purposes and dances. None of these tribes ever used this type of headgear until they found that the white people expected every Indian in native costume to wear such a war bonnet. As a Seminole remarked to me, "White men don't believe we're Indians unless we wear war bonnets at our dances."

Sometimes genuine war bonnets, made as carefully as though for the head of an Indian with many coups, are given to prominent white men when they are made honorary chiefs or members of one of the Plains tribes. Occasionally these are true coup bonnets, the feathers, down, and tufts of hair commemorating deeds or important acts or services on the part of the tribe's adopted white man.

When I was made a member of the Oglala Sioux tribe, a Plains group, I was given an Indian name, Tchanku

Tanka (Big Road), because of my many explorations. I was presented with a beautiful bonnet made of thirty-one white eagle feathers, each with its coup-down and hair. These were honors which the Indians bestowed upon me for my various books and articles about my travels among Indians, and special services I had rendered them (Plate II, Fig. 12). This is a true coup bonnet.

I was presented at the same time with a double-tail bonnet for use on horseback, with more than a hundred eagle feathers. Other gifts were a chief's otterskin hat (Plate II, Fig. 13) and a bear-clan medicine bonnet (Plate II, Fig. 14). These are all genuine bonnets made for ceremonial use, but are not coup bonnets.

The long double-tailed bonnets are designed to be used when the wearer is on horseback. If you examine one used by an Indian, you will notice that a long, beautifully decorated feather is attached to the center of the cap, or bonnet proper. This is very seldom seen on a bonnet made for sale. It is known as a guide plume (Plate II, Fig. 11, A). It is not purely ornamental, as one might suppose. It has a very definite and important purpose. When an Indian wearing one of these bonnets rides swiftly, the tail feathers of his bonnet would fold together and lie flat, were it not for the guide plume. This plume creates a draught of air between the "tails" and causes them to spread apart beautifully.

In the old days a coup bonnet was made of feathers taken from an eagle which had been captured alive by the warrior himself. Nowadays Indians are not so particular. Most of them are satisfied with feathers from eagles

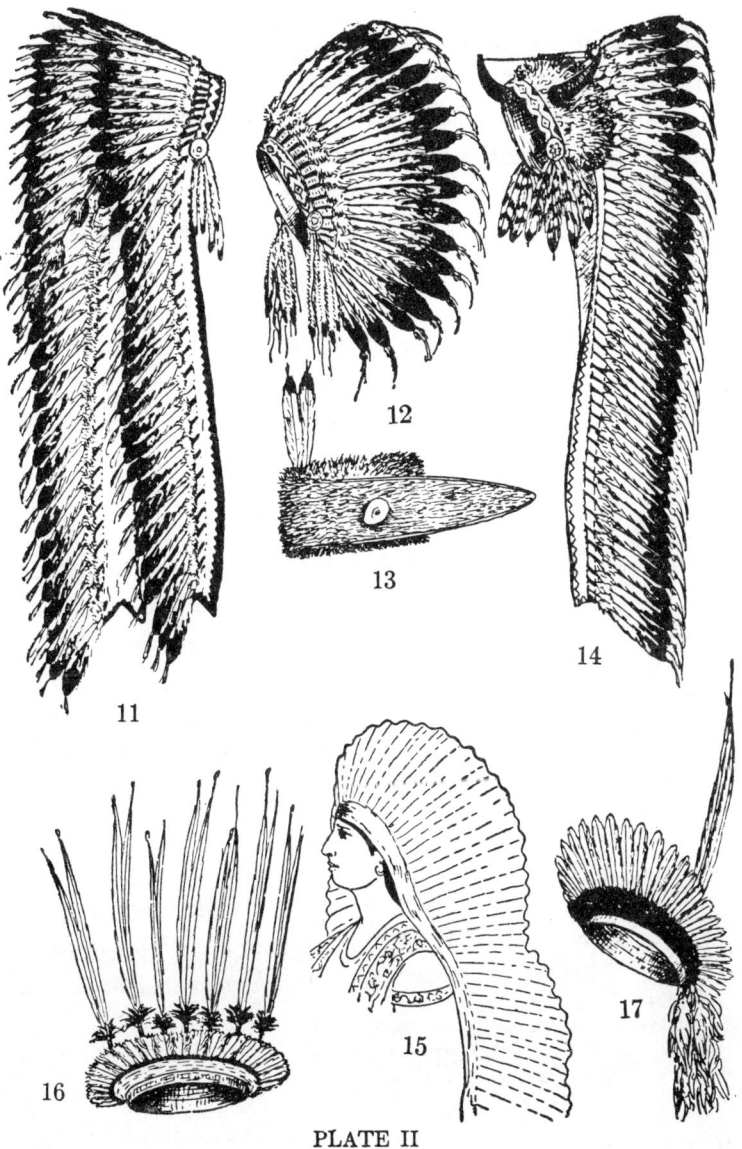

PLATE II
11 coup bonnet with guide plume (A) 12 gift bonnet given to author 13 chief's otterskin hat 14 bear-clan medicine bonnet 15 Tehuana headdress 16 and 17 feather head adornments

STRANGE HEADDRESS

which have been procured no matter by whom. The war bonnet has become a commercial article.

Although these so-called war bonnets are typical of the Western Indians of North America and are always associated with them, other races have somewhat similar headdresses. The Tehuana Indian women of the Isthmus of Tehuantepec in Mexico wear beautiful headdresses which at first sight appear to be duplicates of the bonnets of these Western Indians. But the Tehuana headdresses are made of cotton cloth, frilled or pleated, instead of being made of feathers (Plate II, Fig. 15). And in Europe, in French Alsace, women wear a similar headdress on special days, although it does not extend down the back as does that of the Mexican Indians.

It seems strange indeed that three races so widely separated should have developed, independently, similar forms of headdresses. One might almost assume that one was copied from the other, yet the Tehuana women were using their peculiar headdresses when Cortez arrived in Mexico; the Alsatian women had been wearing theirs for centuries before anyone in Europe ever heard of America; and the first white men to visit the Indians of the North American Western Plains found the feather bonnets widely in use.

Throughout the world, primitive races are very fond of feather headdresses. In South America the Indians have most gorgeous and striking feather headpieces. The North American Indians use the feathers of eagles, hawks, owls, or turkeys, while the headgear of South American tribes displays brilliantly colored feathers from parrots, macaws, and other tropical birds. Many

South American headdresses have long bobs or tails composed entirely of skins and feathers of gorgeously plumaged birds.

The variety of styles of these South American millinery creations is very great. Every tribe and often the individual as well has particular ideas on the subject and tries to have something distinctive in the way of feather head adornments (Plate II, Fig. 16 and 17). One tribe, the Chokoi Indians of southern Panama and northern

18

Colombia, uses very remarkable crowns made of wood. At first glance these would be mistaken for feather crowns, for the numerous thin plumes of wood are shaped and painted to resemble feathers (Fig. 18).

When Dampier, the buccaneer naturalist, crossed the Isthmus of Darien with Captain Sharp's men, who were on their way to sack the old city of Panama, he found these wooden crowns in use by the Indians and described them in his journal.

Many of the Indians of the American far Northwest

STRANGE HEADDRESS

use wooden headdresses. Some of these are immense, grotesque affairs. They often combine a head decoration and a mask for the wearer (Fig. 19).

Very remarkable among American headdresses are those used by some of the Aymara Indian tribes of Peru and Bolivia. Made of brightly colored feathers in the typical South American crown form, the headdresses are

19

topped off by plumes of great size. These plumes are made by splicing together the long tail feathers of macaws until the built-up plumes are often six or eight feet in length (Fig. 20).

None of these ornate or cumbersome headdresses is intended for everyday use. Like the war bonnets of the Western Indians, they are worn only for ceremonial purposes and during tribal dances. Very often each kind of dance calls for a certain form of headdress. The same

Aymaras who wear the enormously long, plumed, feather headdresses in some of their dances employ very different headgear in other dances. In one of these the men wear a most unusual headdress in the form of a huge hoop which resembles the shell of a drum attached to a

20

skin cap. In addition to this strange contraption they don peculiar stiff capes of jaguar skin, painted rawhide, or other material (Fig. 21).

Unusual as is this dance costume, we find it duplicated among the Dyak tribes of far distant Borneo in the East Indies, where the head-hunting warriors use stiff capes of the same form and materials as the Aymaras of

STRANGE HEADDRESS 13

Bolivia (Fig. 22). They do not, however, wear the hoop headdresses.

Striking and peculiar as are many of the headdresses used by the Indians of America, we must go to Africa and the islands of the South Seas to find millinery

21

creations which are really amazing in size. Like the American Indians, the aborigines of these distant lands are partial to feathers as ornaments for headgear. This is quite logical and natural, for feathers combine color, lightness, and showy possibilities to the very highest degree. Some of these tribesmen build up their head-

14 STRANGE CUSTOMS

dresses on frameworks of light basketwork, bamboo, or rattan. By using such lightweight material and even lighter feathers, they are able to build up an enormous headdress weighing only a few pounds.

22

African tribes, in particular, favor great size when it comes to their headgear. The men of the Kavirondo tribe of Kenya use tower-like structures of spires topped with fine plumes (Plate III, Fig. 23). Some of the Zulu peoples of South Africa prefer a huge mass of waving

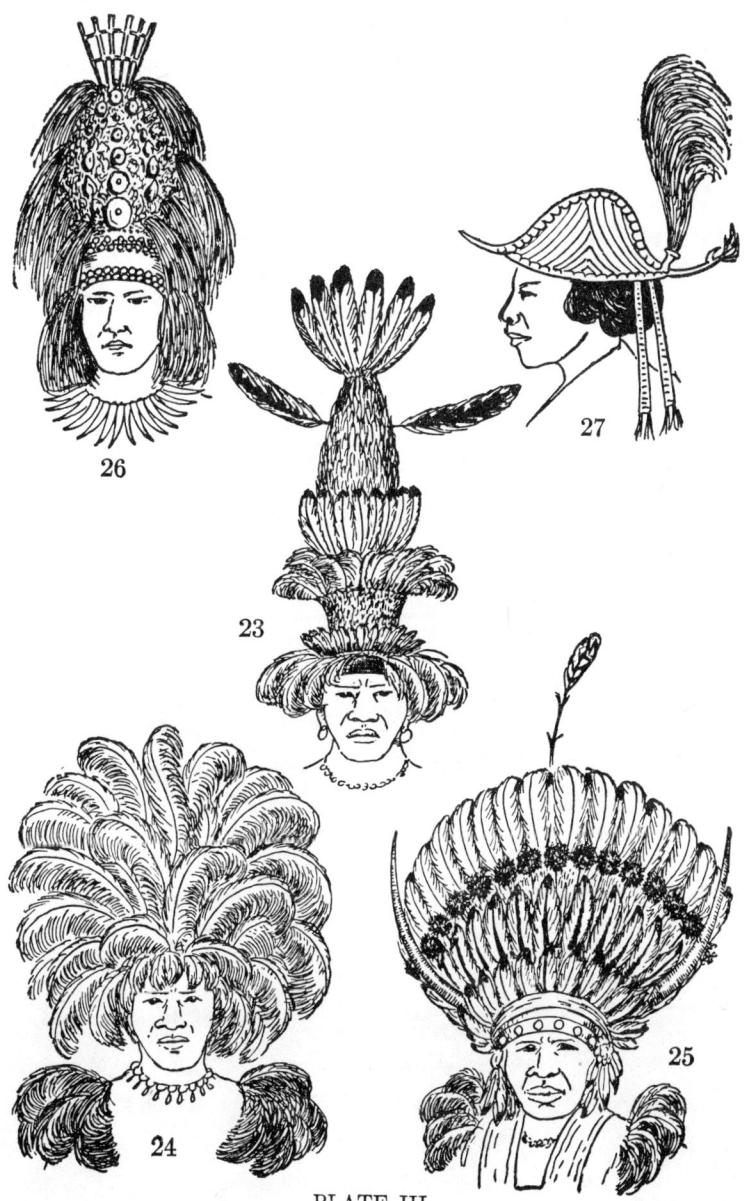

PLATE III
23 Kavirondo headdress 24 Zulu headdress 25 South African headdress
26 Samoan headdress 27 Mindaya hat

STRANGE HEADDRESS 17

black and white ostrich plumes (Plate III, Fig. 24), while the Kaffir rickshaw "boys" of Durban and other South African cities wear most striking and picturesque headdresses of feathers and the polished horns of steers (Plate III, Fig. 25).

Another strange and truly beautiful headdress is worn by some of the people in the Samoan islands (Plate III, Fig. 26). Made up of bright feathers, bleached human hair, mother-of-pearl, seashells, and brilliant flowers, it is artistic and striking and is very becoming to the wearer. A Samoan chief or village belle often adds to the headpiece a number of small, scintillating mirrors and shiny beetle wings. Sometimes antennae-like branches several feet long and adorned with shells dominate the headgear.

Very different indeed is the cocked-hat-like affair favored by the warriors of the Mindaya people of the Philippines (Plate III, Fig. 27). But the very ultimate in headdresses, an amazing creation that makes all others seem smaller by comparison, is the stupendous headdress of some of the Papuan tribes of New Guinea. It is built up to an exceeding height and is made from brilliant feathers of such birds as cockatoos, lories, and birds of paradise, along with plumes of cassowaries, pheasants, and other birds. These examples of savage millinery are often taller than the warriors who wear them (Fig. 3, Frontispiece).

From such gigantic and gorgeous affairs to the strange headdress shown in Fig. 28 is a drop from the sublime to the ridiculous. These hat-like, upturned baskets are worn by noblemen beggars of Japan. They are designed to conceal the face of the wearer so that he will not be shamed by being recognized while begging on the streets.

Most of the headdresses so far mentioned, other than those worn by Alsatian women and Mexican Tehuana women, usually are reserved for use by men. Among

28

savage or primitive races it is the male rather than the female members who wear strange and elaborate millinery finery. But there are other races whose women are as fond of striking head coverings as are the ladies of modern Western civilization.

Odd, pagoda-like, metal-covered hats are worn by the women dancers of Siam, Bali, and Java, but how about the strange hat worn by another type of woman of Siam, as shown in Fig. 29? Surely no modern up-to-the-

STRANGE HEADDRESS

minute monstrosity worn by the fashionable women of Paris or New York can outshine this combination of a basket and flowers! Yet is it any stranger than the bridal

29

headdress of a Druse woman of Lebanon in Asia Minor (Fig. 30)?

Not so striking, although more unusual, is the faldetta, worn since earliest times by the women of Malta, an island in the Mediterranean Sea (Fig. 31). The faldetta has a redeeming feature, which is more than can be said of the majority of women's headgear—it is really useful, and it does protect the wearer from sun and rain.

The Bedouin woman of southern Palestine often wears her dowry of coins as a veil, in Moslem style. The coins hang in close strings from the middle of her forehead down over the center of her face, and often the

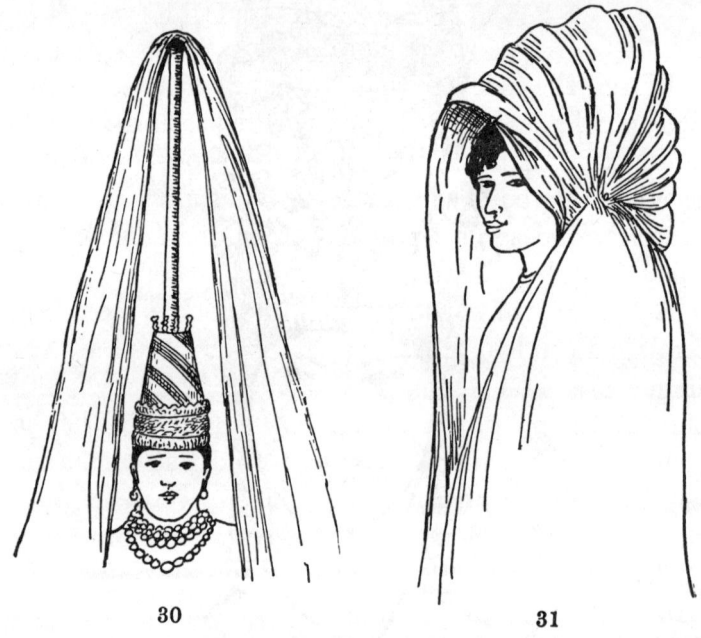

lower ends of these strings are fastened upon the shoulders of her robe.

In head coverings, human tastes and fancies seem to have few limits. Whether or not a hat is attractive or ugly, whether it is becoming, comfortable, or useful to the wearer or is purely decorative, never seems to make much difference. A certain type of millinery is the fashion—no further explanation is necessary.

Chapter II

BEAUTY IS SKIN DEEP

When the modern girl rouges her cheeks, paints her lips, plucks and pencils her eyebrows, and stains and polishes her nails, she feels quite up-to-date. But pre-Incan girls who lived over three thousand years ago did precisely the same thing and with the same idea—to enhance and emphasize their beauty.

A mummy of a pre-Incan girl which I took from a tomb in Peru had plucked eyebrows, bobbed hair, tinted fingernails and toenails, reddened lips, and rouged cheeks. In the woven vanity bag buried with her were somewhat the same things one would find in the handbag of a living girl of today. There were the powder puff, the feather compact, the tweezers, the orangewood stick. There, too, were the lipstick and the rouge, the red paint and the powder used by the girl of a thousand years ago.

Some workmen excavating for a new building in London a few years ago came upon the remains of an ancient Roman beauty parlor. They found jars filled with creams, pomades, coloring tints, skin bleaches, and aids to beauty much like those that are popular with women of today.

Perhaps the Roman beauty culturist gave certain

kinds of permanent waves and marcelled hair to his patrons, for when it comes to aids to beauty there really is nothing new under the sun. Members of every race think that they can improve upon nature by some means or another and seldom seem to be satisfied with what Mother Nature has bestowed upon them.

Quite frequently what one race deems ugly or undesirable is considered beautiful and desirable by others. As my West Indian camp boy once observed, "It is so very strange that white women spend time and money trying to have curly and even kinky hair, while Negro women spend time and money trying to have their hair straight."

The white woman smears her face with light powders in order to look fairer; in Equatorial Africa the women of various tribes, including the Kavirandos of Kenya, although already dusky in color, powder themselves with fine charcoal in order to look blacker than they are—a sign of beauty. Instead of commercial cold cream, they use the fat of the hippopotamus.

Among most civilized people it is usually the women who use aids to beauty. To be sure, some men do patronize beauty parlors and submit to facial, hair, and scalp treatments in order to enhance their appearance; and many men have their nails manicured regularly. But plucked and penciled eyebrows, artificial eyelashes, painted lips, and mascaraed eyelashes among moderns are still woman's exclusive adornment.

Quite the opposite is true among the majority of savage and primitive races. Here it is the men who seek most of the aids to beauty, if beauty it can be called. No

BEAUTY IS SKIN DEEP 23

doubt these dandies consider their decorations irresistible. The damsels probably think themselves beautiful, too, even if some of their bodily adornments appear ugly and sometimes even repulsive to more civilized persons.

It is all a matter of taste, whether of race or individual. Many persons, for example, think that a rouged and mascaraed girl with plucked eyebrows and with imitation eyelashes projecting like black wires from her eyelids is the acme of loveliness. But to others a woman adorned in this manner is as unattractive as a brown or black-skinned savage with a pin in her lip, a ring in her nose, and her neck tightly wrapped with brass wire.

Men in the armed forces of the United States in the Second World War were astonished to find that Melanesian males in many of the South Pacific Islands bleach their black hair with coral lime. Natives of New Caledonia, for example, appear very blond. This practice is not alone for enhancing the appearance, but for the purpose also of discouraging hair vermin. Yet no boy is allowed to bleach his hair until he has passed the age of childhood and has become a man. There is considerable fanfare surrounding the first bleaching of the young lad's hair, ceremonies which officially usher him into a place among adult men.

Many Africans like to use rouge, the red powder being obtained from certain tropical trees. The red powder is ground out of the trunk of the tree, and then it is mixed with either water or oil to form a thick red paste. This is shaped, allowed to dry in the sun, and then pressed into a powder. The African man or woman anoints the body with a mixture of this powder and palm oil, or sprinkles the powder itself over the body. A very bright red coloring is thus attained.

Sometimes, indeed, face paint has been considered modest and retiring rather than bold and daring. In olden days, for example, no respectable Chinese woman thought of appearing in public unless her face was heavily painted. The heavier and more obvious the paint, the more respectable and modest the woman.

Some of the beauty aids used by savage races seem very strange indeed to us, but we must remember that to the savages the make-up of civilized persons appears equally odd. We marvel that any human being could endure such agonies as female Chinese infants used to suffer in having their extremities bound in order to produce the tiny feet which formerly were deemed beautiful by high-caste Chinese. But modern women more or less cheerfully undergo a great deal of suffering in wearing high-heeled shoes that are too small for them. They also submit to certain tortures in order to possess dimples, a clear skin, or arched eyebrows; or to reduce or add weight or shapeliness to their figures.

In fact, whether savage or civilized, most persons who wish to beautify themselves seem to feel that the more pain or inconvenience endured in the process, the more effective it must be. This isn't so surprising when we stop to consider that primarily many of the aids to beauty in use by savage races were associated with self-torture. Thrusting a sharp object through his flesh and letting it remain there proved the wearer's stoicism, his ability to endure pain; and while earrings as worn by civilized women of today do not cause suffering, they

BEAUTY IS SKIN DEEP

are merely leftovers of self-tortures practiced by our primitive ancestors.

Earrings are one of the most ancient and widely used aids to beauty. Long before human beings discovered the use of metal, even before they had learned to chip stone weapons, they wore earplugs, which are ornaments inserted into apertures pierced or cut in the ears. Many of the most ancient ear ornaments are of shell or bone, and many are true earrings. But by far the greater number are earplugs.

Ear ornaments were first intended to be marks of honor or distinction either to the individual, his family, or his tribe. Usually a ceremony of some type, sometimes religious in character, attended the piercing of the ear lobe. Among some tribes, such as Alaskan Indians, perforations were made around the entire rim of the ear, and bits of shell, metal or bone were inserted in each. Long pendants sometimes were used, that reached nearly to the waist. These often were made of lengthy woven bands of dentalium, with an abalone shell dangling at the lower end.

Primitive man rarely uses halfway measures. As a rule, when a savage decides to wear ear ornaments, he wants them fairly large and conspicuous. Many of the earplugs used in the past and still in use today are an inch or more in diameter; many are several inches in diameter; and some are much larger. The lobes of the ears are constantly pulled down by these large, heavy ornaments until the lobes themselves become long rings of flesh often hanging below the shoulders.

Among Eskimos of the North Pacific tribes an

26 STRANGE CUSTOMS

opening was cut in the lip, at one or both corners of the mouth, when the boy, for example, reached the age of puberty. Into these holes slugs were inserted and as time passed were replaced by larger ones. Eskimos also had nose piercings into which feathers, bark, or rings were inserted. Strange to say, after the first shock of surprise which the newcomer to their village experienced

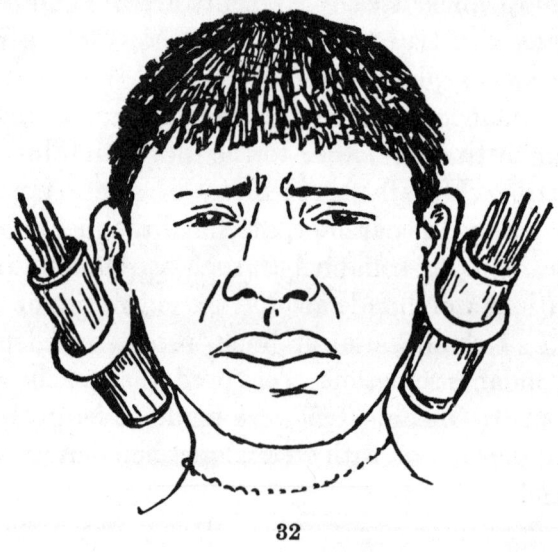

32

upon seeing them, these nose and ear ornaments appeared really artistic and beautiful.

As I have said, the custom of wearing very large earplugs is very common, and while it is primarily a decorative matter, many savages combine the ornamental and the useful. By thrusting sections of bamboo, old cartridge shells, tobacco tins, or other hollow contrivances through the apertures in their ears, they provide themselves with aural pockets (Fig. 32).

BEAUTY IS SKIN DEEP

In Yap Island in Micronesia in the South Pacific it is still considered fashionable among the native Kanakas to pierce the lobe of the ear and then stretch the opening sufficiently large so that sizable objects or parcels may be carried in it. When empty, the loose, dangling flap is tucked out of the way by looping it conveniently over the rest of the ear.

A Masai woman of the Kenya district in Africa does not feel that she is up to standard unless her distended ear lobes are very long indeed. Quite frequently they are stretched to such an extent that they may be brought beneath the chin and over the head, where they meet (Fig. 33).

Many races pierce the lower lips as well as the ears and wear a lip pin, or labret, thrust through the slit. The labret may be of bone, wood, pottery, stone, or metal; it may be a tuft of feathers or even a chain or other heavy type of pendant.

The Masai people of African Kenya are partly Negro, but it is difficult to make out whether the hair of the women is woolly or not, for they shave it close to the scalp, using razors of iron, flint, or glass. Then the heads are polished with grease, so that they fairly shine in the sun. Even small infants are shaved.

Many of the Masai men carry with them tweezers of iron with which to pull out the hairs on their chins, cheeks, and nostrils, and thus keep themselves shaved until they are old enough to be warriors. When the age of manhood is reached, they let the hair grow and wear it plaited in pigtails over the forehead, often soaking it in oil and adding red clay as a further aid to beauty.

28 STRANGE CUSTOMS

To increase her attractiveness further, the Masai woman loads herself with chains and beads. Some women have great rings of brass wire coiled around the neck in connecting circles, wire after wire being used until the whole extends out as far as the shoulders. In time, of course, the neck becomes heavily laden.

33

These women also have brass wire woven about their arms from the wrists to the elbows and from the elbows to the shoulders, and also great coils of similar wire fastened by strings to the lobes of their ears. Aside from this, a skin draped around the body and falling to the knees is usually their only clothing.

BEAUTY IS SKIN DEEP

Quite frequently a Masai woman will wear twelve to fifteen pounds of wire on each leg and almost as much on her arms. But she pays a penalty for her wire finery, for an old Masai custom prescribes that she cannot remove even one coil of the wire as long as her husband is alive.

This fondness for wire adornment was a constant annoyance to white men who in modern times installed telegraph lines across Africa. No sooner would a section of line be strung between posts than it would be stolen by the natives to be used upon their persons. Strenuous measures in punishments by fines at last became necessary in order to maintain the lines intact.

Wire coils are very popular adornments among various other tribes, in Africa and elsewhere. It reaches its extreme among the women of the Shan tribe of Upper Burma in Asia. In addition to having their legs encased in wire rings, they have their necks tightly wrapped with wire and gradually stretched out to abnormal length.

The first coils are wrapped about the girls' necks when they are mere infants. As the neck muscles lengthen, more and more rings are added until the neck has become so greatly elongated that the woman has the appearance of a human giraffe (Plate I, Fig. 9).

Recently some of these women became modernized in their tastes and had the copper rings, thus worn for years, removed from their necks. It was found that in many cases the neck muscles were much too weak, at first, to support the head without artificial aids.

As a rule such ornaments are worn only at ceremonials or dances, while at other times the pierced lower lip may be used as a convenient sort of wallet. It is not unusual to see a man or woman with an empty brass rifle shell thrust through the lower lip.

Members of the Carib tribes of South America use their pierced lower lips as pincushions. They are fond of pins and needles. Since their regular costumes, or rather lack of costumes, offer no available pockets for carrying such objects, the Indians thrust pins through the pierced lower lip. Many of these Indians can remove or replace the pins by means of the tongue. It is fascinating to watch the pins and needles appearing and disappearing through a Carib's lips as he talks.

Although many primitive people are content with ordinary earplugs and labrets, there are some tribes which use ear and lip ornamentation of an amazing size. The Mobira woman of the African Congo wears a large disc in the upper lip, which extends the lip outward like a circular shelf for several inches beyond the nose (Fig. 34). The Botocudo Indians of the interior of Brazil gradually stretch the apertures in ear lobes and lips until they hang down sufficiently far to accommodate discs of wood five or six inches in diameter (Fig. 5, Frontispiece), giving the wearers an appearance that never fails to astound a visitor.

But the real champions of lip-stretching are the Ubangi women of Equatorial Africa. Early in life the lips of some of the Ubangi women are perforated and a round disc of wood is inserted in the aperture. The size of the disc is increased from time to time, and thus eventually the lips are stretched to enormous size, some of the discs being around twenty inches in diameter. Discs of wood, tin saucers, or round mirrors are used to distend the lips, which project horizontally instead of hanging down as do the lips of the Botocudo Indian women of Brazil.

Sometimes one of the Ubangi women will remove a disc temporarily. Then the upper lip falls down over

34

the mouth and chin, leaving a gaping hole through which the teeth are visible beneath the nose. And to add to this surprising effect, the women have a habit of licking the outer edge of the lip by thrusting the tongue through the opening.

Very appropriately have the Ubangi been called the "duckbill people," for the distended lips give the women the appearance of having large, duck-like beaks instead of mouths (Plate I, Fig. 10).

Why any race should ever have resorted to this custom of deforming the lips is a mystery. One tradition is that something over a century ago a woman of the Ubangis had naturally deformed lips and was rejected by slavers. In order to protect themselves from the raiders the other women started the custom of artificially deforming their lips. This explanation may or may not be true; but even if it is, it does not account for the fact that a similar custom is prevalent among the Botocudo Indians of Brazil. It is equally possible that personal adornment was the original motive.

It is a different matter with distended ear lobes or even moderately sized nose rings, which are not particularly troublesome to the individual thus adorned. The distended platter-like lips of the Ubangi, the pendant lower lips of the Botocudos, and the jutting upper lip of the Mobira women seem to us to be a tremendous handicap when eating, drinking, or speaking. But what woman ever took into consideration an inconvenience when it came to a matter of self-beautification?

A moderately sized nose ring may not be a very great nuisance, but the huge nose rings worn by Hindu women of India and other Oriental women must be very much in the way at times. Many a time I have seen a passing Hindu woman with a five-inch gold ring dangling from her nose.

Nose rings are a favorite form of self-adornment in many parts of the world. Those worn by the Kuna and San Blas Indian women of Panama are symbolic of serv-

BEAUTY IS SKIN DEEP

itude. Long ago, before these Indians had ever seen a white man, they made part of their living by raiding other tribes. They were not actually at war with their neighbors. They merely wished to secure a supply of fresh meat, for at that time, like their relatives, the Caribs, they were cannibals.

On these raids they killed any man who resisted capture, carried male prisoners to their villages to be kept and fattened for future food, and brought the female captives home to serve as slaves or wives of their captors. It was not easy to keep these women from running away, so the cannibal Kunas pierced their noses, passed cords through the holes, and strung the captives together for safe keeping. Today, civilized farmers keep strong bulls under control by a similar nose ring and rope method.

Having thus been provided with a hole in her nasal septum, even if she had no say in the matter, it was second nature for the captive woman to make good use of it later by adorning it with a ring or a pendant. At first, of course, it was a badge of servitude, for it indicated the wearer had been literally "led by the nose." But after a time the women changed all this. Compelled by necessity to learn the language of their captors, these women preserved their original dialect by teaching it to their daughters. This led to a dual language for these tribes, that of the women being unknown to the men.

The result of this was just what might have been expected. Almost before they knew what was happening, the men discovered that the women were gaining the upper hand. They could understand everything the men said, but the men could not understand a word of what the women were talking about when they conversed in their feminine tongue. Before very long the women were the real rulers of the tribe, as they are today. They may truthfully boast of having been the first to establish women's political rights!

Today, the Kuna and San Blas women own everything the tribe has except the weapons of their men. The women select their own mates. They lay down the law to the chiefs, who are mere figureheads in tribal affairs. Thus the nose rings worn by the women would seem eventually to have become signs of superiority instead of badges of servitude.

BEAUTY IS SKIN DEEP

The nose rings of these Indians are very modest affairs, being only small triangular ornaments of gold wire. The women, however, make up for the small size of their nose rings by wearing enormous gold plates in their ears (Fig. 35). These are worn like ordinary earrings in use by civilized women and are suspended from small holes pierced in the lobes of the ears.

36

These ear ornaments are large, but they are quite modest pieces of jewelry when compared with the great silver ear pendants used by the Mapuche (Araucanian) Indian women of southern Chile (Fig. 36). The Mapuche women, however, have never adopted the nose-ring or lip-pin fashions.

When it comes to ornaments inserted in the nasal

cartilages, natives of New Guinea and of neighboring islands must be awarded first honors. Mere rings, or even plugs, are not sufficiently appealing to these savages. They wear huge pieces of bone or the tusks of wild boars thrust through slits which have been cut through the sides of the nostrils (Fig. 37).

37

The Dyak women of Borneo in the East Indies are addicted to wearing hoops. But in their case the numerous rings encircling their bodies from hips to armpits are fairly light in weight, being made of rattan wound with fine copper, brass, or silver wire (Fig. 38). What the Dyak woman saves in the weight of her hoop-corset

BEAUTY IS SKIN DEEP

costume, however, is more than offset by the weight of silver coins and other ornaments added to the structure. As a finishing touch she wears a huge, elaborate head comb of silver filigree ornamented with shells, bangles, and feathers.

38

Native Sepik warriors of African New Guinea, when dressed for a dance, are really stunning, with headdresses of enormous, waving white cockatoo feathers, armbands of vegetable fiber decorated with long, gay grasses, large cowrie-shell buttons, and necklaces of animal teeth.

The costume is topped by a long, highly decorated stick, suggestive of the baton of the leader of a drum corps.

From the point of view of decoration, Mother Nature was not very generous. She gave human beings so few features. Two ears, one nose, and two lips do not provide nearly enough projections upon which to hang ornaments! But the savage, whether dandy, warrior, or woman, isn't to be deprived of aids to beauty merely because of lack of protuberances.

Many tribes have found additional opportunity for beautification in decorating the cheeks. Among some South American Indian tribes it is the custom to pierce the cheeks, to thrust skewers through the apertures and then tip the skewers with bright-hued feathers. (Fig. 4, Frontispiece). History, or rather custom, repeats itself in Africa and the South Sea Islands, where cheek ornaments of one kind or another are quite widely the vogue.

At one not too distant period of the civilized white man's history it became quite a fad for wealthy ladies to have diamonds inserted in their front teeth. Not only did this afford an opportunity to show off more jewels, but it was supposed to enhance the brightness of the smile. In modern times women of less means (and also not a few men) have paid to have gold fillings inserted in perfectly sound teeth, merely to be in style and to attract attention.

They were really centuries behind the times, for many primitive races had been ornamenting their teeth for ages. Some of the skulls taken from pre-Incan, Incan, Aztec, and other ancient South American Indian tombs

BEAUTY IS SKIN DEEP 39

contain teeth which had been decorated. Some were merely perforated in fancy designs; others were inlaid with gold and semi-precious stones; while far more had been chipped and ground to needle points.

This custom of sharpening the teeth is still common among many races. Sometimes it is an indication of can-

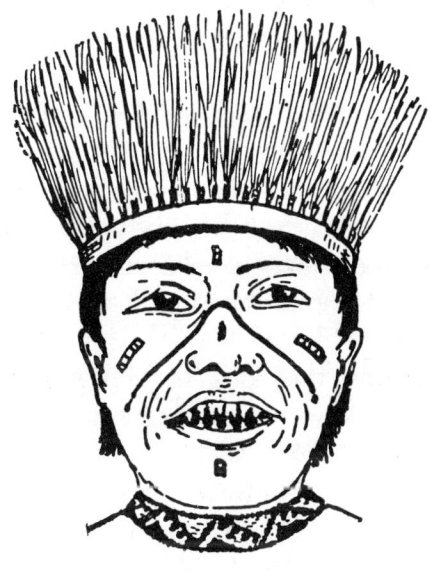
39

nibalism; but because a savage has needle-sharp incisors does not necessarily mean that he is a cannibal.

Several tribes of Central American Indians sharpen their teeth (Fig. 39). They claim that this prevents decay. Perhaps it does help preserve the teeth, since bits of food cannot lodge between them. At all events, I have noticed that among these Indians, men and women with the pointed teeth usually have better teeth than those whose teeth are left in the natural shape. The majority of persons, however, would prefer to lose the incisors and wear a plate rather than to endure the torture that must be endured during the process of sharpening. The teeth are not filed or ground away, but are chipped by means of stone or steel implements.

The same effort to beautify the person goes on throughout most of Africa. Among the Banyoro, who live north of Uganda in Equatorial Africa, young men and women have the six front teeth of the lower jaw knocked out. The Jaluo women of the same section follow a similar custom. The neighboring Buvumas have two of the incisors struck out, the price for such an operation being four cowry shells, or a fraction of a cent. The Masai and Nandi tribes of East Africa also follow these fashions.

Whence came this idea of separations among the teeth? No one knows for a certainty. The story runs that when tetanus or lockjaw was a scourge in East Africa, it was easier to feed a victim if there were gaps in his rows of teeth. The explanation hardly seems adequate, because the custom of knocking out teeth is widespread among savage races in other parts of the world as well.

Civilized women like to try new styles of "hair-do," and so also primitive women and men have a wonderful time inventing startling fashions in hairdressing. Usually a primitive person sticks to one particular coiffure, once it satisfies his ideas of what the human head should look like.

We can scarcely blame him when we see the amazing

PLATE IV
40 hair wad, southeastern Uganda 41 Mangebetou umbrella-like coiffure 42 Fanti hairdress 43 Fulah hair arrangement 44 hair style of Nusu women of China

BEAUTY IS SKIN DEEP

and intricate results some of them accomplish, where it would be a difficult and time-consuming undertaking to undo and rearrange their locks. In fact, it is quite impossible in many cases, such as, for example, the hair of the Teso and Turkana tribes of southeastern Uganda in Africa. Among these Negroes it is the custom for the eldest son to inherit the hair wad of his deceased father. This, together with his own hair, is mixed with blood and cow dung. Then it is molded into a great bun or wad hanging at the nape of the neck and is decorated with small feathers and brass hoops (Plate IV, Fig. 40).

Naturally this pile accumulates as parents die off and the mop of hair is passed on to the eldest son, until in a few generations the "hair-do" reaches enormous proportions.

Almost as unwholesome and quite as impressive as these coiffures of the Uganda savages are the great outstanding masses of hair favored by the "Fuzzy Wuzzies" of Kipling's poem. There is the Somali Fuzzy-Wuzzy, who gets a far more impressive hair display by gumming his hair to a light wicker-work frame (Fig. 1, Frontispiece).

Many of the tribes of Somaliland in Africa are of mixed Hamitic, Negro, and Arab blood. Most of them are magnificent in appearance, very tall and dark, with well-formed features and martial carriage. The effect of the high-topped hair upon these already lofty individuals is arresting, to say the least—as it is undoubtedly intended to be.

Equally as striking is the inverted umbrella-like coiffure (Plate IV, Fig. 41) which is the prevailing style among the Mangebetou women of Central Africa.

The Fanti women of the Gold Coast oil and gum their kinky wool into two sharp, pointed horns protruding from the head above the temples (Plate IV, Fig. 42).

A far more attractive result is attained by the Fulah women of the French Soudan. They add bangles, coins, and wooden combs to their carefully arranged and heavily greased woolly hair (Plate IV, Fig. 43).

Still stranger than any of these forms of hairdressing is that of the Nusu women of China. They add black wool to their own abundant tresses and braid and mold the whole into a huge mass which forms a permanent hat extending far over the forehead (Plate IV, Fig. 44).

In contrast to this, the Bulgarian peasant woman of Europe spends considerable time in carefully plaiting her long hair into twenty-four distinct braids. These are decorated with rows of silver or gold coins (Fig. 45). The general effect is pleasing and becoming.

It is rather strange that North American Indians cared little for fanciful hairdressing. Perhaps the Western Plains Indians arranged the hair itself in simple style because they needed space for their ornate, separate feather headdresses. Certain North American tribes shaved their heads and left an upstanding roach, or crest. Others cut their hair short with the exception of a tuft of long hair which served for attaching feather ornaments and was not a "scalp lock," as is generally supposed. The majority of the Indians was satisfied with plain braids, bobbed hair, and feather ornaments.

Among the South and Central American tribes it

BEAUTY IS SKIN DEEP 45

was much the same. As far as I am aware, only one tribe of Indians has a truly unusual method of hairdressing —the Warraus of the Orinoco Delta and the near-by swamps. They knead honey into their hair and plaster it with silvery, iridescent fish scales.

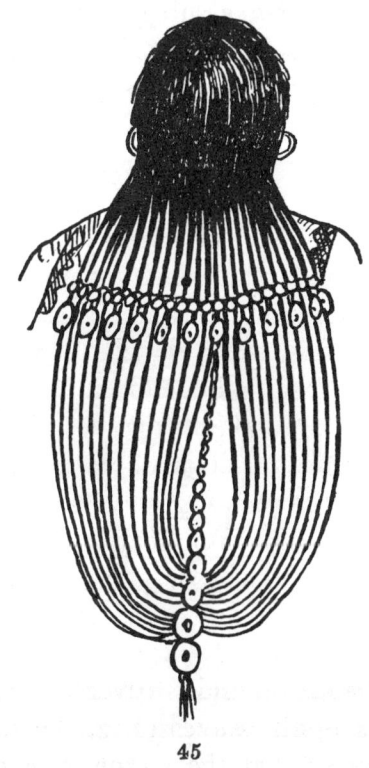

Some Sudanese tribes of Africa dress their hair in long, even curls which hang out like the snakes of Medusa. The Zulus of Africa put up their hair in mighty towers which often extend a full foot above the crown of the heads. In Natal, a province of South Africa, a bridegroom goes out to court his sweetheart with a pair of real cowhorns tied upright upon his head so naturally that they look as if they had grown there.

One of the strangest of hairdressing customs is that of the Solomon Islanders in the South Seas. When a youth attains marriageable age, his hair is thoroughly

soaked in cocoanut oil and is covered with a tightly fitting cap of sago-palm leaves (Fig. 46).

Custom decrees that the young man must wear the container constantly for a period of two years. At the expiration of that time the hair has grown until it completely fills the cap. It has expanded the cap to such an extent that it cannot be removed except by cutting off the hair close to the man's head. What a sigh of relief the poor chap must breathe when at last he is free to scratch his scalp!

One might suppose that personal vanity would be satisfied with the possibilities for decoration that are af-

forded by ears, nose, lips, cheeks, teeth, and hair. But there are no limits to the ambitions of human beings when it comes to improving upon Nature. The men of several African tribes wear tight belts, or stomachers, which result in ridiculous wasp waists. These "beautifiers" make the purposely deformed native appear as if he might break in two at the slightest exertion (Fig. 47).

White civilized women need not smile at this custom, for it is only recently that they themselves ceased to lace their waists much too tightly for health or comfort.

The woman of the Kavirondo tribes along the shores of Lake Victoria Nyanza in Africa, wishing to extend the rear of her anatomy in appearance, wears a variation of the civilized woman's bustle, that peculiar style which lasted for so many years in Europe and America.

The white woman's bustle was made of various combinations of wire, pads, ruffles, and ribbons. The Kavirondo woman wears very little clothing in her warm climate, but, if married, never fails to wear a flouncing tail or bustle made of palm leaves or grass or fibres of the papyrus plant. This bustle is attached to a woven belt which also holds up a little apron in the front. Except for beads and bracelets she has no other clothing.

The Flathead Indians of the American Northwest considered a long, sloping forehead a most attractive feature. They bound the heads of young babies between boards and artificially flattened the skulls, thus achieving the desired effect (Plate I, Fig. 6).

In South America ideals of head contours were exactly the reverse. In the graves of the Parakas people of Peru many skulls have been found which were so distorted that they formed tall, narrow domes (Fig. 48).

Among artificially deformed heads, those of the Negro tribes of Nigeria in Africa are most remarkable. By binding ligatures about the foreheads of their infants

BEAUTY IS SKIN DEEP

they produce heads which bulge out and might well belong to inhabitants of some other planet (Fig. 49).

Even after the head has been distorted; when every available portion of the anatomy has been bedecked with

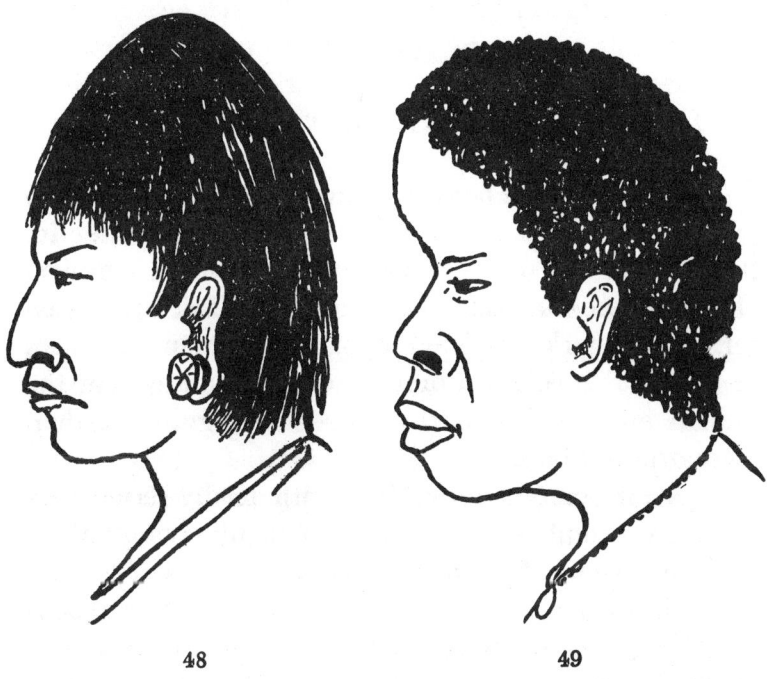

rings, chains, wires, earplugs, labrets, or nose ornaments; when the hair has been fearfully and wonderfully arranged and an amazing headdress has been added—still the mania of man for beautifying himself is not satisfied. There is still a considerable area of bare skin to be adorned, and this is where painting and tattooing come into play. So wonderful and so widespread are these customs that another chapter has been devoted to them.

Chapter III

TATTOOS AND TABOOS

TATTOOING of the body by man is a custom which by no means was established for decorative purposes alone. Its background and use over the years is far more complex. Behind these curious, sometimes beautiful, and often terrifying marks inflicted upon the human skin, lies history that involves a number of other motives of the human mind and soul that are more significant than mere ornamentation.

That tattooing is indulged in with deadly seriousness by many primitive peoples goes without saying. Why otherwise would they endure the forms of self-torture involved in this weird art? Both tattooing and taboos are closely tied up with self-torture in one form or another. For that matter, many other seemingly unreasonable customs of human beings, including some even of modern man today, involve certain phases of self-torture, as will be mentioned later in this chapter.

Tattooing, as it is done today with electric needles and other up-to-date appliances, is not a particularly painful process; but primitive tattooing, by means of sharpened bones or bits of sharp stone, or by thorns or fish spines, is exceedingly painful. So when we see South Sea

TATTOOS AND TABOOS

natives covered from head to foot with tattooed designs, we may rest assured that the proud possessors underwent hours and days of intense agony while the patterns were pricked into their skins.

Polynesian tattooing expresses an appreciation of beauty early created among races which had no metals, no clay, no cotton or silk, and who possessed only very primitive tools. Tattooing among them also displays endurance of pain, is a mark of personal worth, and proves quality of manhood.

In Samoa, tattooing is the crucial moment in a man's life, when he wins community esteem. The tattooer's art is accorded deep respect and the tattooer himself holds an enviable position in the tribe, next in importance to that of the chief himself. After each tattooing the artist is ceremoniously fêted with food and drink and gifts.

More painful even than tattooing is another primitive kind of skin decorating called cicatrization, which means the raising of a scar by means of a wound. This beautifying consists of cutting deep gashes in the skin and then keeping the wounds open for a considerable time, thus producing eruptive scars. These cuts often are arranged in beautiful decorative patterns.

Many of the natives of the Pacific Islands, Africa, South America, Malaysia, and other parts of the world follow this custom. One sometimes sees a native with his body almost completely covered with such scars or cicatrices. Sometimes these are open cuts which are made more conspicuous by filling them with colored earth or clay. Sometimes they are raised ridges which are produced by sewing the edges of the wounds tightly together over a cord, a piece of hide, or other object, and then allowing them to heal (Fig. 50).

It is difficult to say which tribe or race of the earth is the most addicted to cicatrization. After all, it is a crude form of tattooing. Some of the aborigines of Aus-

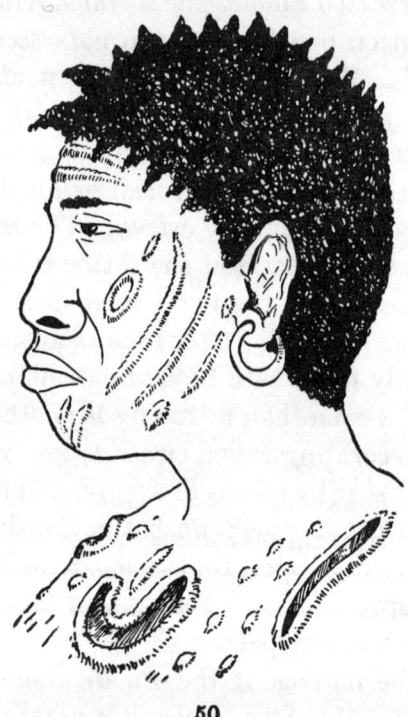

50

tralia, from the civilized viewpoint, are terribly disfigured by these supposedly beautiful, decorative cicatrices. Many of the African Negroes display wonderful examples of the art, if art it may be called. Their artistic patterns of scars are original, arresting, and sometimes almost awesome.

TATTOOS AND TABOOS 53

Cicatrizing is common more or less over all of West Central Africa. Some of the patterns are so elaborate that a great deal of suffering is undergone by the individual over a long period of time before they are completed.

In the Congo regions of West Africa many of the women use large shell patterns on the lower part of the torso, with somewhat smaller markings on the face. But there are others who are lavishly cicatrized not only with the shell patterns but with intricate markings that resemble many strings of beads or that are carried out in an elaborate herringbone pattern.

Sometimes these markings cover all of the body. There is no question but that the greater the ornamentation, the more popular the beau or the belle and the more desirable for marriage. Cicatrization is of course becoming a thing of the past, as the white man continues to import to these tribes gaudy, cheap clothing and tinsel trinkets to take its place. But it is still common enough to have astonished thousands of servicemen who visited various distant parts of the globe during the Second World War.

I do not think there are any people who bear more cicatrices or larger ones than the Bush Negroes, or Djukas, of Dutch Guiana in South America. Among the magnificently built males of these tribes it is impossible to find an adult whose torso, and often his limbs as well, do not bear numerous great welts and deeply incised scars. Often these are of contrasting colors and are arranged in a definite order, so that the skin has the effect of having been elaborately painted. Even the women bear similar scars, which sometimes cover the shoulders and breasts in raised welts, or in other cases are arranged in such a way that at first sight they might be mistaken for necklaces of colored beads.

Although these cicatrized Bush Negroes dwell side by side with the Guiana Indians, the Indians have never adopted the African type of incisions, but prefer true tattooing.

The design which they wear may be purely decorative. Then again, the tattooing of these Guiana Indians may be tribal marks. Sometimes these marks on the Indian's body tell a brief story of certain valiant deeds he has performed, and he carries them proudly, much like medals of honor.

It is safe to say that the happy possessor of these indelible records of courage does not realize that tattooing had its origin in the same purpose thousands of years ago.

But how, one may well ask, did such a custom as scar-decoration originate?

Probably, in the first place, it was an accident. Some ape man or Stone Age man may have been badly mauled by a cave bear, a saber-toothed tiger, or some other wild beast, or perhaps painfully cut by a jagged flint knife wielded by some caveman enemy. To prove his bravery and his superiority to his fellows and his womenfolk, he may well have laughed at the injuries, endured the pain without a moan, and chanted a savage song, while the others looked on in wonder and admiration.

What followed was natural, the result of human pride and ambition. The injured man knew that if the wounds

TATTOOS AND TABOOS

healed without leaving prominent scars, his bravery would be soon forgotten, and he would have no tangible proofs to remind his tribe members that he had suffered stoically. So, to keep ever alive the memory of his bravery and his exploit, he kept the wounds open long enough to leave conspicuous scars upon his person.

In other words, the evidences of what he had suffered and of his battle with a wild beast or a human foe, were, to all intents and purposes, badges of courage. And was it not natural that on gala occasions, at tribal dances, and when going forth to battle with an enemy, he should render his scar badges more conspicuous by filling the gashes with colored clay?

Of course, there would be more than one man who had received bad tears and cuts in hunting or in war. After one man had set the example of perpetuating prowess and bravery by producing indelible scars, the others would quickly imitate him. But there would also be many who returned from hunts and fights unscathed and who naturally felt envious of the other fellows with their scar-tissue medals. So, to prove themselves equally valorous, they deliberately tortured themselves by slashing their tough hides and producing scars equal to those of their fellow tribesmen. Then other clans and tribes would adopt the custom and it became a regular matter for the men artificially to produce magnificent scars upon themselves.

Since primitive man is always seeking new forms of self-adornment, before very long some savage with an inventive mind and an aesthetic sense would conceive the idea of producing fancy designs and patterns with the scars. However, tribal jealousy was strong. It would never do to allow an enemy to wear the same scars as the fellow members of one's tribe. For that reason, scars of a special arrangement or form became tribal marks.

From patterned scars to tattooing was a very short step. Even the best of raised welts and incisions do not lend themselves to finely carried out designs; so punctures, short cuts, and pricks supplanted the larger, coarser gashes.

That tattooing is a very ancient custom is proved by the fact that it is, or was, in almost universal use in all parts of the world by nearly all races. Many of the mummies from graves thousands of years old in Peru still bear elaborately tattooed designs upon the shriveled skin of faces and limbs. Also, the art has been so long in vogue that each race or tribe addicted to tattooing has developed its own technique and style.

Even if we consider it a barbarous custom, we must admit that some tattooing is a true work of art and very beautiful. Among many of the natives of the Pacific Islands tattooing reached a very high stage. Although each tribe or each island has its distinctive designs, yet all are similar in the lacelike complex patterns and delicate tracery of fine lines.

Very different from that of others is the tattooing of the Maoris of New Zealand, who employ fairly heavy lines in the form of curves, scrolls and circles (Fig. 51). And here it is interesting to note that almost identical designs are used in tattooing by some of the Indian tribes of the headwaters of the Amazon. Moreover, both the Maoris and these Indians preserved the heads of the dead and decorated them by covering the faces with elaborate tattooing.

Curiously enough, the artistic body-scarifying done by South American descendants of imported Africans in

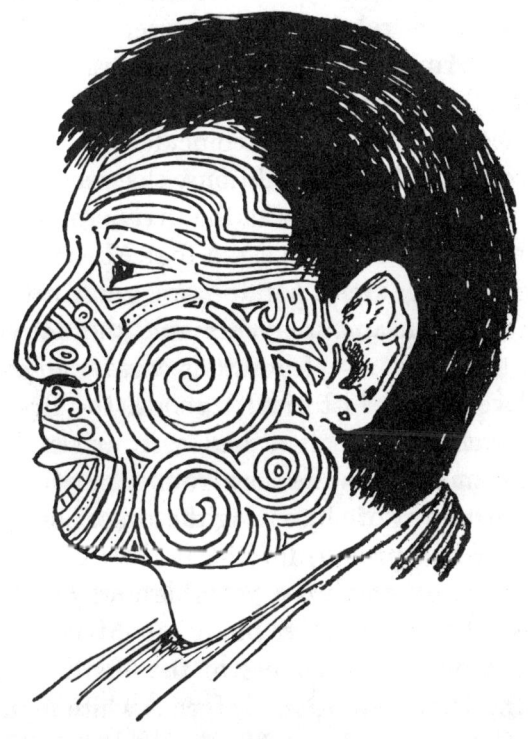
51

Guiana is very similar to that of the Maoris, who live around on the other side of the earth. The Maoris are a Polynesian people of New Zealand. Vigorous and athletic, tall in stature, they have handsome faces and are brave and warlike. Their elaborate tattooing is as famed as their wood carving and their poetic nature myths. Formerly cannibals, they are today civilized citizens of New Zealand.

That Maori cicatrices are like those of the Guiana Negroes may be merely a coincidence and may not be any evidence of relationship between the Maoris and the South American tribes. But, strangely enough, there are other matters which can scarcely be explained on the theory of chance and coincidence.

According to Maori traditions, the greatest event in the history of their race was the arrival of the *cumara,* or sweet potato. Whence came that Maori word?

In Peru, where sweet potatoes were cultivated by pre-Incan races thousands of years ago, the native Indian name of the "dry" sweet potato is *camot cumara.* If we can believe Maori historical legends, the first of their race to reach New Zealand had been driven for an immense distance across the seas from their original home, and had sustained life by eating the sweet potatoes which their leader had provided.

Of course, all this may be fable and nothing more. But if so, how can we explain the Maori use of the Peruvian word and their use of the identical sweet potato of the Peruvians, ages before a white man set foot on New Zealand's shores? We feel at liberty to imagine an ancient tribal connection in their identical forms of body decorations.

To return to the subject of tattooing. Just as some races adhered to the more primitive, cruder welts and cicatrices, while others abandoned decorative scars in favor of the more artistic and less painful tattooing, so certain other peoples gradually supplanted tattooing by using painted designs.

Tattooing was indelible, it could not be changed at the whim of the wearer or to suit various ceremonies and conditions. Painting, however, could be put on and taken off again. Among many races only the eldest members are ornamented with tattooed designs, the others contenting themselves with painting. In most cases, the painted designs are very similar to those which were formerly tattooed. Since the same colors are used, it is often impossible to say whether a man or woman is

52

tattooed or painted, unless one examines the designs closely.

Many of the tattoo markings have a special significance or meaning. Since it is rather difficult to copy these over and over again by painting, many races conceived the idea of duplicating designs by means of stamping. The ancient Mayas, Aztecs, Incans, pre-Incans and other early tribes as well as some that are living today have made stamps out of pottery clay. Sometimes these were designed to be pressed against the skin, in the same way as a modern rubber stamp would be. Others were made in the form of engraved cylinders which could be rolled over the skin. In fact, these were the original cylinder printing presses (Fig. 52).

Other races cut their stamps from wood. The Guaymi

53

Indians of Panama use a great number of arbitrary designs for facial painting, each design having a definite meaning. Thus there is the tribal mark, the individual name mark, the mark denoting the rank of the wearer, marks showing whether a man or woman is married or

TATTOOS AND TABOOS

single, and marks indicating the ceremony in which he is about to take part, or the purpose of a journey, a visit, or a mission.

As these must be very accurately made and must always be exactly the same, the Guaymis use small wooden stamps. While among the Guaymis, I collected more than one hundred different types of painting stamps, yet a great many more are in use by this tribe (Fig. 53).

Many races and tribes that adopted facial painting to supplant the older tattooing still retain certain tattooed designs which had long held distinct significance. Among Hindus and other Orientals tattooed caste marks are very widely used. Many races wear their clan or tribal marks tattooed upon their skins as distinguishing marks; while others have faith in certain tattooed markings as charms to ward off evil or sickness. The Arabs, Syrians, Armenians, and others, as well as natives of Australia, Africa, Asia, and the New World are often protected by tattooed charms from mishaps they may encounter in life.

Tattoo charms or talismans are quite common, and sometimes they serve a double or triple purpose. Here is one example: Many tribes of Indians of northern South America (such as those in the Guianas) are much addicted to the use of a slightly alcoholic drink known as "paiwari." This favorite beverage of Guiana tribes is far from delicious in appearance, resembling weak coffee and milk with numerous black particles of scorched cassava bread floating in it. Its taste may best be compared to a mixture of vinegar, stale beer, and yeast.

If a stranger becomes familiar with the manner in

which it is prepared, considerable moral, mental, and gastronomical courage is required for him to drink it. The method of making paiwari leaves much to be desired. It is made by scorching bread or meal made from the cassava plant, which is then chewed by the women and expectorated into a wooden trough, where it is left to ferment.

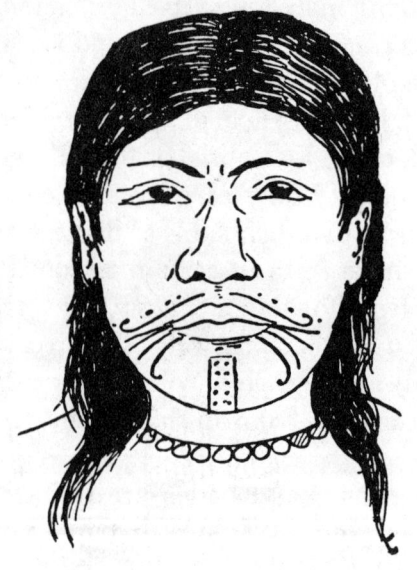

54

Unappetizing as the process appears, yet it is not quite so bad as might be imagined. The women selected to masticate the cassava are, in a way, professionals, and are distinguished by tattooed paiwari "beena," or drink-charm marks, about their lips (Fig. 54). These marks not only identify the women as paiwari makers, but guarantee their health and cleanliness and at the same time are supposed to prevent evil spirits from entering the cassava flour as the women masticate it.

Among North American Indians tattooing was far more prevalent than is generally supposed. When Eu-

55

ropeans first reached Florida and Virginia, they found the Indians elaborately tattooed. This was particularly the case with the Florida Indians, who went about almost nude, but whose nakedness was scarcely noticeable because of the tattooed designs which almost covered their bodies and limbs (Fig. 55).

Many of the North American Iroquois Indians were tattooed. The designs were pricked in colors upon their skins and were tribal or clan marks. This custom was also quite prevalent among the tribes of New England.

The North American Indians, however, much preferred painting as a means of personal adornment and for ceremonial purposes. Each dance or ceremony called for certain colors and designs painted upon the skins of the participants. Each man's part in the ceremony or dance was indicated by the painting he wore.

The meanings of the so-called "war paint" were various, however. Although most persons think that Indians donned war paint in order to make themselves hideous and to terrify their foes, this was not at all its original purpose. War paint, as used by the majority of North American Indians, was a form of camouflage. A warrior who was painted with stripes and spots in various colors easily blended with the lights and shadows of brush, weeds, and trees. A painted torso was far less conspicuous than a naked bronzed body. In other words, the Indians followed the example set by Nature when she gave the tiger its stripes, the leopard its spots, and the fawn a white-spotted coat.

The Indian brave, painted to protect himself from enemies and to enable him to approach his foes unseen, appeared frightful or hideous, but it was not intentional on his part. No doubt a naked Indian, painted half green and half black and daubed with red and white, or with yellow patches and stripes, would present a terrifying appearance to his white enemies, even if his war paint had been donned with the original purpose of self-protection and concealment.

The Uapes Indians, who live along the Uapes river in the Amazon Basin, use tattooing very little. Most of them, however, have a row of circular punctures along the arm, and the members of one Amazon tribe, the Tucanos, have three vertical blue lines on the chin. The Tucanos also hang three little threads of white beads through holes in the lower lips. Most of the Uapes bore their ears, the hole serving as a handy place in which to carry little ornamented tufts of grass to which are attached small waving feathers.

Perhaps the most perfectly tattooed nation in South America comprises the very warlike Indians of the Amazon region who are called the Mundrucus. Their tattoo markings cover the complete body. The skin is pricked with the spines of a certain palm, after which soot from burning pitch is rubbed in. The result is an indelible blue color.

Frequently, an Indian's tattooing or painting is a form of "medicine." In other words, it constitutes a powerful charm or fetish, certain colors or designs presumably having magical power. Some are supposed to be pleasing to the good spirits, others are supposed to ward off devils or evil spirits, while still others are believed to make the wearer invisible and to insure his success in securing game or destroying an enemy.

Probably no other race on earth has had more implicit faith in medicine than the Indians, and "medicine painting" as well as "medicine tattooing" has been very prevalent among them. Even today many of the jungle tribes of South America wear tattooed charms. Among these are the peculiar moustachelike designs tattooed upon the upper lip of the Carib Indian (Fig. 56).

If people believe in good charms they will, of course, believe in "spells," the "evil eye," and other harmful

56

magic. They mentally argue, unless "bad medicine" also exists, how can "good medicine" help one? This is excellent logic, even if based on false premises. In it lies the basis of the fetishes, proxies, medicines, effigies, and other magic and taboos of primitive peoples.

Taboos undoubtedly had their beginnings in connection with tortures, and especially self-inflicted tortures. Probably—in fact, almost certainly—some of the first taboos were instituted in connection with the honor gashes and cicatrices of ancient man. There was no distinction to be won by displaying an accidental or a purposely inflicted scar upon one's person, if every Tom, Dick, and Harry had similar wounds. Therefore, the individual prognathic caveman declared it dangerous for anyone else to duplicate his own particular scars, upon which he therefore placed a taboo.

If he was the most powerful fellow or the best fighter of the tribe, his commands were doubtless obeyed; but if some better man should disobey and call the other's bluff, the taboo would have been off. To offset this possibility some clever chap who lacked brawn evidently thought of enforcing his own special taboos by the aid of magic, or spirits. He announced that evil would befall any and all who did not respect his taboos—and the game was on.

In time, the system of taboo grew and was extended to innumerable matters and for countless reasons, as well as for no reason at all. Without doubt, after tattooing became popular, there were many followers of the custom who took it up solely to avoid appearing conspicuous by its absence. "Keeping up with the Joneses" is by no means a recently developed human weakness.

Very largely, taboos were and still are employed mainly by medicine men or witch doctors. These men are believed to possess magical powers which can make a taboo efficacious where mere brute strength might fail.

If for any purpose, whether personal or otherwise, primitive man wishes to prevent his fellows from doing something, going somewhere, performing some deed, or following out any objectionable idea or project, a taboo puts a quick stop to it. The taboo may be a very real and tangible thing—a war, a fight, or an artfully administered poison for the one who disregards the taboo. But usually it is something which to the primitive mind is far worse—some vague, unknown penalty of a supernatural character.

It is a poor rule that does not work both ways, so the witch doctor or other individual who wishes to get something done, again employs the taboo as a threat of what may happen if a certain act is not accomplished. The more mysterious a taboo is, the more potent it must be, hence it is rarely anything concrete, but so intangible and indefinite that even the tabooer himself could not explain it. As a result, any ill luck or misfortune, whether quite natural or not, which may follow the breaking of a taboo can easily be attributed to its violation.

A taboo, however, may be wholly symbolic. Oftentimes a rudely formed or repulsive image supposed to represent a demon or evil spirit will indicate a taboo. It may even be a stick, a bit of rag, a few feathers, a piece of string, or a daub of paint.

In the jungles of South America I discovered that an open camera was a most effective taboo to use for my own protection. The staring, unwinking eye of the lens peering from the mysterious black box, and also that mysterious click impressed the Indians with great fear and respect. Merely by placing my camera in plain view, I could leave camp and be absent for days, quite confident that my taboo would prevent any curious aborigine from meddling with my possessions.

Among various tribes of South and Central America as well as in the Pacific Islands and in Africa I have often seen valiant warriors turn back with fear on their faces when they found a slender string stretched across the trail leading to a house or a village. But in the majority of cases the taboo consists of spoken words or threats or a magical incantation. Yet a taboo may persist indefinitely and be meticulously observed years—ages in fact—after it was first decreed. In a great many cases the original purpose or object of the taboo will have been completely forgotten.

A stick with a split end and with a shorter stick placed crosswise in the slit is a most powerful taboo among primitive people. In the republic of Haiti in the West Indies even today civilized native farmers, walking along to market on a narrow mountain trail with heavy loads upon their heads, will detour into the prickly brush rather than step over or around two little sticks laid in the form of a cross in their path.

On one occasion, while travelling down a jungle river in South America, I noticed that my boatmen suddenly veered away from one shore and paddled to the other side of the stream. A mile or two farther on they worked back to the western side where there was less current. As far as I could see, there was no reason for this. It merely added to their labors, and there was certainly swifter water on the eastern side than there was on the western side of the river.

I asked their leader why the men had made the detour and was informed that this particular stretch of jungle-covered shore was *peai*—in other words, it was taboo.

He hadn't any idea why it was taboo, when it was declared taboo, or who had first originated the taboo. Yet nothing on earth would have induced him and his fellows to navigate the tabooed area, much less to set foot ashore at that spot.

The savage who does not dare venture within a certain area without wearing certain regalia or carrying certain charms or fetishes is not so different from the civilized man who would not dream of appearing at certain social functions unless attired in absolutely correct formal dress.

The savage who would not dream of using a certain color because it is taboo may be compared to the civilized man who would be horrified at the thought of appearing in brilliantly colored evening clothes.

Basically, a great part of modern life is governed by taboos. We cling to some of them with the greatest tenacity, even to the point of self-torture. Modern man's social fear of relinquishing the tight collar and tie, even in the most sweltering hot weather, is but one example of a modern taboo, the original purpose of which is undoubtedly unknown to most of the sufferers. Also, how about the taboo on oysters during all months of the year that do not have an "r" in them?

We uncover another modern taboo in the report of the United States Navy that only a small proportion of the women who joined the American armed services in the Second World War had normal feet. The physical torture of heels-too-high and lasts-too-narrow has been patiently endured by millions of women and girls as a sort of social taboo from which they cannot escape, even though it has deformed their feet.

Therefore, do not for a moment think that taboos are confined to primitive races. Civilized persons are not by any means free from superstitious fear, faith in charms, and taboos. How many men and women carry a lucky coin or a rabbit's foot? How many will knowingly walk under a ladder? Few are those who do not feel a slight sinking of the heart when they break a mirror.

We may pooh-pooh our superstitions and declare we have no faith in them, but I venture to say that there is not one person in hundreds who does not have his or her favorite ones. And when it comes to taboos, we have many of them. Broadly speaking, a taboo is merely a belief that a person must not do or say certain things or appear in certain places in certain garb or under certain conditions.

We may call our taboos "conventions, etiquette, customs," or what you will, but they are as much taboo as any superstition of a South Sea Island savage and usually have no more reason for their existence. It will perhaps take thousands of years of educating even to free the modern civilized man of his own peculiar taboos.

Chapter IV

STRANGE SUBSTITUTES

ONE of the strangest customs of many groups of people is the use of proxies, or substitutes. No one knows when or how man first put into practice the strange idea of using effigies, or images, to represent human beings and animals, but the custom is very ancient. It had been developed to a high degree in the days of the earliest Pharaohs in Egypt. In the ancient tombs of that country have been found many buried proxies.

These proxies are models, often beautifully made, of favorite wives, servants, slaves, animals, boats, utensils, and other objects. The ancient Egyptians believed that the spirit of the dead person would require in the next world many things of which its owner had been fond, while alive, or with which he had been closely associated in his daily life. The miniatures were provided in his grave to supply this need.

Originally, among some peoples, slaves, servants, wives, or domestic animals were buried alive with the master's body. Curiously enough, it is not on record that the poor human beings concerned made many or any objections to being thus horribly interred while still alive.

Later on, some brilliant genius must have conceived

STRANGE SUBSTITUTES 73

the idea that effigies might serve quite as well and at the same time be far less costly. Among the ancient pre-Incan Indians of South America, this inadvertently more humane custom was followed. Images, often very crude, of dogs, llamas, men, and women have been found in the tombs and graves beside the mummies of the masters. Sometimes even imitations of the food which it was supposed the spirit would require in the next world also have been supplied; but, as a rule, real food was easy to provide (Plate V, Fig. 57).

The use of proxies was not restricted to burials. Many races in many lands used images of human beings and of deities for a great variety of purposes. The Incan people buried in their fields little figures of Inti, their sun god and principal deity. The idea was that by so doing they would draw or attract some of the god's favor to his images, and he would then give the farmers large and bountiful crops (Plate V, Fig. 58).

The Incan Indians often buried another type of special charm or amulet in the field to insure good crops. These were little rectangles or squares of baked clay or of carved stone. Some of these can be seen in museums today. They bear symbolic designs representing such things as tilled fields, corn, potatoes, or human hands filled with crops. Even at the present time amulets like these are planted by the Peruvian Indians and some may be purchased in modern-day Peruvian Indian markets (Plate V, Fig. 58A).

At first thought this may seem a childish, ridiculous custom. Civilized Christians, however, follow out much the same custom by carrying a sacred image or medal on the person for protective purposes. In each case the proxy is more or less symbolic. About the only difference is that the more primitive people believe that these effigies are actually possessed by the spirits of what they represent. In the case of both primitive and modern man, however, a special type of blessing or spiritual power is believed to be carried in the images.

Many primitives who believe that a miniature image actually possesses certain powers have little religious respect for the proxies themselves. Among the Kuna Indians of Panama, very crudely made wooden effigies are very common and serve many purposes.

Upon one occasion I noticed a particularly large figure standing in a building where the tribe's corn was stored, the proxy serving as a guardian of the corn. While taking a photograph of the effigy, I noticed that a woodpecker had chipped out a hole in the back of the figure.

I called the attention of some of the Indians to it. Instantly the Kunas removed the proxy, angrily chopped off its nose, and otherwise mutilated it. Then, having suitably punished the image for being so inefficient, they erected a new and more perfect proxy in its place (Plate V, Fig. 59).

The Kunas include the so-called San Blas Indians of Panama. These belong to several sub-tribes and, with the true Kunas, constitute a confederacy. Among these Indians images play a very important part in the curing of sickness. Every medicine man or "doctor" has a supply of a little wooden figure called a *neli*, which is supposed to represent himself. When the medicine man

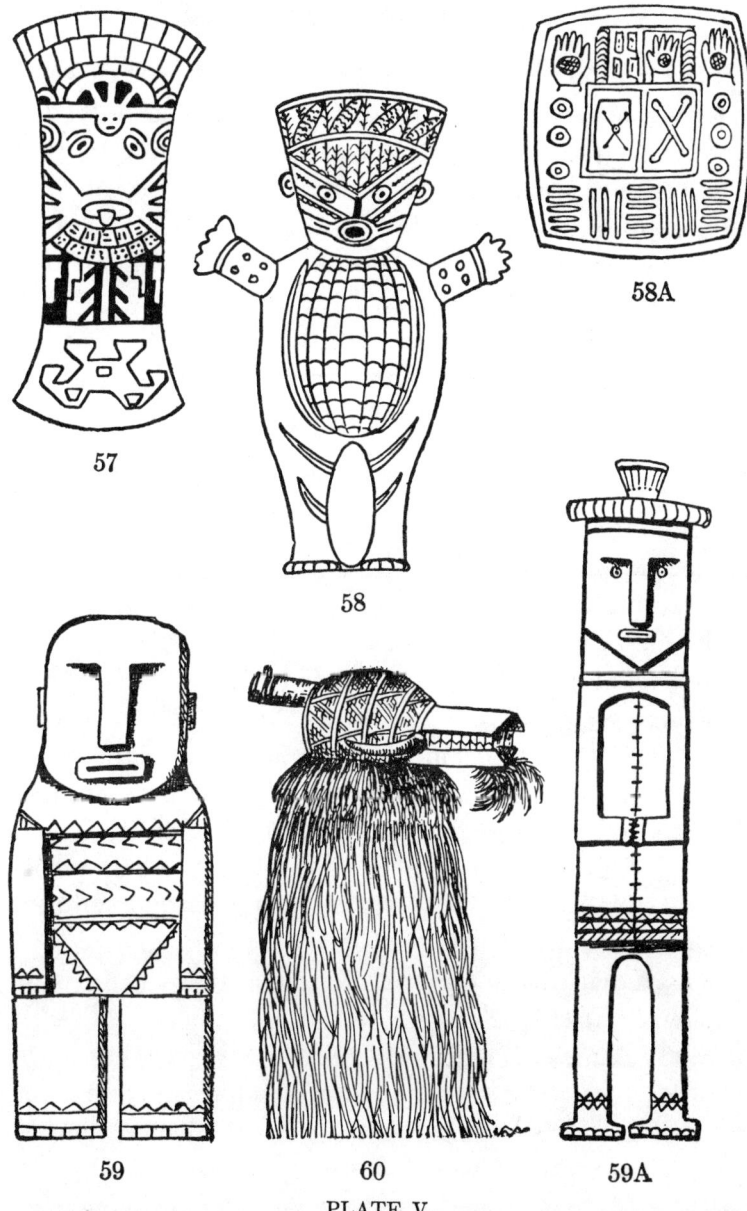

PLATE V

57 pre-Incan symbolic image 58 image of Inti, the Incan sun god 58A Peruvian amulet for insuring good crops 59 Kuna effigy 59A Guaymi wooden image 60 Fanti village fetish

STRANGE SUBSTITUTES 77

visits a sick or injured member of the tribe, he leaves a *neli* to look after the patient. If the man or woman shows no improvement, another *neli* is placed near. It is not unusual to see a sick Indian with a dozen or two of these small carved figures beneath his hammock, each personifying the medicine man.

But the Indian medico goes still further in his absent treatment. Having placed his own proxies beside the patient, he carries an image of the sick person to his own home. There he doctors the patient's proxy instead of the patient himself.

This method of exchanging proxies saves the medicine man a great deal of time and trouble and also relieves him of all responsibility. If the patient fails to recover, the Indians reason that the proxies were not up to their job. Perhaps if our medical practitioners would adopt this form of treatment, they might be able to reduce their fees! In many cases, no doubt, it would be just as efficacious as are some of the quack cures against which civilized persons must protect themselves at all times.

Probably no race on earth carries the use of proxies to such length as do the Guaymi Indians of Panama. When a Guaymi leaves his home unoccupied, he places a wooden image of himself at the doorway in full faith that no one can or will enter while he is away (Plate V, Fig. 59A). He also is convinced that should anyone by an extreme chance disregard the proxy and enter the house, he, the owner, will be aware of it and will see the trespasser through his proxy's eyes.

The most remarkable use of proxies by these Guaymi Indians is at their ceremonial dances. Within the dance house the men, savage-looking figures in closely packed rows, are seated at one side of the temple, smoking their ceremonial pipes. In the center is a fire of huge logs over which some of the women cook thick, unsweetened chocolate and tend immense pots of boiling rice.

Girls, moving silently about, serve the rice and chocolate to the men. On the opposite side of the temple the remaining women are seated with eyes fixed upon the floor and their long black hair falling over their faces.

Placed all about a sort of altar are small earthenware figures of birds, beasts, and reptiles. There are also a few figures of humans, some of them monsters that resemble ogres, or devils. Other pieces resembling miniature pots, dishes, and plates are placed near by or upon the altar.

The ceremony begins with a slow wailing chant, haunting and weird in tempo and melody, while the old dance chief takes his place beside the altar, devil-stick in hand. Then, in perfect rhythm, the Indian men dance and stamp all around the altar. Every now and then one of the dancers shouts the name of some bird, beast, person, or spirit. Leaping aside from the line of dancers, he seizes a handful of food from the altar, thrusts some into his mouth, drops some into one of the tiny clay dishes, and tosses the remainder into the fire.

The dance chief then picks up the image of the being or creature whose name has been called, together with the dish of food, and breaking them into bits, casts them into the flames.

Here we have the strange custom of a proxy for a proxy. The clay figures represent persons who cannot

STRANGE SUBSTITUTES

attend the ceremony, owing to illness or some other cause. They also represent animals which are either sacred to the tribe as a whole or are the clan animals of individuals. The Indians believe that even if not present in person, the absentees will be present in spirit through the medium of their proxies.

Since a clay proxy cannot partake of ceremonial food and drink, even if it does house the spirit of the original, certain Indians, delegated by the dance chief, act as "proxies for the proxies" by calling the names of the proxies and swallowing the food and drink which have been prepared for them.

Thus, an Indian may possibly say to himself: "My friend Totu is not here; therefore my spirit shall enter the clay figure that represents him. I shall eat for him, drink for him, dance for him, and attend these ceremonies for him."

In order that devils may not take possession of the originals through the medium of the clay proxies, the images are burned after being broken to release the spirits of the originals.

Although these Guaymi images, as well as those of other races, are well made and are excellent representations of the originals, yet some other races seem to feel that anything will serve as a proxy so long as it is addressed by the original's name. Sticks, lumps of mud or clay, feathers, stones, or other small objects may be used as proxies. The Huichol Indians of Mexico employ pebbles as proxies for animals they kill. Placing these upon the ground, they make symbolic offerings to them to appease the spirits of the slain creatures.

A similar use of proxies is in vogue among the Mapuche Indians of the Andean regions of Chile. These people regard the puma, a large, catlike animal, as a semihuman creature inhabited by an evil spirit. Hence, when a Mapuche has killed one of these animals, he uses a small stick or a pebble as a proxy for himself. He coaxes the evil spirit of the puma to enter the stick or stone, which is then broken or burned, thus obviating any chance of the beast's "devil" taking possession of the hunter.

All of the proxies mentioned are employed for the purpose of benefiting the beings they represent; but there is a different class of proxies which are designed and used to harm or to destroy the original.

Just how man happened to think of bringing pain or disaster upon an enemy by the indirect method of using proxies is uncertain. Probably some weakling who dared not attempt physical violence upon a foe vented his anger by breaking or otherwise injuring a crudely made figure or drawing of his enemy. Then, by chance or coincidence, the subject of his wrath probably fell ill or met with some accident or misfortune. Thus the power of revenge by proxy would have been firmly established in the mind of that primitive man.

On the other hand, it may have been the result of simple logic. The savages may have reasoned: "If we can use images of gods and people to get good things to transpire, then maybe we also can use others which will harm our enemies!"

Regardless of how the custom originated, it opened up a wonderful new phase of life. Instead of lying in

STRANGE SUBSTITUTES 81

wait for some enemy or raiding his camp and banging him over the head with a stone axe—with the chance of being smartly banged in return—it was much safer and easier to make a little image of one's foe and batter its unresisting head. It was much simpler to model or carve a figure and gash it with a flint knife or otherwise maltreat it, than to do the same to a flesh-and-blood foe.

Once initiated, the custom spread far and wide until there was scarcely a race anywhere that did not follow the practice. Many still do. In scattered backwoods sections of the United States there are individual, so-called civilized persons who secretly make a doll figure of an enemy or a person they fear. They stab it with pins, forks, or knives, and then sit back and wait for harm to come to that individual. In the natural course of life, some illness or misfortune is bound to come in due time to the individual in question. This gives the secret doll-maker great satisfaction and encourages a firm belief in the power of the little figurines. In certain parts of Pennsylvania, for example, placing a curse upon a person in this manner is called "hexing."

Spells put upon the proxy are believed to react upon the original of the image. An enemy thus could be made to suffer physical pain, to have bad luck, to be afflicted with sickness, or even to die, because of tortures given his proxy. The image may be broken or otherwise destroyed in order to bring death to the one it represents. It may be mutilated with the expectation of inflicting similar injuries upon the original, or it may be stuck full of thorns or pins to cause the original intense pain or other bad luck.

As these proxies are made for the sole purpose of being injured or destroyed, very little care is bestowed upon their design or their making. In the case of a savage, he probably reasons that the more grotesque and imperfect such a proxy is, the more harm will be done the person it is supposed to represent. Very often such an effigy is a shapeless lump of clay or mud, or a stick. Sometimes it is merely a roughly drawn figure traced upon sand, stone, or some other surface. Neither its material nor its shape matters much. It is enough if the figure or object represents a certain person and is addressed by the name of the one to be injured.

We may laugh at such a preposterous belief, but whether ridiculous or not, it is certain that the curse very often fulfills its purpose, especially if the victim is aware that a curse has been laid upon him. Naturally, the object of the evil curse is not actually harmed by having his image pierced by thorns or otherwise mutilated. But if he himself believes in such things, his faith may, and often does, result in his mind producing the desired effect. It is, in a way, a form of indirect autosuggestion. Even if the human mind is incapable of producing actual physical injuries such as gashes, punctures, or broken bones, it is still capable of producing illness and even death by mental suggestion.

As I have already indicated, this means of bringing disaster upon an enemy by proxy is by no means restricted to pagan savages. Although more widely used by so-called savage races than by others, yet it is employed by many supposedly civilized or modern people. It is very prevalent among the Gypsies. It is in use by

STRANGE SUBSTITUTES 83

some Italians and Spaniards. It is not unusual in Ireland, and it is an everyday means of "getting even" with an enemy in some portions of Scotland.

This custom may sound very silly to us, very heathenish and superstitious, but consider the mobs of so-called civilized persons which sometimes find intense satisfaction in hanging men in effigy or in seeing them "roast" in cartoons. These, after all, are mild forms of the same practice, even if the perpetrators lack the belief that the originals actually will be harmed.

Indirectly, the proxy idea was one of the most beneficial inventions of mankind. The naked caveman who first evolved the scheme should be honored as a real benefactor of humanity, for the idea of using an image instead of a human being was a great factor in abolishing tortures and human sacrifices. Instead of inflicting pain upon a living man or woman, the savages hit upon the idea of inflicting the tortures upon an effigy. Instead of slaughtering one's own children or one's fellows as sacrifices to the gods, proxies were used.

No doubt the first human beings to try this experiment did so with fear and trembling, not feeling at all certain that the deities would accept a substitute. But when there was no sign of the gods' anger at being served a proxy in place of the real thing, the custom became firmly established among many tribes.

Today, proxies are used by the followers of voodoo and other cults in Africa and in some West Indian islands, notably in Haiti. Voodoo worship requires the sacrifice of the "goat without horns," which means a human being; but very seldom is this demand followed out to the letter. The worshippers follow the customary rites and ceremonies attendant upon human sacrifice, even to placing the selected victim upon the altar; but at the appropriate moment the human offering is whisked out of sight and a genuine goat without horns is sacrificed in its place.

In the Biblical story of Abraham we find an account of a similar procedure. Abraham, about to sacrifice his son, used an animal instead. We must not forget that when devout Christians light candles before the altar of a church, they are carrying out the symbol of making a burnt offering by using a proxy in the form of a candle. The bread and the wine, sacred to the communion services of Christian churches, are symbols of the greatest Sacrifice of all.

Thus, down the dim and distant years man has legitimately inherited from his forebears the sign, the image, and the proxy. He has put them to strange or wonderful uses, according to his enlightenment and his real or imagined needs.

Chapter V

CHARMS FOR LUCK

When a civilized man carries a lucky coin, a rabbit's foot, or a four-leaf clover, he is following a very ancient custom common to a great many races. How many of us really believe that the bunny's foot, the worn money, or the pressed cloverleaf has any power to bring us good fortune or protect us from harm?

It doesn't seem to matter to a person, whether civilized or not, what the charm is. Very often there appears to be no reason why a certain object is considered a charm. For that matter, why should a rabbit's foot be any better than a cat's foot; or an old worn silver coin be superior to a newly minted one?

Many a hardheaded business man or matter-of-fact scientist would feel very much disturbed if he should lose his favorite talisman. Aviators, soldiers, and sailors have their various collective and individual signs and talismans. And there are countless other persons who carry such charms and actually have faith in them, although many may hesitate to admit it. Primitive man, however, not only has implicit faith in charms but is not at all ashamed to admit the belief. Frequently some peculiarity of a common everyday object may cause a primitive man to regard it as a charm. A stone, a stick, or even a plant that is of unusual appearance may be carefully treasured as a most potent talisman, even as civilized persons treasure a four-leaf clover.

In many parts of the world the fossil remains of living creatures are looked upon as charms. They are unlike anything with which the people are familiar, and hence they are regarded as being supernatural in origin. The Western Indians of North America consider the fossil mollusks known to scientists as belemnites as very powerful "medicine." The Indians call these fossils "thunder stones," for they believe the conical objects fall from the sky during thunderstorms.

There is some excuse for attributing celestial origin to such objects, but there would appear to be no reason on earth why anyone should believe that ancient stone axes and clubs have dropped from the sky. Yet this is a widely spread and almost universal belief among many races. In the West Indies some colored folk cannot be convinced that the stone implements they find are not produced by lightning, and they prize the "thunder stones" accordingly. Some tribes of Indians, whose ancestors made stone weapons, have the same belief.

At one time when I was in the northern part of South America, I saw some fine stone implements, or celts, in the hut of an Arowak Indian. I tried to buy or trade for them, but the owner absolutely refused to part with the celts, declaring they had fallen from the sky and possessed supernatural powers. He even assured me that he actually had seen the stones strike the earth during a heavy shower. Of course that was pure imagination, although he doubtless did find the ancient implements soon

CHARMS FOR LUCK

after a thunder shower which had washed away the earth and exposed them to view.

Pretending to share his belief in the occult powers of the stones, I asked him if he did not know that thunder stones would draw lightning. I added that if he kept them in his house it might be struck and burned. For a few moments he gave this phase of the matter deep thought. Then he wanted to know why I wished the stones, since they were likely to attract lightning to my home.

"I live in a stone house," I told him, "so I will be perfectly safe."

That was enough. Hastily gathering up the implements, he threw them out and informed me that if I desired such dangerous things, I was quite welcome to take them.

The North American Plains Indians did not consider the stone implements of their grandsires as anything other than what they are, but they used to place great faith in "buffalo stones," or fossil mollusks. They believed that these would lure or call the buffalo during the hunt. They carried these stones in highly decorated skin covers which were provided with a hole so that the stone could "look out." Most Indians of the present generation, of course, have been educated in schools and colleges and are aware of the true character and origin of such fossils.

These fossils were distinctly hunting charms, for the early Indians, like most primitive races, believed in carrying certain charms to insure success in battle, charms to safeguard the owner from harm, charms for hunting various kinds of game, and charms for many other purposes. Very often an assortment of charms was kept together in a "medicine bundle." The faith of the Indians in such talismans was profoundly rooted.

Among other charms the North American Plains tribes had medicine shields—tiny, useless, highly ornamented affairs which the Indians believed rendered their owners both invulnerable and invisible. If an Indian carrying one of these shields was wounded or killed, it did not in the least shake the tribal faith in the charm. Instead of questioning the power of the magic shield, the Indians blamed its maker. They were convinced that the shield had failed in its purpose because some rite had been bungled or some "medicine" had been omitted while the shield was being prepared.

Some South American tribes believe that capes or mantles made of the black feathers of certain birds render the wearer invisible. If, when wearing such a cape of darkness, an Indian is seen and recognized, it does not alter his belief in the least. He feels sure that the person who saw him possessed some charm which gave him the power to see things invisible to others.

Among the Amazon and Rio Negro jungle tribes of South America, charms, or beenas, play an important part in the lives of the Indians. Like their North American cousins, they have a beena for nearly every purpose. No self-respecting jungle Indian will undertake anything of importance without making use of a beena to insure success or safety.

These are, usually, the leaves of certain plants of the caladium or "elephant-ears" family, the particular

CHARMS FOR LUCK 89

species to be used depending upon the purpose in view. Thus, if the Indian is starting on a hunt for deer, he will use a variegated leaf; and if he wishes to kill a tapir, he searches for a leaf with white spots.

Having secured the proper leaf for the charm, he scratches or cuts his wrists and rubs the leaf into the wounds. The juice of the plant is acrid and causes sharp pain, but to the Indian mind this signifies that the beena is powerful.

Another potent charm used by these Indians is a dead toad, whose mucus is rubbed into the lacerations. For certain dangerous undertakings the Indian burns a frog in the fire and swallows some of the charred remains. He also rubs some of the frog's ashes into scarifications in his body or limbs.

The most powerful and potent of all beenas are the ant beena, the centipede beena, and the nose beena, for the jungle Indian believes that the power of a charm depends largely upon the amount of pain he suffers by its application. The ant and centipede beenas consist of light grids or frameworks of palm leaf. Savage warrior ants or centipedes are placed in the grid, their heads protruding from one side. These are then pressed firmly against the Indian's body and limbs.

The nose beena is an even more agonizing device. It consists of a long, fine braid of palm fibres tapering from a point at one end to a large tuft or tassel at the other. A bit of sticky wax is pressed upon the pointed extremity and a biting ant is affixed to this. The Indian then inserts the captive ant in his nostril and pushes the affair into his nose. Biting fiercely as it goes, the ant crawls through the nasal passage until it emerges in the mouth. The Indian then grasps the tip and draws the entire thing through his nose and out of his mouth.

He suffers greatly, of course; but he shows no sign of suffering, for he feels certain that so much pain proves the charm most potent. Incidentally, his stoic endurance also proves his own valor.

Oddly enough, an Indian who neglects to use a beena before starting on a hunt is rarely successful, whereas if he employs the charm, he is almost certain to bring back game. Not, of course, because the beena possesses any occult power; but because, having used the charm, the Indian has far greater initiative. He feels elated, strong, and certain of success. If he has failed to invoke the aid of a charm, he has no faith in his own ability, hangs back, and is beaten at the start by lack of self-confidence.

These Indian braves possess many other charms for more ordinary purposes. There are the little good-luck bundles, or packages, for example, containing bits of hair, fingernail parings, bones, teeth, certain seeds and dried flowers, bulbs, and other miscellaneous objects.

The women also have their personal charm-bags. No man is permitted to see or touch them, and no woman is permitted to gaze upon the objects which a man carries around as luck providers. In fact, among some tribes a hunting beena is regarded as absolutely ruined if so much as the shadow of a woman falls upon it.

Among many African and Pacific Island natives almost any strange or unusual object is regarded as a charm or talisman. Old cartridge shells, small china

CHARMS FOR LUCK

dolls, mirrors, peculiarly shaped pebbles, the knuckle joints of animals, certain plumes or feathers, skins of night-prowling animals, dried bats and frogs, snakes— almost anything may become a potent charm in the imagination of these savages.

I once stayed for a while among some remote tribes of Guiana, in South America. These Indians regarded my pocket electric torch as a most powerful charm. One chief was so obsessed with the desire to own the white man's shining beena that when I was preparing to leave his village, I presented him with the coveted torch. No doubt he gained tremendously in tribal prestige through being the possessor of such a wonderful talisman.

I have often wondered what happened when, in due course of time, the batteries were exhausted, and the magic eye ceased to shine at the will of the chief. Probably he merely sighed and threw it away.

Another chief whom I met cherished a broken alarm clock as a most potent charm and never ventured away from his village without it. A Carib chief, who became my blood brother, regarded a Turkish bath towel which I gave him as a marvellous charm. He was never parted from it for a moment.

In Dutch Guiana (Surinam) one may sometimes see a gigantic bush Negro, or Djuka, carrying a lantern in one hand and a lady's handbag in the other. Not that he ever uses either object; but since white men always carry lanterns when in the bush, and as white women carry handbags, the Djuka reasons that lantern and handbag must be charms, or talismans; and so he acquires them if possible.

The medicine bundles of the Western Indians of North America may contain real charms, as well as being true fetishes in themselves. There is a distinction in the meanings of the words "charm" and "fetish." A charm is an object which has magic powers. A fetish is an inanimate object of actual worship.

Among African tribes a stick, a stone, or other object may be both a charm and a fetish or only a fetish. But as a general rule the fetishes of the Negro tribes as well as those of the South Sea Islanders are idol-like figures of animals, birds, or semihuman monsters. These may be personal fetishes, which occupy a prominent place in the hut of the owner, or they may be tribal, affecting the whole community.

Among the Fanti tribes of Africa every village has its fetish consisting of a weird figure with a grotesque wooden head, long jaws fitted with savage teeth, decorations of feathers, and draped in a voluminous mantle or skirt of palm leaves or shredded bark.

Very frequently the tribal fetish or personal fetish may be intended to represent the spirit which is connected with it. But just as often it represents some animate thing, such as a fish, bird, or quadruped, especially when it is supposed to bring success to hunters or fishermen (Plate V, Fig. 60). In fact, a preserved animal, a skull, or a skeleton may become a fetish. Many of the gruesome trophies of war which are collected by some savage tribes are regarded as fetishes.

Love charms are widely used among many primitive races, as well as among a number of civilized races. To attract love is one of the most common uses of old-

CHARMS FOR LUCK

fashioned charm objects. Sometimes love charms are merely scents or perfumes; at other times they are mysterious medicine bundles supplied to the individual by the tribal witch doctor or medicine man, and usually, of course, they are paid for in money or gifts. Very often they serve their purpose, too—since they are mentally suggestive to a high degree.

Among some of the South American Guiana tribes the young women employ the dried and pulverized flowers of a certain vine as a love charm. The belief is that if the charm is placed in a man's hammock or upon his person, he will either marry the girl who made use of the charm, or as a punishment for refusing her advances he will become insane. (As among civilized persons the "woman scorned" is deadly!) As a result, he nearly always does marry the scheming female. Being firmly convinced that he will go mad if he fails to respond to the charm, he chooses the lesser of the two evils.

Here let me say that whether or not one believes in the occult, in matters bordering upon the supernatural, or in spiritual manifestations and powers beyond our comprehension, some facts must be recognized. One cannot be long with primitive peoples without becoming aware that there are among them certain mysteries which cannot easily be explained. Strange, uncanny things do happen, seemingly without natural causes. Many of the Indian peai or medicine men seem to be gifted with weird powers. They are also expert hypnotists. But hypnotism alone will not explain some of the mysterious results of the medicine man's power among superstitious subjects. This is particularly true of the inexplicable happenings in daily life which in the West Indies are attributed by superstitious colored folk to the brand of African magic called "obeah."

Belief in obeah magic was brought along with the Negroes from Africa in the old slave days, and it persists. Obeah was once a religion, and it was widely practiced among Negroes of the West Indies, the Guianas in South America, and the southeastern parts of the United States. The old obeah was characterized by sorcery and magic ritual which were sometimes attended by fatal results. Obeah doctors (men and women) were clever users of poisonous plants, ground glass, ground fibers, and the like; and they were past masters in instilling mortal fear in their followers.

Most obeah charms are supposed to insure good fortune or safety to the owners, but there are other charms which are intended to bring disaster or misfortune to one's enemies.

As a rule, these evil charms are perfectly harmless and often even ridiculous articles. A red rag tied about some human hair and a few bones, a bottle containing a lizard in "magic" rum, a crudely carved miniature coffin, or almost any sort of junk may cause a burly primitive Negro to tremble with deadly fear if its curse has been "put upon him" by an obeah man. What is more, many a so-called civilized white person also trembles at the sight, though the fear in either case, of course, may consist largely of dismay at the discovery that he has a secret, mortal enemy.

Obeah is not to be confused with voodoo, although the two are hopelessly mixed up in the minds of many

CHARMS FOR LUCK

persons. Voodoo is a form of African religion or serpent-god worship in which, originally, a human sacrifice was called for. Today, a goat or other animal is substituted for the human victim of sacrifice.

Obeah, as practiced today, has little connection with any religious rites, but is merely a form of witchcraft or black magic. Very largely it is pure "bunk"—the obeah man or woman of the West Indies depending upon the gullibility and superstition of the Negroes and of many white persons and their faith in the obeah practitioner's supernatural powers.

This kind of obeah often thrives today in crowded Negro settlements in the United States. Traces of it are often found in New York's Harlem section, where often smart charlatans collect secret revenue from among the less educated thousands who pay gladly for "protection" through obeah magic and charms. Sometimes the obeah practitioner, for a price, will resort to poison to accomplish the desired results. Although this revolting feature has been almost eradicated by drastic laws and penalties, the milder forms of obeah are more difficult to stamp out by laws and force. Only thorough education of the masses will accomplish the end of obeah and free its modern-day slaves of fear.

Quite aside from all the nonsense surrounding it, the fact remains that at times the obeah men do perform inexplicable feats. Undoubtedly, much of the success of obeah and many of the strange occurrences sometimes resulting from its practice are due to autosuggestion and the power of fear. It is an indisputable fact that there is a certain weird power possessed by some of these people.

It enables them to thrust pins, needles, or other objects through the flesh of their subjects without causing the least pain or even drawing blood.

By a reverse process, this power also may be used in such a way as to cause a person to suffer the agony and exhibit the symptoms of being cut or otherwise tortured, although neither touched nor injured.

Many obeah practitioners unquestionably have a strange mental hold on their subjects. So greatly do some victims fear them that death has been known to result from some harmless charm or spell; for, once a believer in obeah feels that he or she is doomed by an obeah doctor, death often does follow.

It may seem incredible that a healthy man may actually be frightened to death merely by a threat, yet such is the case. Any resident of the West Indies can furnish examples to verify this.

CHAPTER VI

LEOPARD MEN AND BLOOD AVENGERS

We are prone to think of hypnotism and autosuggestion as rather modern phenomena, but primitive races have known and practiced them both for innumerable centuries. Many savages have gone far beyond us in their knowledge of these strange matters which even today are so little understood generally.

We hear a great deal about the stoicism of the Indian, his ability to endure pain. In reality it is not a question of his enduring of physical agony, but of his possessing the power to put himself into a partially self-hypnotized condition so that he does not feel pain.

Primitive man, of course, feels pain as quickly and suffers as much from it as any white man, when the cause of pain is unexpected; but if he is prepared for it, he can voluntarily make himself to some degree immune to the suffering. I have seen an Indian step on a sharp thorn and let out an agonized howl of pain, yet the same Indian permitted me to extract an ulcerated molar without flinching. This was despite the fact that my only dental instrument was a pair of pipe pliers which slipped from the tooth again and again so that I actually had to worry the tooth from the jaw.

Another Indian showed no symptoms of pain and even

laughed and joked while I cut away his thumbnail and dug deeply into the quick in order to remove a big splinter. But when that same Indian accidentally sat down upon a live hornet, he felt the pain and did not hesitate to let everyone in his vicinity know about it.

Whether or not the primitive Indian suffers depends upon whether or not he has an opportunity to render himself insensible to pain by autosuggestion. He has acquired to a marvellous degree the power of making mind triumph over matter.

While this ability saves the savage from a vast amount of suffering, it also has disadvantages. His mental processes are as susceptible to hypnotic control and autosuggestion in other matters as in immunity to pain. The powers of the medicine men, or witch doctors, depend very largely upon this fact. By means of mental suggestion or hypnotism, or both, these so-called magic-makers maintain their influence and their reputation for possessing supernatural powers.

As I have already pointed out, primitive man's sublime faith in charms and fetishes is the direct result of his mental reactions to suggestion. If he convinces himself or is convinced by someone else that a certain charm, incantation, prophecy, or "medicine" will work, nothing will shake his faith in it. Insofar as he is capable, he is subconsciously instrumental in making it a success.

Because the South American Indians have absolute faith in their hunting charms, or beenas, they are better able to secure game. Because a man is convinced that he will go crazy if he does not marry the girl who has placed a strange love powder in his hammock, he marries her.

And because savages have implicit faith in the efficacy of their medicine shields and weapons, they are inspired with a courage and reckless disregard of danger and death beyond anything that would be possible for them without such stimulating props.

At the time of the Zulu uprising in South Africa in 1906 a white man was killed by the blacks and the soles of his feet and other parts of his body were made into "war medicine" by the witch doctor. The decoction was sprinkled over the warriors. They were told that the charm would make them immune to bullets, which, as soon as they struck, would melt and run like wax.

Having perfect faith in the power of their witch doctor and his medicine, three thousand Zulus, armed only with short assagais, or spears, hurled themselves with ferocious confidence at the British batteries of machine guns and the British troops with their rifles. Needless to say, they were mowed down almost to a man.

Does disaster like this cause primitive man to lose faith in war medicine? Not at all. He merely believes that something went wrong with the medicine; or that the white man's medicine used by the enemy just happened to be stronger.

North American Plains Indians, when carrying their "medicine shields," were completely devoid of fear. Armed only with bows and arrows, they would attack many times their numbers of cavalrymen armed with carbines, feeling certain that their charmed shields were ample protection from the soldiers' bullets.

When an Indian of the Gran Chaco in South America becomes very ill and believes that someone has bewitched him or cast the "evil eye" upon him, the tribal medicine man cuts a gash in the man's side, fills the wound with stones, animal claws, and teeth, and closes the incision. There is danger, of course, that the man will die; but he is perfectly willing to endure the operation. He feels certain that by means of this powerful medicine the culprit responsible for his illness and death will be discovered and duly punished.

This is supposedly accomplished in a manner as strange as the charm itself. The Indians believe that in due time a shooting star will flash through the sky carrying with it the claws, teeth, and stones that were placed in the side of the afflicted man, and that these celestial missiles will strike the guilty one and bring death in the most agonizing way.

Completely ridiculous as this seems to us, it is very often successful in bringing about the enemy's demise. The culprit, who may have poisoned the other, or who may have placed a curse or mutilated an effigy to injure him, feels certain that the star will fall and destroy him. Everyone suspects him, avoids him. Frequently, he commits suicide or runs away.

Perhaps the most remarkable example of this amazing effect of mental suggestion and a faith in charms is the strange cult of Africa designated as that of the Leopard Men. Mysterious, almost uncanny, these human leopards have been a terrible menace in Liberia and several other parts of Africa. Assuming all the savage ferocity of the spotted beasts for whom they are named, these men prowl through the forest, imitating the actions and cries of leopards and wearing leopard skins. On hands and feet they wear false feet with leopard claws or huge claws of iron. They stalk and kill their human victims by pouncing upon them and severing the carotid artery with their teeth, exactly as do leopards with their prey.

No one knows how many of these fearsome leopard men there are. No one knows who they are. An apparently harmless native may become transformed into a leopard man quite easily. An ordinary Negro can become a leopard man by partaking of the "medicine" of the cult. Worst of all, the luckless man may unwittingly and involuntarily become a member of the horrible, revolting sect.

Using a human skull as a container, the leaders of the band prepare a potion composed of the blood of one of their victims. They administer it secretly to some man whom they have chosen to become a member of the cult. Having mixed a little of the medicine with the fellow's food or drink, they afterwards inform him that he has swallowed the magic charm and is now a leopard man.

Convinced that the brew possesses magical power to compel him to become a human leopard, his entire character is soon transformed. When he is commanded to lure even one of his brothers or sisters into the forest, where he or she will be murdered by the leopard men, he obeys without question. After this initiation, the new recruit must hunt and kill for himself.

Just what the ultimate purpose of the band may be, or what its basic idea, no white man knows. It is a secret cult. No member will reveal his own part in it or the names of others. A few years ago ninety suspects were arrested and placed in jail, and all committed suicide by poison they had secreted upon their persons. In some of these African communities the natives live in deadly, superstitious terror of the leopard men, and the toll of deaths at their hands is considerable. In many districts no one dares venture forth after nightfall for fear of falling victim to a leopard man.

The Kenaima, or blood avenger, of the Guiana Indian tribes in South America is another strange example of mental suggestion and faith in charms or "medicine" and a proxy. Kenaima, in Indian mythology, is the avenging spirit, an invisible being who avenges the death of a murdered Indian. The Indians, however, do not leave vengeance to the spirit itself, but select a living, human being as a proxy to act for the Kenaima. It is a terrifying, ancient custom which luckily is fast being blotted out by advancing civilization.

Ordinarily the human Kenaima is the nearest relative of the man or woman who has been killed, but quite frequently some other man will volunteer to become Kenaima, or, as in some tribes, he may be appointed by the tribal medicine man, or peaiman. In either case the proxy for the blood-avenging spirit prepares himself by drinking a medicine concocted by the peaiman. He paints his body and limbs in a certain prescribed manner. He arrays himself in a mantle or cape of black feathers to render himself invisible and sets forth upon his mission of death.

It makes no difference whatsoever whether or not the potential victim is known to be the actual murderer. Very often the death to be avenged is the result of some brawl, and the murderer is known; but quite as often, when an Indian is found dead, the peaiman "makes medicine" and names the one responsible. This of course affords a wonderful opportunity for the peaiman to dispose of an enemy or a rival, although, to do these medicine men justice, it is seldom that any of them take advantage of such an opportunity.

Before the Kenaima starts upon his mission he must decide whether he is to be a jaguar Kenaima or a boa constrictor Kenaima. If he chooses the former, he paints himself with spots like those of the jaguar and must hunt down his victim and kill him with a pounce or blow, in the same manner that the tiger or jaguar kills its prey. For this he generally uses a short heavy club. If he chooses to become a boa constrictor Kenaima, he paints his body in imitation of an anaconda or boa and goes forth unarmed, for he must strangle his victim after the manner of the serpent. He can use only his bare hands.

The law of the Kenaima decrees that he must destroy not only the murderer but every member of the doomed one's family as well; but actually, this is rarely done. He must not be seen by any human being until his mission has been fulfilled but must range the jungles alone until he has wreaked vengeance.

According to Indian belief any person who happens to see the Kenaima, whether by accident or not, will be transformed into the creature the Kenaima represents. To prevent this the avenger always warns others of his presence by uttering a peculiar whistle.

Many a time when I have been camping in the depths of the Guiana jungles in South America, I have seen my Indian boatmen and hunters cower in terror at the sound of a strange, quavering, thrice-repeated whistle from the depths of the surrounding forest. Wild-eyed and trembling, they would turn their heads away from the sound, muttering "Kenaima! Kenaima!"

Yet I always doubted if we ever actually heard a Kenaima's warning whistle, for the Indians are in such fear of the avenger that any strange or unusual note of an insect, bird, or animal may be mistaken for the whistle of the Kenaima.

If the Kenaima follows out the rules of his vengeance to the letter, he does not kill his victim at once when he finds him. Instead, Kenaima is supposed to maim the victim so badly that he cannot move. After a lapse of several days, the Kenaima is supposed to put the victim to death by plunging a pointed stick into his heart; and his orders are to lick the blood from the point.

In practice, however, the Kenaima very rarely does this. There is always the chance that the wounded man may be found and rescued. In that case the Kenaima can never fully resume his human personality, but must forever wander in the forest, killing anyone whom he meets; for until he has tasted the blood of his victim, the avenging spirit cannot leave his body, and he becomes a maniacal killer. Hence, in order to insure himself against such a fate, the Indian avenger kills his victim at once and tastes his blood, thus releasing the Kenaima spirit; after which he becomes an ordinary human being again and returns to his home.

Naturally, as every killing demands a Kenaima to avenge it, the destruction of one victim brings another Kenaima on a mission of vengeance. On more than one occasion in the past, entire villages and even whole tribes have been completely wiped out by Kenaima killings!

If one avenger is killed, another immediately takes his place. Once a Kenaima is on a man's trail, his doom is sealed, unless he can manage to elude the avenger until he reaches a locality known as Kenaima*pu*. Then he is safe, for this locality is taboo to the Kenaima who, baffled, must forever be possessed of the terrible spirit of the avenger.

In this one strange custom we find a combination of superstitions—an implicit faith in the charm, or medicine, which causes the man to become the embodied spirit; a belief that unless the spirit is released he will be forever doomed to kill his fellow men; faith in his supernatural powers as a proxy for the spirit of the vengeance; and faith in the power of the taboo.

In recent years, as the Indians become more and more civilized and the practice of Kenaima is frowned upon by the governing white officials, another custom has entered into the practice of Kenaima. Instead of having an Indian set forth on a mission of vengeance, an effigy of the wanted man is made. The medicine man sprinkles it with a magic brew; the head of the image is smashed to pieces; and everyone is satisfied by having wrought dire vengeance by proxy.

Chapter VII

MEDICINE MEN

EARLY man and many savage and primitive races of later days believed that illness was caused by the entrance of evil spirits or "devils" into a person's body.

They hit the mark pretty well in this belief; for are not the living, active germs of disease real "devils" in accomplishment? Small wonder that primitive man deeply fears these unseen, unidentified, and powerful causes of illness and death, and that due to fear he invests them with spiritual personalities.

Medicine men, usually the wisest individuals in the tribe, attempt to drive out or destroy these spirits in order to cure the patient. Charms, fetishes, incantations, chants, and dances are all employed for this purpose. Very often the noise and excitement are sufficient to upset the nerves of a perfectly healthy person, let alone a sick man.

If the patient dies or does not improve, the medicine man sadly decides that his magic was not powerful enough to oust the devils; and he attempts to concoct stronger and better "medicine" for the next occasion.

To us this seems lacking in common sense, but we must remember that only a few centuries ago many civilized doctors held similar beliefs. Medical science and treat-

MEDICINE MEN

ment as we know them today are really very recent. They are only in their beginnings even now. Every year brings its revelations—its great improvements and innovations.

Primitive races do not always treat their sick with magic incantations. Many individuals among them possess a deep knowledge of medicinal plants and are actually very successful in curing various maladies.

Quinine was known and used by the Peruvian Indians many centuries before a white man ever knew that America existed. The use of the coca plant, from which cocaine is derived, was common knowledge among the Inca Indians. Sarsaparilla, ipecacuanha, sassafras, arnica, boneset, mullein, burdock, gentian, viburnum, gold thread, liverwort, quassia, ginseng, mandrake, and hundreds of other plants were employed by the Indians for curing diseases and maladies. What is more, the Indians used them long before civilized white men recognized these plants as valuable sources of remedies.

There are a number of Indian medicines, unknown to white doctors, which effect such remarkable cures for certain illnesses that even the best of our physicians are baffled. Indians of Brazil, for example, use extracts of a root in a concoction which rarely fails completely to cure amoebic dysentery. An American doctor in Ecuador told me of a case of leg ulcers which he could not cure until an Indian woman gave him an ointment of her own manufacture which produced almost miraculous results.

Years ago when I was traveling in the French West Indies, I was afflicted with an ulcer in my foot which had been caused by minute parasites. Despite every effort of the best physicians on the island and by the doctor of a steamship, the ulcer grew steadily worse.

I had about resigned myself to undergoing an amputation, when a Negro woman insisted she could cure the ulcer. Gathering some plants and leaves, she brewed these over a fire, made a compress of them and applied it to the ulcer. Within three days the ulcer was completely cured and the wound was healing well!

The North American Indians were famed for their knowledge of medicinal plants and herbs. Many a white settler owed his life to the medical skill of Indian friends. Usually it was the Indian woman who prepared these medicinal concoctions. The curative power of Indian medicines are so famous that many popular patent medicines have been labeled "Indian" in order to create a demand for them, whether or not they ever were known to the Indians. There was no hokum in Indian remedies made from medicinal plants. Their value was real even though the plants were most ordinary.

On the other hand, many peoples both in America and in other lands have resorted to most strange and unusual medicines and treatments. Some Chinese still have great faith in rhinoceros horns, "dragons," deer antlers, teeth, pearls, and various other oddities as medicines. Among many races such things as fingernails, dried frogs, dried bats, dried lizards, and other mummified creatures are used as medicines or medicinal components and are supposed to be very potent. And who among us, the civilized, has not seen common mud applied to a bee or wasp sting? or pipe smoke blown into a child's aching

MEDICINE MEN

ear? or chewed-up tobacco tied onto a sore as a poultice?

In the native markets in the Andean villages of western South America one finds many strange medicines. The Andean Indians, who have never seen the ocean, have an idea that anything from the sea must be good medicine. Dried starfishes, cuttlefish, sea squirts, seashells, sponges, sea fans, and sea rods—all are highly

61

prized as medicines by these people and are shipped inland to them in quantity.

The Chinese have used many strange methods of doctoring. Some believe that almost any ailment or ache may be cured by pricking the skin with sharp needles or pins, the spot to be pricked depending upon the ailment and its location (Fig. 61).

An even stranger practice is found among several

tribes of Australia and the neighboring Pacific islands. Native primitives sometimes actually amputate the joints of their own fingers in the belief that the mutilation will cure sickness! Perhaps the pain acts as a counterirritant, and the loss of blood may be beneficial.

When the means is employed to cure others, however, it is a difficult matter to see how the self-sacrifice is of any benefit. These people have sublime faith in the system, however, and some have been known to sacrifice all but one or two fingers in the process.

It is certainly lucky for our doctors that they are not called upon to lop off a section of their fingers each time they happen to be summoned to the bedside of a seriously ill patient.

Medicine men of the island of Madagascar off the coast of Africa seek the causes and cures of illness in signs perceived among seeds which they arrange in "magical" groupings upon a mat. They boast many successful cures.

Certain races believe in the old adage that an ounce of prevention is worth a pound of cure. They keep in good health by taking tonics or medicines regularly, even when not suffering from any ailment. This custom is not uncommon among modern civilized persons. Many individuals among them dose themselves regularly for imaginary or real prevention of disease.

A custom which used to be rigorously followed by all true North American Sioux Indians decreed that raw kidney and raw liver should be eaten at least once a week. Undoubtedly this diet was beneficial, even if some of us today cannot appreciate a taste for the raw meat.

MEDICINE MEN

Many white people believe thoroughly in Turkish baths as a health measure, and North American Indians as well as primitive races in various other portions of the world have used sweat baths for untold centuries.

We must not forget that the Incan and pre-Incan Indians were remarkably able surgeons. They successfully performed trepanning operations, amputated arms and legs, and removed eyes that were badly injured. They used the crudest sort of stone and bronze instruments, but used them with great skill.

Some races resort to most unusual and often amusing methods for curing or attempting to cure various ailments. Among the strangest are some which are used by the Kuna Indians of Panama. In a way, these people are dyed-in-the-wool homeopaths, for they believe that "like cures like." In other words, it is faith based upon the theory of using "a hair of the dog that bit you." Moreover, they place much faith in the benefits derived from external applications.

According to the code of their medicine men, if a man has a headache or has received a head injury, his head must be rubbed with the skull of some animal, the particular skull to be used depending upon the patient's clan. Thus, if a sufferer is a member of a fish clan, it would never do to employ the skull of a land animal, or vice versa. In the same manner, a lame leg or an affliction of the leg must be treated by rubbing the limb with the leg bone of some creature.

As there are many clans among these Indians, and as any portion of a person's anatomy may be afflicted, the medicine basket of the tribal doctor holds a bewildering assortment of bones, skulls, claws, teeth, ribs, and other animal remains.

Usually, too, there will be several old stoneware doorknobs and some electric light bulbs. These are highly prized medicinal properties. The Indians explain that the glass bulbs must be good for sore or weak eyes, for they shine so brightly and "see" in the darkness; while the doorknobs are so hard and durable that they must be excellent for healing broken bones and injured joints. Faith of this sort is both pathetic and amusing.

Many of the skulls and other objects in the medicine baskets which I collected were worn to a high polish from repeated applications. Having rubbed the afflicted portion of the patient's anatomy with the proper bone, skull, or other object, the medicine man places a wooden neli, or proxy, beneath the sick person's hammock. The neli is supposed to keep watch and see to it that no devils come near, as described in Chapter IV.

Among the Uapes of the Upper Amazon in South America the medicine men have considerable success in curing diseases by strong blowing and breathing upon the person who is ill, and by singing certain songs of incantation.

Such strange methods of treating the sick or injured may seem very peculiar and ridiculous, but it is an accepted piece of general knowledge that the efficacy of many cures depends largely upon faith. If the Indian has faith in the medicine man's nostrums, in rubbing with skulls, bones, doorknobs, and electric light bulbs, the treatment may, as it often does, effect a cure, or at least may help in effecting it.

MEDICINE MEN

After all, are the strange medicines of primitive and savage races any stranger or more ridiculous than some which are used by intelligent and educated members of modern society? Many civilized persons rub a stye on the eye with a copper penny to effect a cure. Some persons carry raw potatoes in their pockets, firm in the belief that the tubers are a sure cure of rheumatism as well as a preventative of its recurrence. Others fasten their faith to a horse chestnut or a lump of sulphur, while still others tie pennies to their ankles. There are plenty of so-called educated persons who have implicit faith in a black velvet ribbon or a string of gold beads as a cure for goitre.

Amber beads about a child's neck are supposed to prevent a sore throat. To guard against contracting fevers, a bag containing an asafetida is sometimes worn about the neck. Some residents of New England insist that warts may be removed by rubbing the growths with a toad; or if that fails, rubbing with string beans, which must then be thrown over a fence.

In some parts of the Middle West in the United States one rubs a wart with an old, damp dishcloth, which must be buried in the ground immediately thereafter if the wart is to disappear. Since many warts do finally disappear, these quaint beliefs persist.

All pure bunkum, we may say, but how do we know? How can we feel sure that there may not be real curative powers in some of these strange "medicines"?

Centuries ago, European doctors had faith in bee stings for curing rheumatism. To moderns the idea seemed as preposterous as to cure a sore eye by rubbing it with an electric light bulb or to cure rheumatism by means of a potato in one's pocket. Yet, today scores of educated people are being treated for rheumatism by being stung by bees while under competent medical supervision!

Perhaps some day we may discover that a great many of the strange medicines and weird practices of primitive races were not so silly as they have seemed.

Chapter VIII

DEADLY SAVAGE WEAPONS

The first weapons used by man were undoubtedly stones and sticks. A heavy stone made a handy weapon which could be hurled at distant game. At close quarters it could be used to bash in the head of an opponent. A stout stick also could be wielded with deadly effect.

Neither stone nor club, however, could cut or puncture the tough hides of wild beasts nor could they hew wood; and the apelike men of early times realized the need of sharp-edged implements. A jagged fragment of flint or hard rock or a broken clamshell probably gave them the key to solving the problem, while a thorn or a splintered bone probably was the original awl.

It is quite easy to understand how these simple weapons and implements were improved upon by early man. He was not slow in learning that stones of certain sizes and shapes could be thrown more accurately than others; and that some could be used for hammers and pounders more efficiently than could others. He therefore learned to select those best suited to his needs.

Early individuals of superior mental capacities discovered that by knocking two stones together they could crack and chip off the angles and irregularities of stones and could shape them roughly to conform to their ideas of what stone missiles should be. Practice makes perfect, and it probably wasn't very long before our remote ancestors had become quite proficient in fashioning stone weapons.

In the meantime they had found that the heavier the club, the more deadly were the results from its use. But there was a limit to the size of a stick a man could handle. Then some brilliant genius thought of fastening a stone to his bludgeon, and the problem was solved. Here was the beginning of the war club, the axe, the hammer, the mace, the tomahawk, and countless other weapons and implements of war and peace.

The chances are that these early men managed quite well with their throwing-stones, crude hammers, and axes for many generations before they developed the art of chipping stones into edged tools and weapons. Yet they may have used flakes of flint or of other stones as soon as they invented stone-headed mauls and clubs, or even sooner.

At any rate, man has fashioned sharp-pointed and sharp-edged stone implements since very early times. It was not a long step from a stone blade grasped in one's hand to a stone attached to a bit of wood for a handle. It was another short step from such a crude, short knife or dagger to a long spear. After all, a spear is merely a knife with a very long handle. And it did not require a great deal of intelligence on the part of the savage to reason that a heavy spear could be thrown with considerable accuracy.

Thus very early in the game of life man acquired the forerunners of innumerable forms of axes, hammers,

DEADLY SAVAGE WEAPONS 117

and similar implements, knives of a sort, and the spear, lance, and javelin.

It must have been a true genius who discovered the sling, with which to cast a stone many times as far as by hand (and much more efficiently); and it must have been an even greater genius who invented the bow and arrow. Yet the bow and arrow were known to man in immeasurably ancient times. It was in use among nearly all races in almost every portion of the world while human beings were still little more than beasts in their ways of living.

Probably we shall never know just how many thousands of years have passed since man first fitted a crooked stick with a thong of rawhide and with this crude contraption fired a heavy, clumsy, stone-headed spear a few yards. We do know that tens of thousands of years ago, in what is now the United States, primitive men had perfected the bow and arrow to a very high degree. With this weapon they killed the giant bison, far larger than the bison of the present day, the equally gigantic prehistoric elk, the huge, unwieldy, woolly rhinoceros, the mastodon-like elephant, and other monstrous beasts of the pre-glacial era.

How do we know all this? Archaeologists have found stone arrowheads and stone spearheads lying among ancient skeletons of these pre-historic creatures or embedded in their bones. It was very clear that these animals had been killed by the missiles.

These oldest of all known stone arrowheads yet found in North America are not crudely chipped artifacts (products of early human workmanship), but are beautifully designed and well finished samples of the arrow-maker's skill. In fact, these Folsom points, as they are called (from the fact that they were first found near Folsom, Colorado), are far superior to the great majority of later stone implements of America and also of Europe.

Despite the fact that the bow and arrow were superior to the stone-headed club, the spear, and the stone dagger, it did not by any means supplant these earlier weapons. Rather, these were continually developed and improved (while the bow and arrow remained much the same) and held their own, as they still do, among many primitive races of the world.

During the Middle Ages, battle-axes, maces, war clubs, and mauls played an even greater part than bows and arrows in warfare. Halberds and lances were considered indispensable weapons long after firearms supplanted bows and arrows and crossbows. Today, lances are still in use by civilized white men, while countless primitive people make use of war clubs, spears, and tomahawks, even though these people also possess modern rifles and ammunition.

Our swords, daggers, machetes, knives, and other edged implements and weapons are all offshoots of the original stone knives of our savage ancestors of ages ago. But what a variety of swords have been developed during the thousands of years that have passed! Looking at a large collection of these weapons, one marvels that human ingenuity could have produced such a seemingly endless number of forms by means of a single piece of sharpened and tempered steel.

DEADLY SAVAGE WEAPONS

It is not surprising that man should have devoted so much time, skill, and inventive ability to swords, for swords have been mankind's most prized and trusty weapon for many centuries. The word "sword" has become synonymous with battle and bloodshed and it is also a symbol of heroism and honor. "He who lives by the sword dies by the sword" is a well-known saying. The presentation of a sword is deemed one of the highest honors that can be awarded. When a man is knighted by an English King, the monarch touches that man's shoulder with a sword.

Whether the weapon is the straight-bladed, cross-hilted sword of the Negroes of the African Soudan, the wavy-edged kris of the Asian Malays, the bolo of the native Filipinos, the heavy sickle-shaped weapon of the Ghurkas of India, the yataghan of the Persians, the scimitar of the Turks, the sabre of the cavalryman, or the slender rapier of the Spanish, it is always recognizable as a sword. Even the weirdly shaped, double-curved, scallop-edged blade of the Negroes of the Belgian Congo is unquestionably a sword of sorts (Plate VI, Fig. 62). So, too, is that most useful (I might say indispensable) combination weapon and tool, the machete of tropical America.

But there are swords which are so different from all others that they scarcely can be classed as such, even if they do serve the same purpose. Aside from their use, there is slight resemblance, for example, between a true sword and the strange weapons which are popular among many of the native tribes of the Pacific Islands. Made of wood and with edges studded with the razor-sharp teeth of tiger sharks, with ornate complicated hilts, and often with several short supplementary or side blades, these weapons are truly efficacious (Plate VI, Fig. 63). They are far more dangerous than a clean-edged blade of steel.

Undoubtedly the South Sea Islanders borrowed the idea of their strange swords from the jaws of sharks. But how did it happen that the ancient Aztec Indians of Mexico invented and used weapons that in design were almost identical with the sharks'-teeth-studded weapons of the South Sea Islanders?

Probably we shall never know; but the fact remains that the Aztec maquahuitl, made of hard wood and with keen edge-flakes of obsidian set along both edges, was amazingly like the weapons of the South Sea Islanders (Plate VI, Fig. 64).

While the flint knife had been developing into countless forms of swords and daggers, the original club also had been advancing. Today the styles, types, and forms of clubs, battle-axes, bludgeons, and tomahawks used by primitive men are even more numerous than the types of swords.

No two races, tribes, or even individuals seem to agree as to what is the best form of war club. Some tribes prefer heavy wooden bludgeons studded with bits of sharp stone, iron, or wooden spikes. Others make elaborate affairs in the form of broad-bladed, paddle-like weapons (Plate VI, Fig. 65) such as are very popular among the jungle-dwelling Indians of South America. Some tribes use massive square clubs (Plate VI, Fig.

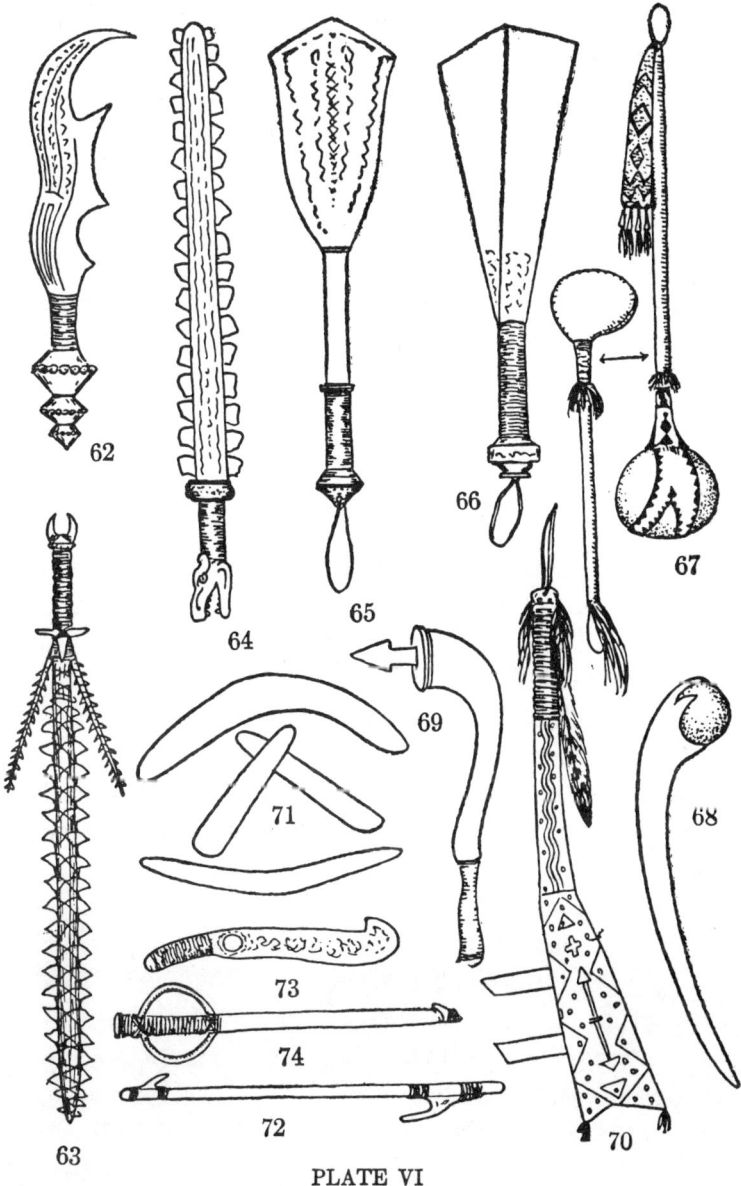

PLATE VI

62 Congo sword 63 shark's-teeth weapon 64 Aztec maquahuitl 65 paddle-like weapon of jungle tribes 66 square club 67 skull-cracker club 68 stone-headed club 69 stone-bladed club 70 club of gunstock form 71 boomerangs 72 spear-throwing stick 73 Aztec atlatl 74 Incan throwing stick

DEADLY SAVAGE WEAPONS

66), while many depend upon stone-headed, axe-like war clubs.

The Indians of Western North America developed the skull-cracker form of club to a very high degree, using either naturally or artificially shaped stones attached to long, strong (often flexible) handles of wood or rawhide. In typical Indian manner they decorated the deadly weapons with feathers, bead and porcupine quillwork, fur, and scalp locks (Plate VI, Fig. 67).

Among the Eastern tribes of what is now the United States, wooden clubs of various forms were in use, some being given added weight by having stones fastened at the tips (Plate VI, Fig. 68), while others were fitted with sharp stone blades (Plate VI, Fig. 69).

Clubs of gunstock form, either with or without stone blades, were widely used by many tribes of Indians, especially in the West and Middle West of North America. With the advent of white men and steel these were often fitted with sword blades, hatchet heads, bayonet tips, or knife blades, which converted the wooden bludgeons into deadly weapons (Plate VI, Fig. 70).

Most persons are so accustomed to reading of Indians with iron-headed tomahawks that they think these were typical Indian weapons. The tomahawk or hatchet headed with iron was unknown to the Indians until they obtained the idea from the white man, who increased the deadliness of the instrument by adding the iron. The tomahawk known to the Indians before the arrival of Europeans in the Americas was an ordinary stone-headed axe or hatchet. It was at first intended for cutting and hewing wood rather than for use as a weapon.

The Algonquin Indians are said to have been the originators of the Indian tomahawk.

Probably no other primitive race ever possessed such a great variety of war clubs as were finally in use by the tribes of American Indians. African natives as a rule were content with simple wooden clubs. They relied upon spears, assagais, and bows and arrows rather than upon bludgeons; while in the South Sea Islands and in Australia heavy wooden clubs known as "knob kerries" were the most popular types.

Bows and arrows vary almost as greatly as do swords and clubs. Some are poorly designed and weak. Others, such as those used by many South American tribes, are enormously long and powerful; while still others, such as those used by the North American Plains Indians, are short, broad, and extremely powerful. Some are flat, some round, others half-round, and still others rather square in shape. Some are made of wood backed with rawhide, sinews, or horn; while others, such as those used by some Eskimo tribes, are composed entirely of horn.

Arrows vary in the same way. Some are short, others long; some are feathered and some are not; while materials in arrowheads range all the way from hardened wood to bone, sharks' teeth, claws of birds or beasts, stone, metal, and bamboo—in fact, any hard material.

Though bows and arrows were common to nearly every tribe everywhere, yet there were some tribes which never used them. This is more remarkable considering the fact that some of these savages dwelt in lands where their next-door neighbor used splendid bows and arrows.

DEADLY SAVAGE WEAPONS 125

In the interior of South America there are several Indian tribes which do not use bows and arrows, although surrounded by tribesmen whose bows are wonderfully powerful and who are expert archers.

Among the Indians of the Goajira peninsula of Colombia, South America, different types of arrows are used. One is like a triple spear and is used for fishing. Another has a heavy, blunt tip which merely stuns an animal.

A harpoon arrow used for rabbits has sharp iron points along the shaft of the arrow, so that the rabbit, bounding away with the arrow in his hide, would be caught in the thick underbrush. A heavy, spear-pointed arrow is used for larger game. These Indians use a poisoned arrow for human enemies only. Its tip contains the tail of the sting ray. The tail has sharp dorsal spines and is difficult to withdraw; thus the arrow is sure to remain sufficiently long for the poison really to saturate the flesh.

The poison used by these Indians differs from ordinary South American poisons, or curares, which are usually made entirely from vegetable matters. These Indians include in the poison animal substances like snake serum, spider glands, and putrefying frogs.

In Australia many of the tribesmen never discovered the bow and arrow, but they invented a far more wonderful weapon, the boomerang. In its simplest form the boomerang is merely a curved club which is thrown as a missile; but through countless centuries Australian savages have developed the weapon to a high state of perfection. However, many of the thrilling tales about the accomplishments of the boomerang are greatly exaggerated.

There are innumerable forms and types of boomerangs, and they are not confined to Australia. The Incan Indian races of Peru used boomerangs, and many of these weapons are found in ancient Incan burial mounds and graves. Several North American Indian tribes knew the boomerang. The Pueblo Indians of Southwestern United States still use these "rabbit sticks," as they are called, for killing small game.

However, no other race ever made so much use of boomerangs as did the tribesmen of Australia. Not only do these people possess many forms of boomerangs, each designed and used for a particular purpose (Plate VI, Fig. 71), but through long familiarity and constant use of the weapons, these Australian tribesmen have become uncannily expert in throwing them. To be sure, not every Australian native tribesman can make a boomerang perform amazing stunts; but there are individuals who seem to be able to control a speeding boomerang and cause it to carry out marvelous evolutions in mid-air.

The most skillful boomerang throwers, however, are not the Australian aborigines, but white men. Some of these experts, who give exhibitions in circuses and elsewhere, will keep half a dozen boomerangs in the air at once, each turning or twisting in a different manner but always returning to the thrower's hands.

If you think it is no great trick to make a boomerang behave, just try it for yourself. Boomerangs may be purchased at some of the sporting-goods stores, and there are plenty of wide-open fields and meadows where

DEADLY SAVAGE WEAPONS

you may try your skill with the contraption. Be sure there are no houses, human beings, or livestock within several hundred yards, and watch your step—or rather, your boomerang.

A boomerang thrown by a beginner seems to possess an uncanny knowledge of the thrower's lack of experience, for it will do most unexpected things. It may sail off and drop harmlessly to the ground. It may rise a few scores of feet, soar upwards, and come gliding down gently at an angle. On the other hand, it may and often does appear to become possessed of diabolical cunning. Just as it seems about to fall to earth, it will suddenly pick up speed and come whining through the air straight toward the thrower.

At such a time it would be unwise to stand there congratulating yourself because you have made the thing return to you. If you do, you may lose your life or receive a serious injury, for a speeding boomerang, light as it is, has terrific force and can easily break a bone or crack a human skull.

Better duck and run! Even then you may not escape. Boomerangs were designed to kill or maim, and they seem to be imbued with that sole purpose, once they go on a rampage. The weird thing may seem to chase you all over the place; but eventually it will slow down and drop to earth, and you may continue to experiment to your heart's content.

No one can instruct you in boomerang throwing. No one can tell you just how you should grasp the weapon or how you should throw it in order to secure desired results. It is all a matter of practice and patience and of learning the idiosyncrasies of the particular boomerang you are using or trying to use. Do not expect a boomerang to return to you, once it has struck its mark. Even the most expert Australian cannot make a boomerang do that (contrary to statements of fiction writers). It is only the boomerang that misses its target or the boomerang that is thrown for sport which comes back to the thrower.

Another important invention of the Australian aborigines is the spear-throwing stick. This consists of a short club-like stick fitted with a handgrip at one end and a hook at the other.

In use the stick is held by three fingers in the palm of the hand. The haft of the spear is placed on top of the stick with its butt-end against the hook and is held in position by the thumb and first finger of the thrower (Plate VI, Fig. 72). By bringing the upraised arm forcibly forward, one can hurl the spear much farther and with greater force than by hand alone, for the throwing stick is, in effect, an extension of the arm, and it gives added leverage.

As in the case of the boomerang, the spear-throwing stick is not confined to the Australians. It also was invented and developed by several races in America quite independently of the Australian invention.

It is a puzzling and strange fact that only in Australia and America are marsupial mammals to be found—those odd creatures equipped with a pouch for carrying the young. Who knows?—perhaps in some period of the far distant past there was some sort of geographical connection between Australia and the New World.

DEADLY SAVAGE WEAPONS 129

Whether or not such was the case, the American races possessed spear-throwing sticks which were far superior to any of those in use in Australia.

Among the Aztec Indians of Mexico the atlatl, as it was called, was a beautifully made and often highly decorated device (Plate VI, Fig. 73), while equally artistic and carefully made throwing-sticks were used by

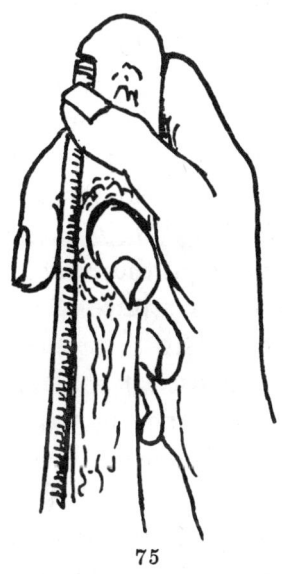

75

the Incan and pre-Incan people of Peru (Plate VI, Fig. 74). Many other Indian tribes used similar implements, but as far as is known, the only American tribe still using the ancient atlatl is the Guaymi tribe of northern Panama.

The throwing-stick in use by these Indians is quite different from that of the Aztecs and Incas. It is a shorter, heavier affair, is usually made entirely of wood, and is provided with a finger hole which makes it much easier to use (Fig. 75).

By means of these implements a Guaymi Indian can hurl a spear twice the distance possible by hand alone. Moreover, the accuracy with which the lightweight throwing-spears can be hurled is amazing. Despite the fact that these Indians possess excellent bows and arrows, they frequently prefer to use the throwing-spear, especially when hunting in thick jungle or underbrush.

Far more remarkable and far more deadly than any other savage weapon is the blowgun. Many persons associate blowguns and poisoned darts with South American Indians, yet these weapons are known in other parts of the world. They are still the favorite weapon of the Dyaks of Borneo in the East Indies, who use the intensely poisonous, milky juice of the famed upas tree for poisoning their darts.

Blowguns are also used by Siamese and Burmese tribes, by the Malays, and by various natives of the Philippines. In the Western Hemisphere blowguns were not restricted to the Indians of South America, but are still in use by some Central American tribes. Blowguns formerly were used by various North American Indian tribes, from the Mississippi River to the Allegheny Mountains; and from Florida to New York State, where they were in use by the Iroquois.

Nowhere in the world, however, has the blowgun been developed to such a degree of perfection and efficiency as in South America. Numerous Indian tribes not only in Central America but in localities scattered from the Atlantic Ocean to the headwaters of the Amazon and

DEADLY SAVAGE WEAPONS

from the borders of the Caribbean Sea to the Gran Chaco in Chile, also use blowguns. The designs and methods of making them, however, vary greatly.

Not all the tribes employ poisoned darts. The Shayshans and Kunas, as well as the Boorabees, of Central America use clay pellets in very short, simple blowguns for the killing of birds and small game. Other tribes use darts which are not poisoned and do not attempt to kill any creatures larger than small birds, squirrels, or marmosets. However, there are scores of tribes that do use poisoned darts in their blowguns. Although the exact nature of the poison varies, the most widely used and the most deadly are the curare poisons.

No white man has ever yet learned the real secret of this most deadly and swift of all known poisons. In fact, very few Indians in any tribe know how it is prepared, what it contains, or what imparts its swiftly deadly character. Only the professional poisonmakers, who usually are medicine men or peai (to give them their Carib name) know all the secrets of curare; and they usually hand down this important knowledge from father to son.

Many a time I have seen the curare prepared and have noted the various ingredients. I have even collected most of them. Yet not a single one of these, nor a combination of them, possesses the intensely poisonous character of the compounded curare.

Some of the substances used are entirely innocuous, and undoubtedly are added to the brew with the dual purpose of confusing those who watch the process and to impress them. Ants, scorpions, toads, frogs, various earths, chips of wood, bark, roots, leaves, seed, fruit, bulbs, flowers, gums, and diverse other things are placed in the mystic pot, which is stirred with a peculiarly shaped paddle made especially for the occasion. Arrow tips are dipped in the molten mass and whatever is left is allowed to harden and is preserved for further use.

According to the belief of some Indians the curare will be worthless if the mystic paddle is not burned in the fire beneath the pot when the deadly brew is finished; but I managed to collect surreptitiously two such paddles. As far as I know, the curare from those brewings was as efficacious and deadly as any other curare, in spite of the theft.

Curare has another South American name, *urary,* or *warali.* Interesting to note is the meaning of this word, which derives from the language of the Tupi Indians of the Amazon: *ur* to come, *ar* to fall, and *y,* relative pronoun; literally, "he, to whom it comes, falls."

Some scientists think that the virulent character of curare may be due to juices of a certain vine of the strychnine family. But most of the strychnine group of poisons are dangerous only when taken internally, whereas curare may be swallowed with impunity, provided there is no abrasion in one's mouth or throat; but it is fatal when it enters the bloodstream directly. It may be just as well that we do not know more about it. Curare is difficult to obtain and is not likely to become a weapon of gangsters or other criminals; yet if its composition were made public, fearful catastrophes and crimes might result.

I cannot say just how long it requires for a man to

DEADLY SAVAGE WEAPONS

die after he has been struck by a curare-tipped dart. Indians who should know have told me that a man rarely lives ten minutes, and that the victim becomes paralyzed, unable to speak or to move, within five minutes after the poison has entered his bloodstream.

The Indians furthermore state that a great deal depends upon the spot in which the victim is hit and upon how deeply the dart buries itself in his flesh. If the missile strikes the neck, throat, chest, or any other spot where it may penetrate a large vein, the victim may expire within a few moments. If the dart buries its poisoned tip in the thigh, arm, cheek, or other portion of the body where the flesh is thick and there are no large veins near the surface, the injured man may even survive and recover.

I know from personal observation that a deer struck fairly with a poisoned dart from a blowgun will fall dead before the animal has run fifty yards. Large birds like the curassow or macaw may fly a few hundred feet before they drop, while a small animal like the coati, or howling monkey, will drop dead almost instantly.

It has been said that there is no antidote for curare. This, however, is not strictly the truth. I doubt if there is an antidote for full-strength curare when it has been thoroughly introduced into the bloodstream, but lime juice and salt, if administered promptly, will save a bird or animal brought down by a slightly poisoned dart.

I have repeatedly seen the Indians secure live macaws, parrots, toucans, monkeys, and other small animals by this means. The Indians admit that the treatment is not always successful, yet a large proportion of the live birds and quadrupeds secured by the tribesmen are obtained in this way.

No one has a greater respect for the deadly character of curare than do the Indians who habitually use it. With them familiarity never breeds contempt. They never take any chances. The darts with the poisoned tips are placed carefully in strips of bark cloth or lace bark. These are then tightly rolled, so that a dart may be abstracted without any possibility of anyone's accidentally touching the envenomed tip.

This roll is kept in a special quiver or a container of basketry which has been smeared with waterproof wax, since dampness or sudden changes in temperature may injure the poison. When not in use, the quiver with the darts and the lump of pitchlike curare (in a small gourd or calabash) are suspended from a rafter of the owner's hut, well out of reach.

When in use, the quiver is slung to the Indian's belt or to a cord about his waist. Attached to it are a tiny basket of silk from the pod of the Ceiba tree and the jaw of a *perai,* or Carib fish (Fig. 76).

These are most essential accessories. A dart to be used has a tuft of silk cotton rolled about its butt end. This makes it fit snugly in the blowgun and balances the dart in flight. The tip of the dart, just above the poisoned area, is twirled between the sharp edges of the fish teeth, which cut a tiny girdle about it. This causes the tip to break off when it strikes an object, thus obviating any chance of the deadly missile's dropping to the ground and being stepped upon later on by a barefooted Indian.

DEADLY SAVAGE WEAPONS 135

Fully as much care is bestowed upon the manufacture of the blowgun as upon the preparation or care of the poison and the darts, although the process varies considerably with the tribe. Some tribes make rather crude guns by hollowing out grooves in two pieces of wood and lashing and cementing these together to form the tube. But the true blowgun addicts—the Caribs, the

76

Macusis, the Arekunas, Central and South American Indian tribes—will not accept or use a weapon that is not perfect.

Oddly enough, the blowguns are never made by the makers of curare, while the poison is never prepared by the makers of the blowguns. Also, as a rule, both poison and guns are made only by certain tribes, although used by others.

In the Guianas in South America the most famed poisonmakers are Indians of the Akawoian and Patamonan tribes; while the best blowguns are made by members of the Myagong tribe. In making their weapons, which frequently are fifteen feet in length, these Indians secure straight, hollow reeds or canes. They are carefully suspended over hot ashes, with heavy weights fastened to the lower ends to keep them perfectly straight.

These reeds form the barrels of the guns. The reeds are inserted into the slender trunks of a certain species of palm, which have been prepared by forcing out the pitch and then drying them. The reed barrels are very carefully centered and secured in position by means of wax and gum.

The Indians test them for possible faults by sighting through them at some mark which produces concentric rings within the bore. If the Indian finds the weapon the least bit out of true, he either destroys it, or, if the defect is near one end, cuts that end off, and makes a shorter and cheaper weapon. Sometimes a mouthpiece of carved wood, bone, or nutshell is added. Sometimes a sight is provided by cementing teeth of the small animal called the agouti to the outer weapon, a foot or two from the breech of the gun.

The power and accuracy of these blowguns are nothing short of amazing. I have seen an Indian put six darts in rapid succession into a visiting card fifty feet distant. I have seen a dart, a slender fragile sliver of palm-leaf midrib, penetrate a quarter-inch pine panel and project half an inch on the farther side. It is not at

DEADLY SAVAGE WEAPONS 137

all unusual for the Indians to bring down with a blowgun tiny, almost invisible hummingbirds from high up among the forest trees.

The use of poison also constitutes a queer method of fishing. In the Amazon Basin of South America it is a general custom among the Indians to use the juice of the bitter bark of the timbo vine to poison the water and thus easily secure fish. The timbo bark is beaten upon rocks with hard pieces of wood until it is reduced to fibers. This pulp is placed in a small canoe mixed with water and clay and thoroughly squeezed until all the juice has come out of it.

The Indians carry this small canoe and its contents a little way up stream, tilt it, and gradually let its contents fall into the water in a quiet spot where fish have been seen. Soon the poison begins to produce effects. Fish jump out of the water, turn and twist on the surface, or even float upon their backs or sides. Indians wade into the stream with baskets and hook out the fish. They dive and swim after the larger fish which may not be fully stunned. The timbo has no effect upon the flesh of the fish.

Scaring a lobster almost to death is a novel manner of catching him. In southern New Caledonia in the South Pacific the residents fish in this manner for spiny lobsters in shallow pools left by the sea tide. A dead octopus on the end of a pole is dragged through the deep waterholes. The lobsters are too startled to move, and fishermen diving for them easily capture them.

No description of strange weapons would be complete without mention of the lasso and the bolas. Although the lasso is familiar to everyone and is now used in nearly all portions of the world, few know that it was an invention of the American Indians. So, too, was the bolas. While the bolas is now used only by the Indians and Gauchos, or cowboys, of the South American pampas, in former times it was known to many North American tribes. For example, it was once used by the Wabenaki Indians of Maine.

Today the bolas is seldom used by white men except for sport in hunting the rhea (South American ostrich) and the llama-like guanaco. The Tuelche Indians and other South American Patagonian tribes, however, depend upon the bolas for capturing certain kinds of game, and formerly used it in warfare.

There are two types of this strange weapon—one with two balls or stones enclosed in leather and attached to the ends of a strong cord or thong, the other with three balls. As a rule the two-ball weapon is used for guanaco and the three-ball type for ostrich. However, an Indian may use only one form for all game, or he may use a two-ball affair for ostrich and one with three balls for guanaco.

Perhaps the most interesting feature of lassos and bolas is that they are strictly American weapons. Primitive man everywhere used war clubs, spears, bows and arrows, and axes; boomerangs were invented and used by the Australians as well as the American Indians; even blowguns and poisoned darts were known to savage tribes in many parts of the world; but only in America did the aborigines employ the bolas and the lasso as weapons.

Chapter IX

GRUESOME SOUVENIRS

WHEN the civilized white man hunts big game, he brings back the heads, horns, or hides of the animals he has killed. He is very proud of these trophies which prove his skill in slaughtering wild beasts. As a general rule he shoots wild animals merely for sport or to secure trophies of the hunt. Rarely does he need the creatures for food or other purposes really necessary.

When the savage warrior of the head-hunting type goes on the warpath, he returns with fragments of the human enemies he has slain and is proud of these trophies of his prowess in war. In a way, he has far more reason to be proud of his gruesome human souvenirs than has the civilized sportsman of his animal relics, for the savage has hunted his game on even terms. His victims have the same general intelligence and the same weapons as himself. They are as anxious to secure portions of his anatomy to add to their collections as he is to remain alive and intact and to obtain his own trophies of the chase.

The civilized trophy-hunter, on the other hand, never gives wild game a chance. With a high-powered rifle or shotgun he kills animals and birds before they can come within striking-back distance. In the majority of cases they are harmless creatures which would never attack him unless he first molested them or disturbed their young.

Some modern civilized hunters prefer to preserve the heads of the game they have brought down. Others are satisfied with the horns or teeth, while still others preserve the hide or the entire animal. The savage who collects human souvenirs of his kill is also various in his choice. Some tribal hunters are content to bring back scalps; others feel that nothing short of a whole human head is adequate, and still others collect ears or ribs.

After all, if we look at the matter quite impartially, the savage for centuries has had to kill humans in order to protect his family. A human scalp, neatly mounted and decorated with beadwork, or a dried and well-preserved human head is therefore no more repulsive to him than are to us the horns of a gazelle, the mounted head of a deer, or the leg of an elephant transformed into an umbrella stand.

We all have hobbies, and the hobby of some savages happens to be collecting bits of the anatomies of his enemies rather than game heads, postage stamps, butterflies, or birds. It is a very widespread and ancient hobby, once common to many races in many lands—and until quite recently, comparatively speaking, most of our own ancestors had the same habit!

We shudder as we read accounts of early American Indian raids and of scalps torn from the heads of white settlers killed by the tribesmen. But the authors of these tales seldom mention how the white men lifted scalps from the heads of Indian men, women, and children.

GRUESOME SOUVENIRS

Yet American settlers took more Indian scalps, all told, than the Indians ever lifted from heads of the whites, for the white men were determined and allowed by law to exterminate the whole Indian race.

Nor did these settlers desire the grisly scalp souvenirs as trophies. They collected them for purely mercenary reasons—for the sake of the cash bounties placed upon them by some of their early governing groups!

Although histories seldom mention the fact, scalp-hunting was a regular and quite remunerative industry of the early American settlers, especially in New England. As one white man put it: "Injun scalps is wuth more'n prime beaver and a sight easier to get. So what's the sense in trappin' beaver when they's Injuns to be killed?"

In 1722 Massachusetts authorities placed a bounty of seventy-five dollars upon every Indian scalp. A little later the reward was raised to four hundred dollars. The governing body was not at all particular whether the scalps were those of Indians or of Frenchmen, both of whom the English settlers were contesting for possession of land. Under date of August 22, 1722, Jeremiah Bustead of Boston recorded: "This day twenty-eight Indian scalps brought to Boston, one of which was Bombazen's (a Christian mission Indian) and one Friar Rasle's."

Whether the scalps were those of men, women, or children made no difference, either, except in price, a warrior's scalp bringing a slightly higher price than that of a woman and a child's being worth less.

During the American Revolutionary War both the

British and the Americans offered bounties on scalps of those on the opposite side—whether white or Indian. Popular heroes like Daniel Boone, Dave Crockett, and other pioneers invariably scalped the Indians whom they killed.

Moreover, it was the white man who started the custom of scalping among many of the Eastern Indians of North America.

Before the European palefaces arrived, the only North American tribes that took scalps were the Iroquois, Choctaws, Creeks, Chickasaws, and Muskohegans. Neither the Eastern Woodland Indians nor the Western Plains Indians of North America took scalps of their foes before the white man began to inflict this particular practice upon them.

Also, when the white men began to offer to pay good money for human scalps, the Indians concluded that if the palefaces valued these trophies so highly, they must possess some magical power to control the spirits of the dead or to protect those who preserved them. As a result, tribes which had never before scalped began to collect scalps on their own account, and the custom spread far and wide among them.

The Indians did not take the entire scalp, as many persons imagine. As a rule only a very small portion of the scalp was removed, each tribe having its particular custom in this matter. Some took a circular piece of skin and hair from the crown of the dead enemy's head. Others removed a narrow strip along the top of the skull or from one side of the head. Still others selected a portion of the scalp above the forehead. But there were a

GRUESOME SOUVENIRS 143

few tribes that did remove the entire scalp, including even the ears.

As scalps were trophies or proofs of enemies slain, the Indians did not purposely remove them from living men, but in the rush and hurry of battle they were not always particular as to whether a man had actually expired or not. Many a white man who had been scalped actually recovered and lived to kill and scalp many an Indian in return.

Such revenges could not have been secured had the white men been fighting some of the more ferocious South American tribes that collect whole human heads as trophies.

Heads are quite popular souvenirs among various races in many parts of the world. In most cases only the heads of actual enemies are collected, but some races have made head-hunting a profession or sport. Such head-hunters are as tireless and avid in securing heads of their fellow men as any white hunter in the pursuit of moose, antelope, or other big game.

The Dyak tribes of Borneo in the East Indies, several races that inhabit the islands of the Pacific and the South Seas, and some African tribes are notorious headhunters. But as the individuals whose heads they desire are also collecting heads, it is a battle that never ends. The savages regard the matter as a sort of game, each trying his best to get the other man's headpiece and keep his own upon his shoulders. Sometimes these headhunters preserve the trophies intact, and dry or smoke or otherwise "cure" them (flesh, skin, and all), while other hunters retain only the skulls.

In former years, the Polynesian Maoris of New Zealand were head-hunting addicts. They devoted a great deal of time and skill to tattooing the trophies as elaborately as they themselves were tattooed.

Although we often read that the preparation of shrunken heads is a secret process known only to primitive minds, this is not the case. There is no secret about this peculiar art. It is neither as difficult nor as long a process as some travelers would have us believe. A head can be perfectly prepared in two or three weeks. The exact process varies somewhat among different tribes.

Several Brazilian Indian tribes collect heads, upon which they lavish a great deal of care. Their art work includes decorating the hair with feathers, placing "eyes" of semi-precious stones in the empty bone sockets, and even inlaying the teeth with colored pigments and semi-precious stones or bright-hued shells.

Strange methods of preserving heads are those of the Jivaro Indians and related tribes of Ecuador in South America, and of the Amunsha and other Indians of the jungles about the headwaters of the Amazon in Peru. These Indians shrink the captured heads until they are reduced to about the size of a baseball and are just about as hard. In fact, a well-prepared, shrunken head bears very little resemblance to a live human head and is not really repulsive or gruesome in appearance. It looks far more artificial than real, and quite often shrunken heads really are artificial—especially those offered for sale to tourists or displayed in curio shops.

The Jivaros remove the skull bones entirely by making an incision in the back of the scalp of the freshly

GRUESOME SOUVENIRS

severed head and then skinning it. Peruvian headhunters, on the other hand, first toughen the skin by soaking it in a decoction of astringent bark. They then break the skull by pounding; after which, they remove the fragments of bone and the other contents through the neck.

After the skull and brains have been removed, the skin is shrunken and toughened by a sort of tanning process. It is then filled with hot sand. As the head dries and the skin shrinks, the Indian moulds and presses the features to preserve something of their natural form.

Finally, very hot stones are placed in the skin, which is constantly moved about until the interior is slightly charred and the entire skin has become as dry and hard as wood. It is then smoked by hanging over a wood fire. In the case of a true trophy head, feathers and other decorations are added afterwards.

A real war-trophy shrunken head always has the lips sewed together to prevent the spirit of the defunct owner of the head from cursing the Indian who collected it. Heads prepared for trade purposes are seldom provided with this safeguard, the Indians feeling, no doubt, that if the spirit of the deceased curses anyone, it will be the purchaser of the head, and it is that individual's business to take precautionary measures.

Originally the Indians confined their head-collecting and head-shrinking proclivities to their hereditary foes and played the game rather fairly and squarely. But when they discovered that white men would purchase or trade for the shrunken heads, a new source of revenue was opened up and a new industry was established.

White men failed to ask whether the heads were those of tribal enemies or not. As the supply of enemy heads was limited, the head-shrinkers became less discriminating and raided the villages of unsuspecting Indians with whom they had no quarrel whatever. Neither were they over-particular as to the race of the person whose head they collected. A head was a head; and not infrequently that of an unscrupulous white man who had displeased the tribe was added to the stock in trade!

If a white trader made a satisfactory deal and was willing to pay the price demanded for the goods which he purchased from the Indians, he was safe; but if he haggled too much, it was sometimes "off with his head." This process had its advantages to the Indian head-sellers, for the trade goods of the too-mercenary deceased, as well as his head, became the property of the Indians. They still had their original stock, with another head added, to offer to the next trader.

As a result of this gruesome business, various controlling governments passed strict laws forbidding the sale, purchase, and even the possession of the shrunken heads.

But it is one thing to make a law and another matter to enforce it. In fact, legal prohibition made the heads all the more valuable. It is a still fairly simple matter to secure some kind of a head; although to obtain genuine, human trophy heads one must visit the remote Indian villages where they are prepared.

The law prohibiting the traffic in these strange curios resulted in an entirely new industry, the manufacture of artificial shrunken heads. Many a tourist who proudly displays a shrunken head and boasts of how difficult it

GRUESOME SOUVENIRS 147

was to secure it, possesses merely a piece of horsetail and hide cleverly moulded into shape over a wax core. Indeed, not a few of these "bootlegged" heads are completely synthetic and are made of wax with hair attached to it.

In addition to human heads the Indians also shrink the heads of monkeys, sloths, and other animals. Also, apparently merely to prove their skill at the process, they occasionally shrink hands and feet. They have been known in the past to put entire human beings through the process of shrinking. Several of these shrunken bodies are preserved in the large museums of the world, notably the Museum of The American Indian in New York City.

Technically speaking, the complete bodies are not as well done as the heads and are far more repulsive in appearance. Naturally, neither hair nor nails shrink, and as a result the hair on the bodies appears greatly exaggerated. This gives the remains an almost monkey-like aspect. The nails, too, appear out of all proportion.

Tastes differ in regard to trophies. Several tribes that are next-door neighbors of these South American head-shrinkers care nothing whatever about the heads of their foes but collect ribs instead. Like the North American Indians, who often carried human scalps as decorations and ornaments, these rib-takers believe in making their trophies ornamental. After polishing and carving these rib bones, they suspend them from bands of cloth or bark which are worn like belts or bandoliers. As personal adornments the rib trophies have one advantage over scalps. Whenever the wearer moves or dances, they strike together and give out a tinkling, rather musical sound.

There are numerous tribes that consider human teeth the most convenient and desirable trophies, worn like strings of beads about the neck. These have one great disadvantage. The possession of a few strings of teeth does not necessarily prove that their original owners were killed; whereas there can be no question that a man is most thoroughly and undeniably dead when his head or ribs are exhibited as trophies.

No doubt the custom of preserving various portions of human beings as trophies will soon be a thing of the past, since civilized men and modern government officials frown severely upon the practice. It has already been greatly reduced and stamped out in many places where it once flourished. Probably before many years have passed the one-time head-hunters will be compelled to content themselves with the heads and horns of peaceful, harmless beasts, as are civilized head-hunters.

Chapter X

PRIMITIVE MONEY

Even if scalps and trophy heads have never been adopted as currency, they have been used for barter and trade. It amounts to the same thing; for anything which has a fixed trade value or which has been standardized in value is money. In other words, money is any medium of exchange actually used—not necessarily paper notes or metal coins. In many parts of the world and among many races some very strange things are used as money or currency.

Americans have used many objects other than minted coins and printed bank notes for money. Wooden money has been used in many parts of the United States, and in the early days of that country an almost endless number of things were used as standard currency in place of coins.

When New England and Virginia were first settled and for many years thereafter, the common money in use was wampum, or Indian beads made from clamshells and winkle shells. The name "wampum" is a corruption of *"wampum peag,"* meaning strings of white beads, but there was blue wampum as well as white. The trade value was fixed at four shillings a fathom for the blue wampum strings and two shillings a fathom for the white.

White men later on learned how to make wampum by machinery far faster than the Indians could make it by hand, and so after a time it became too common to be used as currency.

Then beaver skins became the general standard of exchange. They were the most highly prized of the New England furs and could not be produced artificially. The skins were exchanged for goods at the trading posts and were eventually shipped to Europe. In a short time nearly every New England commodity was priced at "so many beaver skins."

But it was not at all convenient for a person to carry a supply of beaver pelts when going on a shopping trip; and not everyone possessed a supply of the skins or could prove he had any. The traders solved this problem by issuing roughly stamped metal discs bearing the name of the trader on one side and the crude figure of a beaver on the other. These tokens were called "beavers," and each had the trade or currency value of a beaver skin.

The beaver tokens were still in use for many years after live beavers had become almost extinct in New England. Many a time when I was a small boy in Maine my grandmother gave me a copper "beaver" with which to buy candy at the village store. Of course, by that time they were not worth the price of a beaver skin; but they were still accepted by shopkeepers as real money.

In Connecticut, when beaver skins finally became too scarce to be used as currency after most of the animals had been killed off, the colonists had what they called "country money." This consisted of numerous products which were standardized and had fixed trade values among the people.

Lists giving these values were printed and all business and trade was carried on by means of this country money.

According to the old schedule of standards, one pound of buckskin was worth one and one half pounds of oxhide. One pound of oxhide equalled two pounds of old iron. Four pounds of iron were equal to one pound of brass. One bushel of wheat was equal to two buckskins, "the leste buckskin" being four and one half pounds in weight. One thousand bricks were equal to one ox, and so on.

Apparently the early American forefathers got along just as well with this unhandy form of money as modern men do with coins and bank notes. But imagine going shopping today, carrying a load of hides, bricks, and old iron and leading a few live oxen with which to pay for goods purchased!

Ages ago men in many lands discovered that bulky goods were not convenient for currency. So they invented coins. Yet in many lands and among many races coins are never used—except for ornaments—and some very strange and remarkable objects and substances are common currency among them.

Stranger still, even among races where copper, silver, and gold are well-known and quite common, the currency is very seldom made of coin metals. On the Pacific coast of North America tusk shells or dentalium shells were the money of the Indians, while in the South

Sea Islands and in many parts of Africa cowry shells were the standard currency (See *Strange Sea Shells and Their Stories*).

Some of the Indians of California and the Northwest used as currency beads of iron pyrite and also beautifully made obsidian knives. The value of these objects was formerly based or standardized upon dentalium shells. A six-foot string of twenty-five large shells was worth fifty dollars, while the smaller shells known as "kop-kop" served as change. On this basis an iron pyrite bead was worth half a string of the large shells. Nowadays, when the Indians are familiar with white men's goods and money, iron pyrite beads are valued according to size, a fine large bead being considered equal to twenty dollars.

Obsidian knives are often of immense size—far too large and cumbersome to be carried about or used as everyday money. They are worth a small fortune in bead or shell money and are the real standard, serving as a sort of bank deposit of those who own them. Just as modern men have ten-thousand-dollar bank notes, which are rarely or never seen in circulation, so these Western Indians had their huge obsidian knives, which have a definite value but generally are not passed from hand to hand.

This strange custom of having some large bulky object as a standard of money appears elsewhere upon the earth. In many of the Pacific Islands, such as Yap Island in Micronesia, the native currency consists of small stone discs, but the standards upon which the value of the stone money is based are enormous stone discs or wheels

PRIMITIVE MONEY 153

six to twelve feet in diameter and weighing a ton or more. They were brought to the island by an Irish trader years ago. This is truly "hard cash" and perhaps the heaviest money in the world.

The natives of the island of Santa Cruz, of an East Indies island group, go to the opposite extreme. They have the lightest of all money. This consists of rare and

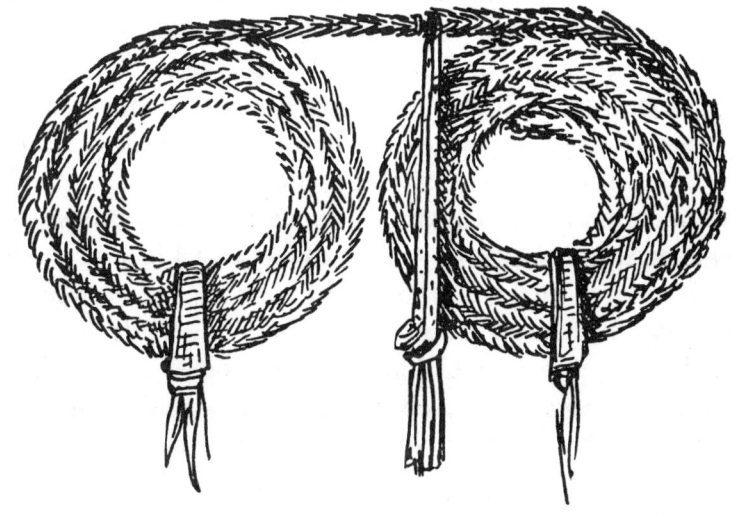

77

beautiful feathers woven into cords which are neatly coiled for convenience in handling (Fig. 77). Among the Amazon River jungle tribes of South America the curare poison described in Chapter VIII often is used as money, while in many parts of Africa, brass or copper wire is the recognized standard currency.

Curiously enough, some very primitive races that never have any use for white men's coins still regard the values of these coins as the standard of trading, even though the coins themselves play no part in a transaction. Several of the Indian tribes of Guiana in South America base all trading on the "bit," the four-penny English coin. Yet they will not accept this currency in payment for their goods, but insist upon beads, knives, and other trade. This odd custom has been handed down from the days when the Guianas belonged to Holland and the Dutch traded with the Indians, using the *betellin,* or tenth of a guilder, as the basis of exchange.

Among the Kuna Indians of Panama, *mana tali,* or five cents in value, is the basis or standard of all trading; yet the Indians do not want and will not accept the Panamanian ten-centavo (five cent) coins, unless by chance they happen to wish to make a necklace of them.

In many parts of the world tobacco has served as money. For many years it was the legal tender of several of the Southern Colonies of the United States. The Virginia Assembly even passed a law declaring that taxes should be paid in tobacco and that individuals must accept tobacco in payment of any and all debts.

Onions have served as currency. At one period in Connecticut's history these popular odorous bulbs were legal tender in the ports of the West Indies and South America. Connecticut River vessels sailing on trading voyages to these tropical lands carried onion money in the form of strings of the vegetables. These were of various lengths, each size having its standard trade value.

Imagine a chin-whiskered Yankee skipper dickering with the swarthy tradesmen of some South American

PRIMITIVE MONEY 155

port, and when the bargain was made, paying for sugar, spices, dyewoods, and indigo with long strings of Connecticut onions and making change with smaller strings!

It may seem strange that American settlers should have made farm products legal tender; that the standard currency of North American Plains Indians was the pony; that the Kaffirs in South Africa bought and sold their goods (and their wives) on the basis of cattle for cash; or that in some of the South Sea Islands a pig is the standard currency. But such customs are far from new. The words "penny" and "pecuniary" were derived from the same custom followed by the ancient Romans, who used oxen as a medium of exchange. *Pecus,* the Latin word for oxen, was the root of the word "pecunia," meaning money; and from *"pecunia"* came "penny."

Cattle are money among thirty thousand Indians living under primitive conditions, quite aloof from the rest of the world, upon the isolated peninsula of Goajira, a part of the Republic of Colombia in South America. Few foreign adventurers have ever visited these Indians, nor has the Colombian government concerned itself with them to any great extent. Hence these Indians still cling to customs which, however odd to the white man, have been satisfactory to their tribes for untold centuries.

They believe, for example, that blood should be paid by blood; that every drop of blood in a human being belongs to his family and tribe, which are jointly responsible for avenging its having been spilt. The strange part of the primitive law is that almost any crime, from petty theft to downright murder, can be satisfactorily settled by the payment of cattle or other livestock to the family or tribe of the injured person. Crafty individuals, therefore, go around with a chip on the shoulder, inviting attacks that can be brought before the native judges.

There is another dangerous side to this arrangement. Every person in a tribe is held responsible for crimes of any one member. Thus any white man whatever can be held responsible for a past crime committed by another white man, even though the two may not even be acquainted.

"You are members of the same tribe," the Indians reason, firmly, "and must pay cattle."

Sly members of these tribes are quite willing to allow themselves to be cheated in a commercial deal with a white man. This gives opportunity for a claim of injury against him; and the white man, of course, pays in livestock—if he wishes to escape with a whole skin; for refusal to pay the amount decided upon by the tribal elders (who are not above accepting a good fee in cattle for their decision) can mean death.

We think that money is an absolute necessity, and there is not a civilized race upon the earth which does not have money of some sort. Yet the citizens of one vast empire, a civilized, highly cultured race of more than twenty million people, never heard of money and did not know that such a thing existed. These people never had or used money, and they did not even have a word for money in their language. They were the Inca Indians of Peru. Yet the Incas possessed vast quantities of silver and gold, and the Incan Empire was the richest community in the whole world at the time of the Spanish conquest of the Americas. Strangest of all, it was the Incas, who never knew or used money, who put the world on a gold standard. The riches in gold stolen from the Incas by the Spaniards enabled Spain to institute the gold standard, which since has been followed by nearly all nations.

Chapter XI

PRIMITIVE MAN AT PLAY

I KNOW a lumberman whose hands, arms, and face are covered with scars from knife cuts, bludgeons, and other weapons. When asked if he received the wounds in war, he replied, "Shucks, no, I just got them a-playing in Georgia, when I was a kid." Then, as an afterthought, he added, "Them doggone Georgia boys sure play rough."

The same might truthfully be said of most savages—they sure play rough. Football and hockey may be rough-and-tumble sports, but both combined do not equal the hazards in the game of lacrosse when it comes to rough play, and lacrosse is an Indian game.

Any lacrosse player will testify that the sport is one of the roughest, yet the white man who plays this game never feels the full force of it. He wears heavy garments, guards, protectors, and even gloves; but the Indian played almost naked, with very little clothing to protect his body, head, or limbs. Casualties were heavy, though luckily they were seldom serious.

Although lacrosse was invented by the Indians and is strictly an American game, there are other popular games which were known to the Indians long before the arrival of white men. Some of them are also known elsewhere in the world. The ancient Mayas of Yucatan were true basketball fans and had huge courts or stadiums built especially for the sport. Instead of baskets the Mayas used stone rings for goals, the object being to throw the ball through the circular apertures. Basketball as played by civilized white men or women may be a rough contest, but when played by the Mayas it was unquestionably much more dangerous.

Rough sport is also to be found in the Far North. Among North Hope Eskimos in Alaska, the rough dance called *Nalukatuck* is a unique performance. The dancer, male or female, usually all dressed up in a brand-new suit of Eskimo clothing, is bounced high into the air from a hide or blanket to the rhythm of Eskimo songs.

If skillful, the dancer remains upright, although tossed up twenty feet into the blue. He moves arms, legs, and body as he jounces up and down. The bouncing mat is usually a large walrus hide stretched over a framework of ropes and small whale jaws. Forty or fifty persons grasp the walrus skin to assist in the strenuous bouncing.

The Aztec Indians of Mexico played a racquet-and-ball game very similar to tennis, and they also played a game very much like baseball. According to the accounts of these sports that have been given us by old-time Spaniards, these games were hazardous indeed. Players frequently were carried from the field or court with broken bones or worse.

Hockey was another favorite game of the Indians, as it is still, and was played by numerous tribes in North, Central, and South America. Among the Sioux Indians of the Western Plains of North America it was played with a soft ball made of moose or elk hair and covered with buckskin. This ball was knocked around with a short stick that had a sharp crook or hook at one end (Fig. 78).

The Navajo and Pueblo Indian tribes of the North American Southwest used a harder ball made of rawhide and a heavier club with a shorter crook; while the Mapuche Indians of Chile still play their hockey game

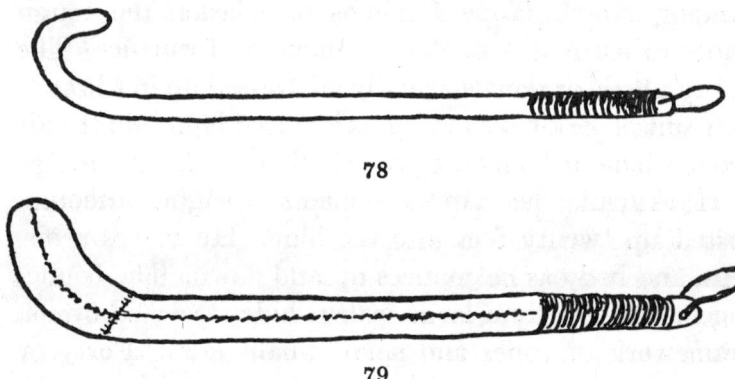

78

79

with hard balls made by covering a stone or a sphere of heavy wood with horsehide; and they use a rawhide-covered club which is as heavy as those used by modern hockey players (Fig. 79).

When two Mapuche hockey teams are engaged in a struggle, our ice hockey seems almost a parlor game by comparison. No self-respecting Mapuche would stoop to donning leg guards, mask, or any other part of the armor worn by North American devotees of the game. Stripped to a scanty loin cloth, and with colt-skin, moccasin-like foot coverings, the players go at it in hammer-

PRIMITIVE MAN AT PLAY

and-tongs fashion. There is no such word as "foul" in their vocabulary.

If the umpire renders a decision which is unpopular, he is usually taken from the scene unconscious. It is every player for himself. If an Indian racing after the ball finds a competitor blocking his way, clubs begin to swing, and one or the other is out of the game for keeps.

Yet there is no hard feeling among the contestants. When at last the playing is over, the Indians limp off, joking, laughing, and poking fun at one another's closed eyes, bruised bodies, barked shins, and bloody heads. They all celebrate together with a sumptuous feast.

Indians play a game for all they are worth, both figuratively and literally, for they are inveterate gamblers and always bet heavily on every contest. Very often they will wager all their possessions on a pony race, a foot race, a game of hockey, or any other sporting event. I knew a Mapuche Indian who bet all his horses but one, his cattle and his flock of sheep, as well as his ornaments, his weapons, and his spare ponchos, on a single game of hockey—and lost. But he took it philosophically and was on the best of terms with the man who won.

Lacrosse may be rough, and the Mapuche type of hockey may be rougher, but a still rougher Indian play in some respects is the stick dance of the Guaymi tribes of Panama. Although called a dance, it is really more of a contest and a miniature battle. In this strange game the most essential requirements are stuffed animal skins and stout sticks about six to seven feet in length, two to three inches in diameter, and with one pointed end. The sticks are used to knock over the opposing contestants.

The stuffed skins are worn on the men's backs to protect their spines from being injured (Fig. 80).

Lots are drawn, and those who are to be the first victims begin to dance about to the beating of drums and

80

the shrilling of reed flutes. As they dance, with arms akimbo and looking back over their shoulders, the throwers hurl their clubs at the dancers, the object being to bowl them over. If a dancer succeeds in dodging the sticks for a time, it is his turn to throw; and the thrower who missed must take the other's place.

To an onlooker there seem to be no order, no rules, no system to the game. Shouting and singing, feather-bedecked and otherwise gaily clad, the Indians dance and prance about, leaping backward and forward; while others rush here and there, waving their staffs or hurling them like javelins at the dancers.

Sticks thud on stuffed skins, crack against shins, or plunge harmlessly into the earth. Dancers stumble and fall, some writhe in pain and struggle vainly to rise. Others lie stretched upon the ground, seemingly dead to the world. When three or four hundred Indians are all at it at once and sticks are flying thick and fast, it seems incredible that any players should survive without broken bones. Yet fatal injuries are rare. Barked shins, bruised bodies, aching heads, and occasionally a broken leg are about the more serious results.

The most remarkable feature of the game is the amazing skill of the participants in dodging the flying clubs. Although to an observer every thrower appears to be striving to kill or cripple his opponent, an experienced Indian never attempts to strike a dancer's body directly with his stick. The trick is to throw the staff in such a way that the pointed tip strikes the ground and the pole swings in an arc, knocking the dancer's legs violently from under him.

Another rough game, erroneously called a dance, is very popular with the Arowak Indians of northern South America. In this contest two Indians take part. Both carry huge shields of palm wood, which is very light, and short-handled whips with six lashes of braided bark fibre. Rushing at each other, they clash shields and ply their whips with all their strength. Great welts appear upon their bare skins and blood flows freely as they leap about. Each strives to get in a telling blow at the other and to protect his own hide with his shields. Finally one of the contestants falls exhausted, or throws aside his whip, drops his shield, and admits defeat.

Whipping is a common feature of many dances, both among Indians and other primitive races. Sometimes the dancers whip one another; but as a rule they whip onlookers or inanimate objects, the idea being to drive out any possible devils that may be hidden therein. Strangely enough, these devil dancers are strikingly similar in costumes, actions, and other details, whether they are African Negroes, Tibetan lamas, Siamese or Malays, South Sea Islanders, or American Indians.

In Panama, the Guaymi and Cocle Indians hold annual devil dances called *kukwah* dances, so called because the participants wear weird costumes of lace-bark cloth, or *kukwah*. The costume includes a loose coat and trousers of the bark cloth painted in various colors and designs. There is a grotesque animal mask built about a real skull, with jaws and teeth and usually with deer antlers or cow horns added, and with a long bark-cloth tail or flap extending to the wearer's heels (Plate I, Fig. 8).

Dancing and prancing about in single file, the devil dancers race through the villages and houses, lashing with their whips at anybody and everybody within reach. Frequently they beat a tree, a post, a stone, or other object which for some unknown reason they feel is the abode of an evil spirit. It is possible that they waste a vast amount of energy by plying their whips, for they

81

are so diabolical in appearance that any evil spirit who caught sight of them would surely take to his heels!

In Bolivia, the Aymara Indians have a similar devil dance, about the only difference being in the costumes. Those of the Bolivian Indians are gorgeous affairs of bright-colored cloth overlaid with silver scales or plates, while their masks are horribly grotesque affairs made of cloth and clay and hideously painted (Fig. 81).

As odd and frightful looking as any other devil

82

dancers are the false-face dancers of the North American Iroquois Indians, especially the Tuscaroras and Senecas. These men today ordinarily are industrious, civilized farmers, wearing conventional American clothes. But upon certain occasions they wear carved wooden masks which are so diabolical and contorted that

PRIMITIVE MAN AT PLAY

they might well be the creations of someone suffering from a nightmare or a disordered brain (Fig. 82).

Garbed in bits of leather or rough cloth, with their faces hidden by the horrible masks, and shaking turtle-shell rattles, the false-face dancers rush about, entering the homes of other Indians and exorcising devils by casting ashes upon the occupants and the furnishings of their houses.

In distant Tibet in Asia are almost exact counterparts of the Bolivian and Panamanian devil dancers and the Seneca and Tuscarora false-faces. Devil dancers in the South Sea Islands and in Africa carry out the same type of ceremony for the same purpose, but their costumes are quite different. The devil dancers of New Ireland go to the extreme when it comes to masks. Nowhere except possibly among the Indians of the North American Northwest are there such weird, complicated, amazing masks as the combination masks and headdresses worn by them. Although no two are alike, all are strange contraptions of wickerwork decorated with feathers, mother-of-pearl, carved heads, teeth, and shells, weird enough to terrify any devil (Fig. 83).

On the other hand, the devil dancers of New Guinea do away with masks but conceal head and body beneath a huge mantle of pandanus leaves and feathers and a lofty, conical spire decorated with feathers, boars' tusks, and other objects (Plate I, Fig. 7). The purpose of these arresting masks and other means of concealment is to prevent evil spirits from recognizing the wearers and to frighten off demons who might otherwise do them harm.

168 STRANGE CUSTOMS

The natives of Ponape, one of the Caroline Islands in the South Pacific, use a peculiar oil upon the bodies of the warriors in their war dances. Women of the tribe prepare the oil in a large cooking pot. They chew dried fish heads, expectorate the mash into the pot, and cook

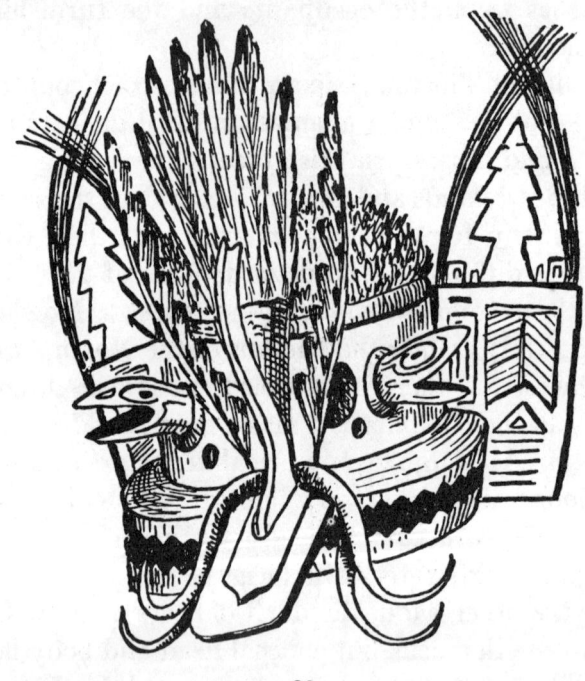

83

it with shredded coconut. The mass is dried in the sun. When rubbed upon the skin, this oil is shiny, slippery, and sun-reflecting. Thus the warrior more easily eludes the "enemy" in the mock battle of which the lively dance consists.

PRIMITIVE MAN AT PLAY 169

Few masks or false faces ever made, however, are more effective disguises than the great mask of the devil dancer of New Britain Island. With huge flapping imitation ears, counterfeit antennae-like horns on his head, a painted leather nose-and-mouthpiece, and with the

84

visible portions of his skin painted to match, the devil dancer of New Britain bears not the slightest resemblance to a human being. He appears far more like some gigantic insect or an imaginary inhabitant of Mars (Fig. 2, Frontispiece).

170   STRANGE CUSTOMS

Apparently some of the African tribesmen feel that they are ferocious enough looking to discourage devils even without masks. They content themselves with

85

painting their faces and donning costumes of palm leaves and feathers (Fig. 84).

The South African Kaffirs wear kirtles of palm leaf,

PRIMITIVE MAN AT PLAY

cover their faces and heads with palm leaves and feathers, and paint their bodies and limbs snow-white, but leave countless spots where the dark skin shows through (Fig. 85). These are not, strictly speaking, devil dancers, for they do not beat or whip evil spirits away. Rather, they are symbolic or mystical dancers, as are the dancers, for example, of the Parasara Indians in the Guianas in South America.

During their own very sacred and mystical dance, these Parasarans wear costumes of palm leaves which cover them from shoulders to feet and palm-leaf headdresses which cover their faces (Fig. 86). At the close of the dance the costumes are hung upon stumps or trees to keep away evil spirits of the forest, while others are placed upon snags in the streams to exorcise the water sprites.

On one occasion, when ascending a river in Guiana, I found a number of these discarded costumes suspended from snags. As a certain museum in the United States had no specimens of the costumes, I collected them. Realizing that if I should chance to meet their former owners there might be trouble, I concealed them beneath my dunnage in the bottom of the boat.

A little later we reached an Indian village. I was getting along nicely, trading for specimens I wanted, when suddenly there was tremendous excitement, and the Indians became as angry and threatening as a swarm of hornets whose nest has been disturbed. Presently I discovered the cause. My men, seized with a spasm of boat-cleaning, had chosen that most inopportune time to remove all the contents of the craft. One of the villagers, happening to go to the landing place, had seen the dance costumes.

For a time matters looked serious; but at last, by dint of various presents, I succeeded in mollifying the In-

dians and promised to put the costumes back where I had found them. Accompanied by a member of the tribe, I journeyed for miles downstream and replaced all the dance costumes. A week later when I sped down river again on my way toward civilization, I once more collected the costumes; but I was careful never again to visit that particular Indian village!

A far stranger ceremonial dance of these Indians is the dance in which each dancer represents some animal. He imitates the actions and sounds of the creature whose part he takes. This is not at all difficult for a man who represents a jaguar, an ocelot, or even a monkey. But the poor fellow who has to imitate an armadillo, a snake, or a mole has a hard job of it.

As strange as this ceremony is the *bimiti,* or running ceremonial. The young men line up and race down a lane between assembled Indians. They run a race toward a huge wooden trough where the customary strong paiwari drink is stored in preparation for a convivial feast. According to the rules of the game the first runner to reach the trough has the privilege of bathing in it.

I never yet saw an Indian reach the goal. Every girl has her favorite runners, and as the contestants dash off, the young women shout encouragement to the men they wish to win and throw red pepper and fine ashes at the others.

Naturally, with several dozen of excited Indian damsels flinging quantities of pepper and dust at men racing past them, the runners cough and sneeze, become blinded, and are soon rolling and struggling on the ground, helplessly entangled, while the onlookers roar in merriment.

Very different from ceremonials so hilariously funny to the onlookers are the self-torturing dances, such as the sun dance of the Poncas and other North American Western Indians. During these dances, if dances they may be called, the Indians cut gashes in their own breasts and backs and thrust pins through the apertures. With these attached to the ends of ropes extending to the top of a tall pole, the dancers swing themselves through the air, suspended by the skin and muscles of their bodies!

Although it appears a most terrible ordeal and one marvels that the participants recover, it is not as terrible as it appears, if we are to believe the Indians. I have been told by an Indian who has repeatedly taken part in the sun dance and who bears numerous scars as evidence, that the medicine man treats the bodies of the dancers with a lotion which renders them almost insensible to pain, and that they suffer very little; not so much as they do from a smashed thumb, as he expressed it. Moreover, my Indian friend stated, the medicine man treats the wounds with secret lotions and ointments so that they heal very quickly.

At all events, the Indians never seem to be seriously handicapped by their torn and lacerated muscles. Some of them take part in the ceremony again and again.

There are many persons who would far rather swing by lacerated muscles in a sun dance than handle live rattlesnakes. Yet the Moqui Indians of Arizona have annual snake dances during which they hold rattlesnakes in their hands and even in their mouths. They permit the poisonous reptiles to crawl all over them. Neither are these rattlers doped nor do they have their poison sacs or fangs removed. Surely, when it comes to "playing rough," no other roughhousing can have quite the zest of dancing with live, healthy, angry rattlesnakes as partners!

Why aren't the Indians bitten? One may well ask. They sometimes are bitten, although not so often as one might expect. For some mysterious reason the Indians seem to suffer no serious results from the poison.

Some scientists claim that they develop an immunity; that they accustom themselves to the snake venom by injecting very small portions of it into their veins and gradually increasing the amount until they are proof against it. Other writers on the subject insist that the dancers prepare themselves by taking some medicine which prevents the snake poison from being effective. Still others feel certain that the Indian medicine men or snake priests know the secret of an antitoxin which they use either upon the snake or upon the dancers beforehand. No one but the medicine men really know how it is done—and they won't tell.

The ceremonial flying dance of the Aztecs, which is still performed by Mexican Indians, is very similar in its purpose and general effect. It lacks, however, the bloodshed and self-torturing features of the sun dance. In this ceremony a number of long ropes are wound spirally about a lofty pole from the summit towards the ground. Attaching their ankles to these ropes, the Indians jump from the pole and, head downward, swing far out in air as the ropes unwind.

In East Africa we find the weird and beautiful ceremonial dance of the Somali Negroes. Unlike some tribal dances, whose performances are restricted to one sex only, both men and women take part, and it is a sight long to be remembered. With bodies gleaming like black ivory and arrayed only in strings of multi-colored beads, the women tread the mazes of the dance with grace and delight. The men, dressed in full warrior regalia, whirl dizzily round and round until perspiration runs from them in streams.

At a near-by well stands an attendant with a large earthen jar filled with water. As the dancers are overcome with heat and fatigue, they stagger to the well. Here they are revived by having the contents of the jar poured over their bodies, at which they mutter a word of thanks and hurry back to the dance.

The Victoria Nyanza aborigines in Africa have a superb war dance. The king is at the head of the dancers, a long tail hanging down from his arm denoting his rank. Two withered elderly dames lead the crowd of semi-naked women and fantastically clad warriors. The dancers wear remarkable headgears of ostrich feathers, eagle wings, baboon skins, shako-like hats, and other colorful garments.

They dance around the village, the women leading the cavalcade. All sing and yell at the tops of their voices. Soon, as the women fall out of the dance, the men start to rush savagely to and fro, exhibiting their valour by sham attacks upon an imaginary foe, to the great delight of the fair sex.

But not all primitive games and savage dances are rough or strenuous. Many of the dances of untutored races are slow, rhythmic, and attractive. There are quiet pastimes such as dice (one of the most ancient of games), jackstones, and games similar to our card games but played with cards made of bark, hide, or wood. Cat's cradle is a game known to nearly every race. Many

PRIMITIVE MAN AT PLAY

primitive tribes are wonderfully expert at it and can form amazingly complicated cradles.

Among the North American Indians a form of hunt the thimble is very popular. The game is played with a stone, a bullet, or other small object. Another favorite game is a game in which the players guess which of two moccasins contains an object cleverly concealed by one of the players. The one who guesses correctly is "it" and takes his or her turn at hiding the elusive object. Among the women, the cup-and-ball game and a form of shuttlecock are great favorites, as is the stick-and-hoop game, in which the player tries to hurl a stick through a rolling hoop.

As a winter sport, many North American Indians have a glorious time throwing, or rather sliding, the snow snake. This is a long, slender strip of wood with one end upturned like that of a ski, and with a slight notch at the other extremity. Holding the "snake" with one finger resting in the notch and extending underneath, the Indian sends it flying with astonishing speed across the surface of the snow, the object being to see who can throw the snow snake the greatest distance.

Savage children have their own games. Youngsters of nearly every race play some form of marbles. There are tops of innumerable forms, some of which are very unusual. The Carib boys of South America use tops made of gourds or nuts, with very long pegs and with holes or slits of various shapes and sizes cut through the hollow body of the top. When these are spinning, they emit loud musical notes.

The strangest feature of these toys is that they are

178   STRANGE CUSTOMS

mechanical tops and are spun by means of a wooden handle with a hole through which the upper portion of the spindle is thrust. About this the string is wound.

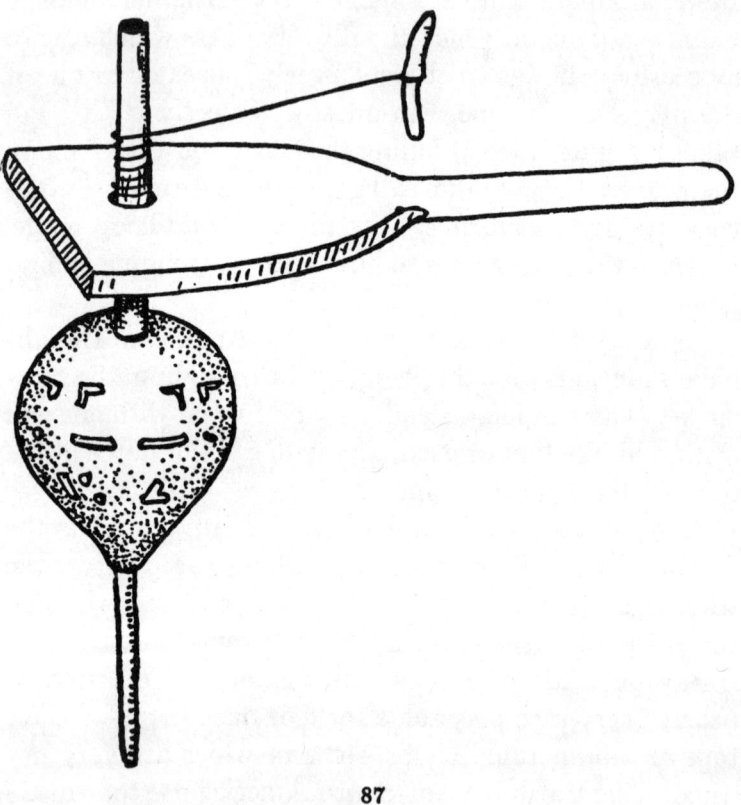

87

When pulled, it releases the spindle so that the swiftly rotating top drops to the ground (Fig. 87), where it continues to spin for several minutes, singing splendidly.

Kite flying is also a favorite pastime of children of

PRIMITIVE MAN AT PLAY

nearly every savage, primitive, or civilized race, and toy boats are great favorites wherever there is water. Savage boys have one great advantage over boys of civilized races. Instead of being obliged to buy their kites and toy boats, they can pick them from the trees. Many tropical trees have very large, strong leaves; and many a time I have seen Indian boys flying these like regular kites. They fly as high and as well as any kite made of paper or cloth.

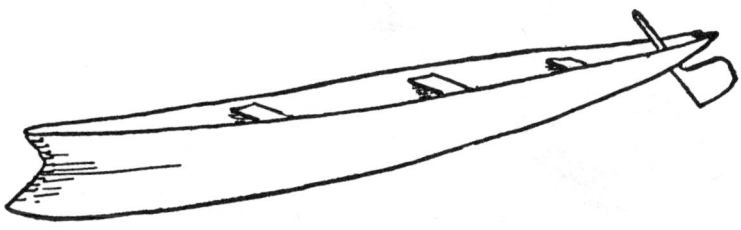

88

When a Carib Indian or African Negro jungle boy wants a toy boat, all he has to do is to search about beneath the coconut palms or climb one of the trees and secure the sheath or covering of a flower bud. These are very strong and woody and when fresh are quite flexible. Lacing together the open, lower end of the bud-covering, the boy forces little pieces of wood between the sides and has a perfect modern-style canoe (Fig. 88).

If he wishes to have a sailing canoe, he fits his tree-grown boat with a bamboo mast. Then he strips some tough, soft, bark fibre from a convenient palm and cuts it into the shape of a sail. He fits a rudder of palm leaf or palm bark to the stern. Now he has a swift, graceful little craft for his play.

Boys of savage races, like boys in civilized communities, are fond of imitating their elders. When they engage in a juvenile game of hockey, a lacrosse game, or a youthful stick dance, they try their very best to be just as actively rough as the grownups.

Chapter XII

STRANGE MARRIAGE CUSTOMS

There is little question that among customs and rites the world over the most universal and the most varied pertain to the marriage ceremony. The evolution of the wedding ceremony may be divided into three phases: marriage by capture, marriage by purchase (which is still very prevalent among some less civilized races), and marriage by mutual selection, which is the "tie that binds" as modern civilization knows it.

Though marriage by capture has gone out of vogue, a pretense of it still remains in the customs of many peoples, even the so-called civilized races. Among some of the Greenland Eskimos, for instance, who certainly have acquired considerable modernizing, the lady in question must appear reluctant to become a bride. She is carried off by force by her bridegroom amid her laughing struggles and gay protests, even though her heart is set upon the marriage. Not to behave in this manner would be very immodest indeed on her part.

In eastern Greenland a young Eskimo bridegroom and his chosen bride are married by the simple ceremony of his catching her by the hair, arm, or clothing, and pulling her away to his home in full view of the assembled village. The girl, usually strong and husky, fights back with violence. Not only is it a custom for her to do so, but it establishes her maidenly modesty, and furthermore, gives the good people of the village a dramatic scene with which to commemorate her marriage.

The admiration of women for strength in men is probably one of the underlying historical motives for marriage by capture. Writers on the subject often hint that among many tribes the women concerned have been excited and pleased rather than angry and distressed at being considered valuable enough to be seized and carried away to become wives.

In Purang, Tibet, it is an ancient custom for a young man to select a girl that he would like to marry and then carry her off by force, assisted by one or two of his friends. Whether or not the young lady is a partner to the plan, she must pretend to be struggling violently against her fate.

The young man keeps her in a separate house, showers her with gifts of food and clothes, and coaxes and woos her. If she decides she does not want him, the village elders or the tribunal of the district chief hear both sides and settle the matter. More often, however, the love affair prospers; and nearly always, of course, the girl of today in some way has indicated her willingness before the actual "capture" takes place.

In the island of Bali in the East Indies it is considered a charming procedure for the young lover to run away with the girl (almost always with her full connivance) and to live with her for some days in a previously prepared and hidden retreat. It is the rule for the lover then to go to her father and pay a fine; after which happy bridal festivities take place in her village.

Among the Lisu tribes of Burma-China the young bride-to-be is carried away by men of her village, kicking, biting, and screaming, while members of her family shriek out for help but do little or nothing to rescue her. The struggling and shrieking continue until the young men have carried her near her future home. Suddenly they let her down to walk, and the whole party goes joyfully forward to a jolly wedding party at the new home.

A less violent custom is found among some of the aboriginal tribes of India, as among the Gonds, where a bride must show herself weeping from time to time before the wedding. It is the proper etiquette for her to indicate that she is not eager to be married off; that she will almost have to be dragged to her own wedding and to her new home. It is not too much to say that the modern custom among civilized people of having the bridegroom carry the bride over the doorstep is a survival of the ancient custom of marriage by capture.

The Uapes Indians of the Upper Amazon follow a custom of marriage by capture which today is nothing more than a pleasant and romantic part of the marriage rites. The young man and his friends are invited for a visit to the young woman's tribal village, the understanding being that the girl is perfectly willing to be married. A festive party is given which lasts for several days. Then the bridegroom's party seizes the girl and hurries away with her in their canoes. No attempt is made to prevent them.

Among the Uacarra Indians in the same section of

South America the young man also has a trial of skill at shooting with a bow and arrow in order to prove that he will be able to support a family with fish and game.

Sometimes the bride herself has a larger part to play in the marriage performance. Among the Araucanian Indians of Chile the carrying away of the bride by pretended violence is a customary event before the wedding ceremony is celebrated. The bride purposely strolls alone past a certain place where she knows her lover and his friends are hiding. They seize her, place her on horseback behind the bridegroom, and rush away to his house, where the relations of both sides are gathered, ready to celebrate the marriage with feasting and presents. While being carried away, the young girl must of course scream with all her might and struggle as if trying to get away. Such dramatics are all part of the game.

An Ipurina Indian bride in Brazil first obtains her father's consent to her marriage. Then upon a certain day she runs away, knowing full well that her young man is pursuing her. When he catches her, they are regarded as husband and wife.

An old Indian tale relates another adaptation of marriage by capture. Hiding outside a girl's lodge, a suitor anxiously awaits for his love to appear, and when she does, promptly seizes her for the purpose of carrying her off for sweet conversation. If she resists, he knows he has made a mistake, that she does not desire him. So he releases her. But if no struggle is made, he finally goes to the father and tells him he is willing to take the daughter off his hands, even though she be lazy, slothful, and generally worthless. The father replies by

STRANGE MARRIAGE CUSTOMS 185

lauding the daughter to the skies and asking an exorbitant price for her; and so the bargaining continues until a satisfactory trade is made.

Actual marriage by capture, however, has never been known to be the universal or normal method of contracting marriage in any tribe. It undoubtedly first appeared as a custom of war, when the victorious males carried off by force and against their will the women of the vanquished foe.

Perhaps the modern custom of throwing rice, old shoes, and various other articles at a departing bride and groom sprang from old primitive customs in which the wedding feast was accompanied by a make-believe or sham fight. Thus, among the Bushmen of South Africa, when a young man marries the girl of his choice, a village feast is partaken of by friends and families of both bride and groom. At a propitious moment toward the end of the feast the young man pretends to drag away his bride. This precipitates a lively fight, with the bride's relations hitting the groom with sticks and trying to get the girl away from him. The young couple is allowed to escape, however, and the "battle" is carried out more or less in a spirit of fun.

Among the Matabele Negro tribes in South Africa the young man obtains permission of the girl's father to marry her. He then kills an ox or sheep, and with his friends brings it to the father's door, shouting that he is bringing "meat for your child."

Immediately, the young men of the girl's tribe (probably ready and waiting for the fun) rush out and try to drive the lover and his friends away. There is a sham fight and a sham chase, but chasers and fugitives all come back and feast together. The girl goes to the young man's town as a bride a few days later.

Among the Banyankole or Bahima tribes of the African Uganda, a British protectorate, the lover and his friends come to the village of the bride. They are led to the bride's home, where she stands waiting. The groom takes her hand and stands beside her while a peculiar contest is held. One of the girl's family ties her up with a rope and holds it, indicating that she has not yet been fully won away. The young men and women of both families and their friends choose sides and with another rope have a tug of war with each other to see which side is stronger.

The bride, meanwhile, is supposed to shed tears because she is being taken away from her family. It is an old custom for her to weep and she must not fail to do so. Her bridegroom remains with her. When his side finally wins (which is the polite ending to the fray) he slips the rope from her and rushes away with her for a short distance to a spot where a hide or blanket is carefully spread upon the ground.

The bride sits down upon this. The friends of her young man lift her in it and carry her away to his home, while her own relatives and friends run after them and try to get her back. The more dramatic the acting throughout the scene, the more successful the wedding has been. A good time is had by all.

Marriage by purchase is still widespread. In most countries, however, it would appear that the marriage custom followed is governed largely by religious, eco-

STRANGE MARRIAGE CUSTOMS

nomic, or traditional reasons. In a country where there are more men than women, brides would bring a high price. When the opposite is true, a man would marry the girl who brought the largest dower.

Sometimes there is an even exchange of presents, either between the bride and groom, or between the two pairs of parents. Sometimes, too, the "purchase price" of the bride is merely a present given to her family by the parents of the bridegroom, or something to help the young couple make a start.

The Nandi tribes of Central Africa consider the price of a good wife fourteen years old at about the value of six cows. Though sometimes betrothed as early as seven, Nandi girls rarely marry before they are eleven. The cows are paid for in installments; if no child is born within a year, the husband may stop further payment, for part of a wife's value is her ability to furnish a new supply of male hunters and female workers.

Among the handsome, coppery-colored Antandroy natives of the southern part of the island of Madagascar the bride most valued is a woman with children, whether or not she happens to be a widow. The reason for this is that many women of those tribes fail to have children, a condition not yet fully explained by medical authorities. Thus a bride who can march to the missionary's altar with a babe in her arms and another toddling at her side is a prize worth having.

Among the Wataveta Negroes in Central Africa, a wife costs a young man one bull, one cow, seven goats, and six jars of beer. The family of the girl comes and feasts at the groom's home for six days, and after the sixth day the bull and cow are taken to the home of the girl's father. The goats follow a few days after.

The honeymoon is spent in the house of the parents of the bridegroom, where the young people are left alone in the house for a month. During this time the bride is not permitted to leave the house for any reason. At the end of that time, the two mothers cut wood for the building of a new house for the young people.

The Masai men of East Africa also pay for their wives. Girls are looked upon as purchasable commodities and are paid for in goats and cattle. After the cattle have been handed over, the girl goes to the husband; and she may not come back to her father's house thereafter unless she is accompanied by her husband.

A Masai may marry as many wives as he can pay for; and if he is a rich man, he will have a hut for each one; if not, he may keep two or three wives in one hut. The first wife is always considered the chief wife and is supposed to rule the establishment. Human nature being what it is the world over, however, a new favorite sometimes supersedes her.

Marriage of a Masai warrior is not supposed to take place until the soldier is between twenty-seven and thirty years of age. Up to that time the youthful warriors and young girls of the tribe live together in a separate establishment managed by the young men's mothers. When the young man is given permission by the elders to marry, and if he chooses a fine-looking girl, she will cost him two cows, two bullocks, two sheep, and some goat skins. This payment goes to the nearest relative of the girl he marries.

STRANGE MARRIAGE CUSTOMS 189

Divorces may be had for laziness and bad temper on the part of the wife, and in such cases a part of the marriage fee is sometimes returned. A widow cannot marry again, but goes back to her mother on the death of her husband, or to her brother, if the mother is dead.

The girls of the Masai tribes have an easy, indolent youth and are required to do little or nothing until they are married. Before that they spend much of their time in dancing, singing, and idleness, not even doing any cooking. This condition continues to a certain extent for a considerable time after marriage and even after their children are fairly well-grown. Then the hard work of the wives begins, however; and from middle age until they die, the older women do all the work of the tribe and become the overworked hewers of wood and drawers of water.

The groom has nothing to do with the selecting of his bride in the island of Ponape, one of the Caroline Islands in the South Pacific. His mother selects a girl for him, gets the girl's agreement to the marriage, oils her and decorates her with flowers, and practically pronounces the young pair man and wife. From then on the wife is under the mother-in-law's thumb at all times.

When girls of Melanesia in the Solomon Islands of the South Pacific are eligible for marriage, they are tattooed, often painfully and at great expense. The relatives who have advanced the money for this beautification expect to be repaid by the groom at the time of the wedding. The payment often takes the form of a great feast and dance.

A variation of the Solomon Islands custom is to delay

the wedding until the purchase money is obtained in full. At the last moment, when the bridegroom has paid the price and goes to collect his bride, the mother thinks of many reasons why she cannot spare her daughter. Her objections call for a final payment known as "the money to break the post near the door." This is a post which is taken hold of when entering the house, and the final payment ends the daughter's going in and out of the old parental home.

White men of all ages have been fascinated more by personal beauty and charm in woman than by any other virtues. Women, on the other hand, have been attracted more by physical prowess in the male. Size, bone, muscle, and courage inevitably suggest the "protector." Sometimes these natural instincts have originated odd customs, as, for example, one manner in which young men of some of the South Pacific islands succeed in impressing their sweethearts.

Men in uniform stationed there during the Second World War wondered why so many New Guinea natives had missing fingers. Here it is considered proper for a stalwart young warrior to offer his best girl a dried finger cut from the hand of some other young stalwart who parted with his finger for a price. The girl proudly wears this strange gift upon a string around her neck.

Around the other side of the world from these young persons, American soldiers of the First World War were astonished to see African Senegalese soldiers collecting human ears from dead soldiers, drying them, and wearing them on a string to carry home as proofs of their prowess in battle.

STRANGE MARRIAGE CUSTOMS 191

Other odd marriage customs seem to be based upon woman's admiration of manly strength. In old tales of nearly every race a lover has to perform feats of valor before he wins a bride. Young marriageable girls of the Western Islands of the Torres Strait, which separates New Guinea from the Australian continent, used to await with great excitement the homecoming of the warriors from a successful foray into neighboring islands. The young man who had fought valiantly enough to bring home the head of someone he had killed could be sure that the girl he had been courting would now finally accept him, as would her family.

It is not too much to say that this was one of many reasons why the custom of head-hunting persisted for so long a time not only in these islands but also on neighboring New Guinea. The young men who failed to bring home heads could still obtain brides among the less popular girls, of course, but it was the best head-hunting fighters who secured the most desirable brides.

When the British settled in these islands and forbade foraging raids and head-hunting, the younger men of some of the tribes complained strongly that the British were preventing them from securing proofs of valor in battle. They insisted that the government was making it difficult for them to get good wives in the good old customary way.

In the island of Madagascar off the southeastern coast of Africa there used to be an odd custom among the Sakalava Negro tribes by which a young man proved his value before being accepted by the prospective bride. He stood opposite another warrior, who cast spears at him from a short distance. The young man had to catch them between his arm and side, one at a time, without showing fear or failure.

We need not look far for other quaint customs which surround the bride and groom, their personal adornment, and their setting up homekeeping together. The Batoros, a Negro tribe which inhabits the country between Lakes Albert and Edward in East Africa, shave and oil their brides before the wedding. The hair on the girl's head is scraped off by the village barber and a razor is run over the rest of her body by some female member of her family. Not a hair must remain. After this she is smeared from crown to toenails with butter and castor oil, the stuff being well rubbed into the skin.

A quaint custom in the island of Cyprus in the Mediterranean Sea is the public washing of the bedding and the filling of the new mattress. The friends of the young couple throw money into the mattress as it is filled. This money may be taken out of its hiding place and spent after the couple has been married for a year.

A parallel of this custom is to be found in Greece, where loaves of bread for the wedding are kneaded in public, and loving friends and relatives throw money into the dough.

The very words used in connection with the modern, civilized marriage ceremony have quaint origins, and in most cases had far different meanings from those for which they now stand. The office of "best man" at a wedding is a leftover from the days of marriage by capture, when a man's closest friend assisted him in snatching a wife from an enemy tribe. What dangers he faced, even to loss of life itself, in the carrying out of the duties of his office! He it was who stood off the assaults of the angry males of the enemy tribe while his friend made a successful getaway with the belle of the village.

The word "honeymoon" is also a leftover from the days of marriage by capture, and while it now indicates the first weeks of a marriage, it was originally a period of hiding, in order that time might soothe the tempers of the outraged parents of the stolen bride.

The throwing of old shoes has had many meanings attributed to it. One version has it that this symbolizes the end of authority by the parents; another, that the shoes might have been thrown in anger during the days of marriage by capture.

Carrying the bride over the threshold is said to have come from the same source, the idea being that the unwilling bride had to be carried over the threshold by force. Then, too, among some races it is considered highly immodest to appear willing or anxious to enter the home of the new husband. As for the word "bridal," it means literally "bride's ale," or toasts which are drunk to the bride.

"Different countries, different customs," but there is one ceremony which might be said to be universal—the feasting and drinking that inevitably precedes or follows the wedding ceremony. Whether the result of tradition or religion, it is probably the one thing that all marriage rites have in common, for marriage is a time of happiness and a looking forward hopefully to the future.

A very beautiful pre-marriage custom is found here and there among South Pacific islands, where the marriage festival is held once a year. The girls are ready for marriage at the age of ten or eleven, and contrary to the custom of most countries, the wooing is done by the maidens.

Their selection of husbands-to-be is preceded by a dance which begins at moonrise on the day of the festival. Wearing behind their left ears the sacred white flowers of virginity, the maidens do a dance symbolic of the mating of man and woman. The waving arms call upon fire to cleanse the body, and upon the wind and waves to bring them long life and treasures.

The dance ends in a frenzy of graceful movement and a crashing of tomtoms. As the maidens fling themselves upon the ground at the close, the men vie for their favor by trying to excel each other in feats of physical strength and daring. After two hours of this the men again line up, and the girls denote their choice by removing the flowers from their left ears and placing them behind the right ears of their intended husbands. Doubtless each young man already knows which maiden will select him.

Not many brides have a human pathway on which to walk, as do the brides of the Cook Islands in the Pacific. During this peculiar ceremony the young men of the village lie face down upon the ground and allow the bride to walk lightly upon their backs, from her own home to the groom's. All the friends and relatives walk in a procession on each side of the human pathway, singing the praises of the bride and the groom and of their ancestors.

In marriage rites or the "tying of the knot" there are similarities and differences among primitive tribes and even among civilized peoples. In some European countries and in many parts of India it is the custom to join the hands of the bridal pair and to tie them as well. In Lahore and Bengal (India) a string of flowers encircles the hands of the young lovers as they marry, while among the Sinhalese of the same country the little fingers of the right hands of the marrying couple are joined together with a little chain. Sometimes it is the thumbs that are tied together; then again, the bride and groom are enfolded in a long piece of clothing during the ceremony.

The bridal couple of the Moriori natives of the Chatham Islands in the South Pacific sit down together in the house, which has been decorated. Their friends, in a circle about them, place upon the shoulders of the married pair a grass rope which they knot together as a signal of the marriage bond.

The Negrito bride and groom of Oceania in the South Pacific can expect to have their heads knocked together by one of the elders of the tribe. In some parts of China the bride exchanges wine glasses with the groom, and then her hair and his are fastened together for a short period as a symbol of marriage.

Marriage is also sometimes shown by the attaching of something to each of the wedded pair separately. Betrothal and wedding rings exchanged between bride and groom belong in this category. In Andjra, Morocco, the young couple send each other gifts of clothing before marriage, which are worn during the marriage ceremony. The Ath Abahthi bride of Morocco gives her belt to her new husband to wear around his head, over his customary headgear; while the bride of Fez (also in Morocco) gives her groom two handkerchiefs, one of which is intended to be tied around his waist.

Sometimes drops of blood of the bride and groom are mingled to indicate union in marriage. In India the Kewats draw blood from tiny scratches on the hands of bride and groom and mix the blood separately in dishes of boiled rice and milk. The bride eats the rice containing the groom's blood and vice-versa.

A Bengalese bride and bridegroom (among the Haris and Birhors of India) are smeared with blood drawn from each other's fingers. Several aboriginal tribes of India have a custom which is undoubtedly derived from the ancient one of blood exchange. The bride and bridegroom mark each other symbolically with red lead instead of with blood.

Sometimes bird or animal blood is used in marriage ceremonies. The Wadders of South India mark the foreheads of the marrying couple with blood from a fowl. The same custom of using blood is observed among the Kayans of Borneo in the East Indies, where both a hen and a cock are slaughtered for the purpose.

The ceremony of eating together from the same dish has a place with many tribes. Among the Navajo Indians of Southwestern North America there was a time when the eating of cooked corn from the same dish constituted the complete marriage ceremony. The Pawnee girl fed her bridegroom from her dish and thus became his wife.

In Morocco, as for instance among the Berbers, the bride and groom feed each other as part of the ceremony

STRANGE MARRIAGE CUSTOMS 197

of marriage. In the Island of Madagascar the bride and bridegroom take alternate mouthfuls from the same dish as a symbol of their marriage.

Sometimes the marriage includes the rite of drinking together, very commonly from the same bowl. Some Brazilian Indian couples drink brandy together; while among the Mindayas of Mindanao in the Philippines the marriage ceremony includes eating together and drinking together by the young couple, who use a common dish and cup.

A New Guinea custom demands that the bridegroom split a betelnut into two pieces, after which he and his bride each chew a half. This exchange of betelnuts is also a marriage rite in various islands of the Malay Archipelago and of the Gazelle Peninsula in New Britain.

The breaking of certain objects into bits to insure good luck to the marriage accompanies marriage rites of some peoples. The ceremonial breaking of eggs at weddings has been found in Morocco, Persia, and in East and West Java. In old days in France the bride stepped upon and broke an egg at the threshold of her new home in order to insure good luck.

Dishes, glassware, and other objects are often part of the wedding festivities and ceremonial rites in Morocco and elsewhere. The Armenian bridegroom throws a plate upon the ground and tramples upon it for luck. The Gypsies in various countries (Turkey, Spain, Germany, and Transylvania) break an earthenware dish as part of a marriage ceremony, while the Gypsies of the Basque country throw a jar towards the sun and afterwards count the pieces.

Sometimes it is a staff, a stick, or a tree that is broken for luck. In South Africa the young Zulu bride breaks the staff of a spear as part of her bridal ceremony, while the Matabele bride, also of South Africa, smashes a gourd or calabash at her own wedding. Among the Yokuts in Siberia the bride breaks across the doorway of her new home two thin, dry sticks, held by two of her friends. With these sticks she then lights the fire inside the house.

Modern society favors the throwing of rice or confetti upon the happy couple, but few brides and grooms of today realize how ancient is that custom. The throwing of cereals or fruit upon the bride or bridal pair for "good luck and many children" has been traced to primitive Indo-Europeans. The custom is common from India, Indo-China, and the Indian Archipelago to the Atlantic Ocean.

The Siamese bridal couple is sprinkled with rice, scented oil, and flowers. The Hindu bridal pair of South India is showered with rice; while among the Mundas of India the bride and bridegroom throw rice at each other. In Tibet the bride is received by her mother-in-law, who holds a mixture of barley flour and butter in one hand and a jar of milk in the other. Sometimes the bride is showered with grain by members of both families.

Sometimes in Slavonic countries the young bridal couple is showered with corn and hops, wheat, nuts, or coins. These ceremonials may even take place in church, as in some parts of Russia, and are always considered a blessing. It may be the mother, the priest, the clerk, or the sexton who does the sprinkling. In Italy confetti has taken the place of the ancient grain, while in some parts of France hemp seed or wheat have been used.

We have now considered marriage rites which, it has been believed, brought good luck or special benefits to the married couple. But there are other ceremonials which people have observed since ancient times that are for the purpose of protecting the young people from bad luck or evil happenings. A few of these customs may prove interesting to describe.

In some parts of Russia, doors, windows, and the chimneys were closed at a wedding to keep evil spirits from flying in and placing a curse upon the bride and bridegroom. The Siberian Yukaghirs used to believe in firing off guns from sledges which followed the bridal sledge, the noise being intended to drive away wicked spirits.

This practice of producing noise and din at a wedding is common to many tribes and peoples around the world. Although it has deteriorated into funmaking, the custom undoubtedly derives from the old idea of scaring away unpropitious influences. Thus, in Morocco, guns are fired, loud music is performed, and groups of women keep up a constant clamor at a wedding.

The power of the odor of gunpowder to drive away spirits was once thought to be considerable. Guns are fired off as the bride is being taken to her new home and again when she arrives there. It is believed particularly lucky for her if the smoke rolls around her or whirls through the doorway and into the house.

Among both the Yukaghirs of Siberia and the Brahmans of ancient India shots or arrows fired at a wedding were intended to pierce the eyes of demons that might be flying around to harm the bride and groom. In China, before the Manchu bride was taken out of her sedan chair at her new home, her new husband fired three arrows at the window blinds.

A curious survival of the custom of noisemaking at a wedding is to be found in parts of the United States, as for instance in the Middle West. This is the *charivari*, or commonly called "shivaree," which is a sort of rough jest in the form of a noisy serenade to the bride and groom.

At a shivaree, friends gather secretly around the home of the bridal couple at a late hour of the night following the ceremony. They make a terrific din with kettles, dishpans, cowbells, and other crude noisemaking implements. The bride and groom are supposed to make an appearance and to greet the revelers or to invite them inside for a brief festivity. Food and drinks are brought by the revelers, or supplied by the bride and groom, who may possibly have been expecting the party to arrive.

The crossing of two swords over the heads of the marrying pair is a common custom. Even today it is in use in modern military weddings among various peoples the world over. This custom prevails in Morocco, where it is supposed that bad spirits are afraid of steel and particularly of steel weapons. There, the bridegroom and sometimes even the bride may carry a dagger to the wedding.

High-caste Hindus of the Punjab in India believe that the bridegroom should carry an iron weapon at the marriage ceremony. At Foochow, in China, it has been the custom for the bride's sedan to have painted upon the outside the picture of a fierce-looking man seated upon a tiger. He holds a raised sword in his hand to keep bad influences away from the bride.

Fire and water have been used as purifiers in marriage ceremonials among a great many peoples. The two lovers bathe in holy water in South Celebes in the East Indies. When the bride arrives at her new home among the Edo-speaking peoples of Nigeria in Africa, a member of her family washes her hands in a basin and her new husband dries them with a towel. Sometimes in Nigeria it is the bride's feet which are bathed.

The Moroccan bride may be purified by milk, water, or henna, which is either offered to her or sprinkled upon her. The bridal pair of Tibet is sprinkled with holy water by the priest, or lama. Among the African Matabele Negroes of South Africa the bride brings a calabash of water to her new home, pours some of it over the bridegroom, and sprinkles his family and friends with what is left. She then crushes the calabash with her foot.

Candles burning at Moroccan wedding ceremonies are supposed to terrify evil spirits. The bride of Fez used to be taken to her new home, not only with noise and fanfare, but with plenty of torches. In ancient Greece and Rome lighted torches accompanied the bridal pair to the new home. Sometimes in modern Greece the bride and groom themselves carry torches. At Hindu weddings lights and other objects are waved around the heads of the marrying pair. It is an East Indian Javanese custom for friends of the newlyweds to enter the bridal chamber with burning torches which they carry to every corner in order to rid the room of hateful spirits.

Sometimes the bride and groom, either singly or together, must walk over or around a burning fire, throw coins into the fire, or throw a firebrand over the threshold. In many parts of Europe and in some places in India the bride is led several times around or before the fire of the hearth.

This circumambulation of the bride or groom is not necessarily around or before a fire. In Poland the bride and groom walk around a table; and among the Little Russians they are led three times around bread and salt which have been placed upon a tray or table.

An old Moroccan custom was to have the bride taken three or seven times around the mosque or around her bridegroom's house or tent. The Bedouins of North Africa lead the bride, mounted upon a camel, three times around the bridegroom's tent, while her women companions make noisy outcries to confuse evil spirits that might be lurking around. The Mundas of Chota Nagpur in India carry both bride and groom around the new home. The Siberian Tartars follow the custom of having the whole bridal procession (usually of sledges) drive three times around the bridegroom's dwelling.

A whole book could be written on customs of these types. Brides and grooms have been ceremonially beaten with light sticks or whips; or thumped upon the back for good luck; or have exchanged clothes with each other in order to deceive evil spirits that might be spying around; or have been represented by substitutes at mock marriages; or have been locked up or closed in, in one way or another, as protection against the evil eye or other danger.

The American bride today wears "something old and something new; something borrowed and something blue"—as truly superstitious a custom as all the rest. In fact, almost every phase of the ceremonials attendant upon the modern girl's marriage can be traced to ancient, hallowed customs whose origins lie far back in the dim, early periods of mankind's existence.

Why are these ties between the old and the modern so difficult to break? Why do we cling to these old superstitions?

The answer is not easy to define. It may be that tribal habit, plus reverence for the ancient, helps us to keep the old customs alive. Perhaps fear holds us to them—fear of the future and the ever-present uncertainty of human life and happiness.

CHAPTER XIII

STRANGE FOODS

What will you have—filet of rattlesnake, baked alligator tail, shark-fin soup, or roast dog?

If you should step into a restaurant and glancing over the menu see such dishes offered, you certainly would think them very strange foods. But if you should feel curious enough to try them, you would find them delicious.

These are only a few examples of many strange foods which are popular with many people. For that matter, they are not confined to "strange" people, for even individual persons of the same country or community eat certain foods that seem strange to others.

Canned rattlesnake is a regular dish in many leading restaurants in New York and elsewhere. The big canneries in Florida find it difficult to supply enough rattlesnakes to meet the ever-increasing demand. It is said that other snakes, too, are good to eat, such as the common black snakes, bull snakes, gopher snakes, chicken snakes, and coach-whip snakes.

The majority of Americans however, feel revulsion at the mere thought of eating snake meat. I have known persons who had no fear of the reptiles themselves, not hesitating to handle them, yet were very reluctant to eat their flesh.

It is a matter of fact, however, that there are few creatures more cleanly in their habits than are snakes. The flesh is white and firm, looks much like a filet of sole, and is free from bones and gristle. It tastes more like quail than anything else, yet it has a distinct and pleasant flavor of its own.

The same is true of alligator tail. Large 'gators are not to be recommended, for they are usually unpleasantly musky in taste; but the flesh from the tail of a 'gator from four to six feet long is as good as any sole or halibut steak, and tastes much the same.

Another reptile whose flesh is served on many tables and is a favorite dish in many parts of tropical America is the iguana (See *Strange Reptiles and Their Stories*). This big lizard, often five feet or more in length, lives entirely upon fruit and insects and is excellent eating, as are its eggs. It is always on sale in most of the markets of the West Indies and of Central and South America. Oddly enough, many people who think iguana a delicious food will refrain from eating snakes, yet one is just as much a reptile as the other.

After all, why shouldn't reptiles be good to eat? We consider the "saddles," or legs, of frogs, a delicacy; so also terrapin stew and green turtle soup; and turtles are reptiles and frogs are batrachians, which are very closely related to reptiles.

I often wonder why we eat only the hind legs of a frog. Of course, many frogs have such a small amount of flesh, aside from the legs, that it would scarcely be worth the trouble of cooking it. But the large bullfrogs, especially those of the Southern United States, have plenty of good flesh on the body and fore legs.

In the West Indies the natives are fond of the large land frogs known there by the French name, *crapaud*. The natives eat the flesh of the entire frog. Many visitors to the islands who would never dream of eating frogs enjoy the delicious "mountain chicken" served in the island restaurants, quite ignorant of the fact that the dish is nothing more or less than *crapaud*.

When it comes to dining, a great deal is in a name. People pay highly for terrapin stew, which as often as not is made from snapping turtles, or "sliders," which are not considered fit to eat if served under their correct name. In Florida the large land turtles known as "gophers" are very common. The meat of these tortoises is most delicious; yet many persons will not eat a gopher tortoise, although they enjoy river turtles or "cooters" and also soft-shelled turtles.

Nothing could be more odd than the peculiar fish found in mangrove swamps in Australia and called by scientists the *periopthalmus* ("mudskipper" to the average Australian). This is a food fish that lives both in water and on land and can climb a tree. In fact, if immersed in water for too long a time, this odd fish will die. It moves along the ground by means of its fins.

In Japan a certain fish, the bonito (*katsubushi*) is preserved for a long time by being boiled, boned, smoked, mildewed, and then dried in the sun until it is nearly as hard as a stone. A piece of well-prepared bonito will keep for ten years, and the older it is, the

STRANGE FOODS

better the flavor. It is expensive, and the Japanese housewife slices off only a few shavings for flavoring the soup or stew. It is a nourishing and appetizing delicacy.

A popular Scandinavian viand which is to be found on Nordic tables toward Yuletide, whether in Europe or America, is a type of dried cod called "lutefisk." Seen in the grocery store, it lies upon the floor or shelf in a great heap of long, salty strips that have been dried so hard "you could hit a man and kill him with a slab of it."

Housewives soak the fish in strong lye to soften it. When steamed, it assumes a delicate, jellylike consistency. Served with melted butter, it is very tasty indeed. It is often a church-supper dish relished by many Americans, whether or not of Scandinavian descent.

The muskrat is an edible animal whose name is offensive to some sensitive ears. Muskrats are not rats at all (See *Strange Animals and Their Stories,* and *Foods America Gave the World*) but are relatives of the beaver. Thousands of these animals are sold in the markets of Washington, Baltimore, and other Southern cities. They are called "marsh rabbit" and are eaten and appreciated by countless people who would never think of dining on flesh called "muskrat."

Woodchuck is even more palatable than muskrat, although few persons would eat woodchuck knowingly; and skunk meat is as delicious as that of a 'coon, 'possum, rabbit, or squirrel. As a matter of fact, the question of what we eat or do not eat is largely a matter of habit and prejudice, so how can we say that some of the very strange foods of strange races may not be just as palatable as many foods we eat every day? The only way we can be certain is to try them, but that is not always possible.

Soldiers of the recent war, tramping through the island of Luzon in the Philippines, were somewhat startled to learn that the large fruit bat (sometimes called a "flying fox") is hunted and shot for food by the natives. It hangs by its feet to a high branch and is easily secured. New Guinea natives also eat the fruit bat.

Nearly everyone has heard that some Chinese eat rats, cats, and dogs. We have incorrectly visualized the Celestials as capturing and cooking house rats or gutter rats, alley cats, and stray dogs. The Chinese are far more fastidious and discriminating than that. The scavenger rats of the cities are never used for food anywhere in the world except in times of extreme famine. In such cases the white man also eats rats, if it means a matter of life or death. During the siege of Vicksburg, Mississippi, in the Civil War, for one example, rats were used as food by the despairing internees.

The rodents which are eaten in China are wild field rats, and they are as tasty as forest squirrels. They are skinned, cleaned, smoked, and pressed flat for marketing. They look much like slabs of ham or bacon and have a somewhat similar taste.

The best dogs for the Chinese table are the well-known chow dogs, a breed developed especially for culinary purposes, the black ones being preferred. Black cats also bring a higher price than others. Both canines and felines dressed for market always have some of the hair left on their tails to prove their color.

STRANGE FOODS

The Chinese are not the only people who eat dog meat. The Igorots of the Philippine Islands used to enjoy dog feasts which, however, are today in violation of the law. Many of the Indians of the United States are fond of roast dog and hold dog feasts regularly. In Mexico the Aztecs of long ago bred a species of weird, hairless dog and fattened it for the table (See *Strange Animals and Their Stories*).

The Chinese use other foods that are strange to us. In addition to dogs, cats, rats, and even mice, they have their shark-fin and bird's-nest soups. While these seem like really strange foods when we hear of them, yet they are not so different from our own favorite soups. The sharks' fins merely take the place of calves'-foot jelly from ham hocks, to supply the soup stock. The bird's nests serve the same purpose as dulse, or Irish moss, in some of our own soups.

The nests are not made of sticks and grass, like ordinary nests, as some people may imagine, but are nests of a species of swift, somewhat resembling the common chimney swift. North American chimney swifts, known as chimney swallows, make nests of twigs glued together and cemented to the bricks of chimneys by means of a sticky, gelatinous substance ejected from the mouths of the birds. But the swifts that make the edible nests do not use sticks, and the gelatinous, gluey substance of which their nests are composed is what the Chinese use in their famous soups (Fig. 89). This substance is clean and wholesome, delicious and nourishing.

The Chinese have still another strange food which they prize highly. They consider ancient eggs a delicacy.

When I say ancient eggs I do not mean eggs a few weeks old but eggs that have been preserved in lime for generations—sometimes for a hundred years or more.

89

These old eggs are not "bad" eggs in the ordinary sense of the word. After they have been kept long enough the contents shrink, become hard as nuts, and

STRANGE FOODS 211

have none of the odor and taste of ordinary "elderly" eggs. They are chemically very different.

Even century-old hens' eggs are not such strange food as the eggs which are a national dish in some islands of the Philippines, for these are eggs which contain good-sized chicks or ducklings. They are served as a special delicacy. And along the Amazon, smoked turtle eggs are common food among the natives. They are often enjoyed by white traders as well.

Tree grubs and ants of the leaf-eating varieties are articles of food among certain peoples. Civilized man should not turn up his nose at these odd items of food, for the white grub and the large ant that consume nothing but green food are certainly purer and cleaner than some of the white man's own preferred delicacies, as, for instance, oysters, clams, or even chicken.

Fat palm grubs are roasted and eaten in many sections of the tropics. I myself ate them and enjoyed them in the Philippines. These grubs, or groo-groo worms (as they are called in the West Indies) are the larvae of huge weevils which infest the interior of groo-groo palm trees (See *Strange Insects and Their Stories*).

Grubs are a favorite tidbit in many parts of tropical America. When they are spitted on a sliver of bamboo and toasted over the coals, they look and taste very much like roasted chestnuts. Personally, I am very fond of them. When cooked, the Australian ghost moth, or "blackfellow's grub," tastes rich and creamy and looks appetizingly cream-colored.

On an expedition into the South American jungles I saw the Indians gathering large, dark-brown sphinx caterpillars which were abundant on the trees about the camp. These they roasted in the ashes of the fire; and they munched them as if thoroughly enjoying the strange food.

Wondering how they tasted, I asked my camp boy to put a pot of grease upon the fire. I gathered a number of the caterpillars and dropped them into the bubbling fat. They tasted like soft-shelled crabs. They were a most welcome change from our ordinary fare of rice, tinned meats, game, and salt pork.

Insects of many kinds are used as food in many lands by many races, so it was not surprising to me to find sphinx caterpillars were fine eating. Grasshoppers and crickets, dried, ground into flour, and baked or fried in the form of thin cakes of bread are a favorite old-time food of many of the North American Indian tribes. No doubt they are nourishing. Personally, I found them rather dry, tasteless food.

But I do like ants! Even common black ants and common large red ants are good to eat. It would take a great many to make a meal, but the body of a leaf-eating ant, when eaten raw, has a pleasant, slightly tart taste which I consider very palatable. There are many species of tropical ants which form an important part of the food of various races.

The Tariana Indians of the Upper Amazon in South America eat a certain type of ants, either raw or cooked. The Indian grasps the ant by the body, being careful not to come in contact with the ant's fierce little pincers. He then bites off the ant's head, which has a distinctly sweetish or honeyed taste.

STRANGE FOODS 213

Catching sufficient of these ants for cooking is another matter. The Indians make baskets of light, openwork withes, over which they smear honey. Then they set the basket over an anthill. When the ants have swarmed thickly over a basket, it is suspended over glowing coals. The ants, quickly browned, taste something like bacon. This dish is by no means unpalatable.

When little else is to be had in the wet season, the Indians along the Rio Negro basin in South America eat large earthworms, which, to say the least, are as clean for eating as are cultivated snails of civilized people. These large earthworms appear when the lands are flooded, ascend trees, and live by the thousands in the leaves of a certain species of tree. Sometimes these earthworms are cooked with fish to give the dish a certain extra flavor.

An edible seaworm, a real native delicacy, is relished in the Samoa and Fiji Islands of the South Pacific. These worms appear in swarms upon the surface of the sea during certain months. They are baked in breadfruit leaves along with sweet potatoes and taste much like crabmeat. Often, too, the natives eat them raw, just as they come from the sea.

American soldiers who visited these islands were surprised to see the natives collecting and eating these worms. Men in uniform stationed in Guadalcanal in the South Pacific were somewhat astonished to discover that natives relished eating the raw eyes of the octopus, and that they found cooked tree-grubs nourishing and delicious.

Several African Negro tribes devour great quantities of the white ants, or termites, which build immense hills often twenty feet in height. These curious creatures breed by the million and burrow through bricks and plaster, eating everything green that stands near the walls. They can destroy in a night the carefully nurtured growth of months.

The queen ant is a round, fat, white termite and is the best eating of all. She is some four inches long, with a head like that of an ordinary ant. A strange thing about these ants is that when burrowing into rooms, they bring with them a red earth deposit. In this deposit there are often tiny mushrooms; and it is not an unusual experience for an East-African householder upon awakening in the morning to find a bed of these tiny mushrooms in the corner of his room, which he eventually can gather and make into an excellent stew.

These white ants are a dainty that is highly prized by the aborigines. It is a common sight to see a native in front of one of the anthills, picking out the creatures. Sometimes the natives cover the anthill with mats and the ants swarm out. Sometimes the Indian burrows into the anthill from the bottom. The ants rush up and then are caught and swiftly devoured by the connoisseur.

Common in Zanzibar in East Africa is a white-ant pie, considered a delicacy among the natives and made by mixing sweet, white ants and banana flour to form a kind of honey nougat. Ants and bees of the sweet types are used in confections of this kind in many places of the world. Candy of this character can be bought, for example, in some of the markets of the Haitians and other island peoples of the West Indies.

In Mexico, honey ants are a great delicacy. No Mexican country wedding feast is considered complete unless these ants are served. Honey ants serve as living honey sources for their fellows and obtain their honey from a species of oak leaf. Clinging to the ceiling of their nests, the insects remain motionless, swallowing the sweet honey-like material brought by the workers until the living storehouses, their bodies, swell to enormous size and can hold no more.

When served at the table, these honey ants look like big yellow currants or gooseberries, for the heads and legs are removed before serving. They taste like a very sweet, delightfully flavored fruit.

The Wataveta Negroes, an agricultural and hunting tribe of East Africa, are quite fond of elephant meat, despite the fact that it is very tough. As one explorer put it, "I boiled it from Monday morning until Friday night, and then I chewed it from Friday night until Monday morning."

The natives consider the flesh of elephant feet a toothsome delicacy. The cook buries the elephant foot in the ground, keeps a hot fire over it for two or three days, and then removes the meat, which inside its tough case is very tender and delicate. It is relished by both natives and white men as much as a dish of tender pigs' feet would be among civilized persons.

Instead of chewing gum, the natives of the islands of the South Seas, including Guadalcanal and Bougainville, chew betelnut, a mixture of areca nut with lime and pepper. The saliva and lips become dark reddish in color and the teeth appear blackened. This red, drippy effect aroused the almost alarmed curiosity of

American soldiers who viewed the natives for the first time during the Second World War.

It does seem strange that Americans should consider carefully raised field snails unfit to eat and yet consider oysters, scallops, and clams excellent food. Most Americans would even draw the line at mussels and the snail-like periwinkles so common on our rocky shores, but in Europe mussels are considered as good as any shellfish, and periwinkles are as popular as are peanuts with us. In fact, they are eaten in much the same way. The little snails are boiled in their shells, and the people pick out the meat and munch it as they walk along the streets, watch shows, or loll upon the benches or beaches at the shore resorts.

Most of us like mushrooms, and some of us who are familiar with the edible varieties of wild fungus find these growths even more delicious than the cultivated mushrooms. But how many of us would care to dine on the favorite fungus of the Pacific Islanders if we knew where and how it grew?

This fungus is parasitic on the larvae of beetles that live in the earth, and sprouting from the head of the grub, sends up a long, slender, cylindrical stalk, or shoot, which is highly prized by the natives and is said to be most delectable. Why shouldn't it be good? Surely there is not much choice between a fungus sprouting from cow manure and a fungus sprouting from a grub.

Even flies are eaten and liked by some races. Of course, these are not common houseflies or horseflies. One is a special kind of fly which feeds on water plants in Mexico. Another is a fly common along the banks of the Nile. Another gathers in great swarms in the swamps at the mouth of the Orinoco River.

As I have never yet eaten flies, I cannot testify as to their edible qualities, but I have eaten the eggs of water beetles, which are gathered on the lakes near Mexico City and elsewhere and are a favorite dish of the Mexicans. These egg masses are fried, and they taste more like fried corn-meal mush than anything else I can think of for comparison.

I have often said that I would try anything once, and I have eaten some very strange foods. Some I have found most excellent and always eat them when I have the opportunity. Others are no better and no worse than our everyday "vittles," while some have such unusual or distasteful odors, flavors, or consistency that I never cared to repeat the experience of tasting them after the first time. But then, I also detest green olives, pickled herrings, mixed pickles, caviar, and many other popular delicacies: whereas I am fond of ripe olives, sardines, shad roe, and other common viands. In order to like certain foods, one must acquire a taste for them.

The people of southern Europe, as well as many inhabitants of the West Indies and South America, the Chinese, Japanese, and others, consider octopus, or cuttlefish, one of the finest of sea foods. Considering the vast numbers of people of many different races who smack their lips over stewed octopus, or *calmares,* as the Spaniards call these mollusks, they must be good. Yet very few Americans are enthusiastic over cuttlefish, no matter how it may be prepared.

In Spain, the favorite method is to boil the octopus in

its own inky-black juices after it has been cut into small pieces. The result is a thick, blackish-purple stew which to some enthusiasts tastes much like a dish of mushrooms. Aside from its dark color—which is about that of black bean soup—and its chewy toughness, there is no reason why octopus should not be just as tasty as clams or conchs, for the creature is a mollusk, like these shellfish.

The Eskimos and many white men who have lived in the Arctic regions consider blubber, or fat of seals and whales, very good to eat. A great amount of fat is necessary for human beings in cold climates. Through countless generations the Eskimos have become accustomed to dining on blubber and have acquired a taste for it. Raw meat or even fish, especially if frozen, also form hearty Northern diets.

Raw fish, if eaten when first caught, is just as palatable as cooked fish. I doubt if one person in fifty could tell the difference between a filet of freshly caught raw kingfish or dolphin and a cooked filet, if he closed his eyes and did not smell the fishy odor.

Eskimos of Point Hope, Alaska, eat raw whale kidneys, tongues, and hearts as special delicacies at feasts celebrating the return of successful whaling expeditions. Parts of the raw skin of the whale also are considered especially palatable.

We confine our sea foods to fish, a few mollusks, crabs, lobsters, shrimp, prawns, and crawfish, but there are many other forms of sea life which are common foods to other races, although strange to us.

In the Barbados and other West Indian islands the people are very fond of sea urchins, or "sea eggs," and

STRANGE FOODS 219

consume vast quantities of them; while in China, Japan, and various islands of the Indian and Pacific Oceans, the big squashy sea cucumber, or beche-de-mer, is a most popular food (Fig. 90).

Gathering and drying these for the Chinese trade and other markets of the East is a very important and valuable industry, for this food is always in great demand and brings high prices.

In many parts of the world which have a very dry climate, jerked, sun-dried meat is a common, almost uni-

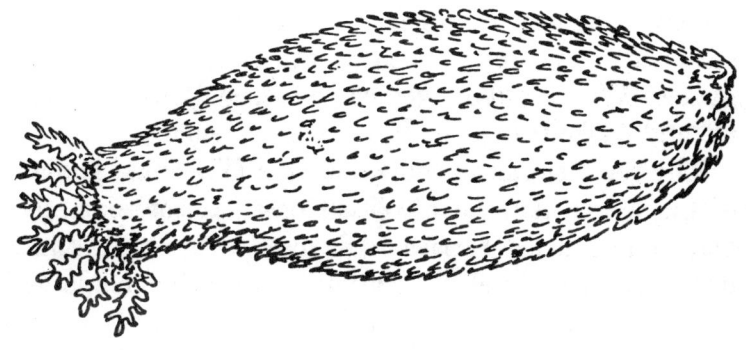

90

versal food. *Charki,* as it is called in Peru and the neighboring countries, when soaked out and properly cooked, is not at all unpalatable. The natives really like it and often eat it uncooked, as Americans sometimes eat uncooked the canned dried beef which is to be found in grocery stores.

The ordinary method of dining on *charki* is to get a good grip with one's teeth and with a very sharp knife hack through the mass as close to the lips as possible.

After that it is all a question of good teeth, powerful jaws, and patience.

In the Western section of the United States, jerked beef is still a common article of food, though strange to Americans in other sections. It tastes like ordinary dried beef, but is perhaps chewier and even more tasty than the regular commercial article.

Pemmican, which also is uncooked meat, is really excellent when well prepared. There are many kinds of pemmican and many ways of making it; but all or at least nearly all pemmican consists of finely chopped or pounded venison or other game meat, slightly salted, seasoned, and pressed into a skin casing with boiling grease. When cold or even when frozen, it may be sliced off and cooked; or it may be eaten uncooked.

The best pemmican is made by the Wabenaki Indians of the North American West Coast. It contains meat and various dried berries, is flavored with herbs, and is well seasoned. Such pemmican, if properly made and fried until well browned, is a dish fit for a king—at least if the king has been on a camping trip in the North woods and has tramped through the forest toting an eighty-pound pack, or has paddled a canoe with frequent portages from dawn until dark.

There is an old and true saying that "hunger is the best sauce," but one does not need to be hungry in order to enjoy roast monkey. Doubtless the overly fastidious person would think it unbelievable that a civilized human being could think of eating a monkey. Even if he does not believe in evolution and scoffs at the idea of men and apes having descended from the same ancestors millions

STRANGE FOODS

of years ago, yet he will declare it is next to cannibalism to eat such human-like creatures. Aside from its appearance, roast monkey is as delicious a dish as anyone could wish, however, and it is widely enjoyed by various classes of people in many countries in Central and South America.

For all I know to the contrary, human flesh may be just as good as that of monkeys. I have been assured by ex-cannibals that it is far better. However, as I have said already, tastes differ, and it is even difficult to find people who agree on the comparative superiority of pork, beef, veal, venison, and other of the commonly used meats.

Fortunately, cannibals are becoming very scarce, and such as still remain are chary about dining in the presence of strangers—at least, when the strangers are present in living form. The thought of devouring human beings is most repugnant to us, yet we must remember that cannibalism was a very widely spread custom until quite recently. Doubtless in the remote past our own ancestors often eked out their larder at the expense of other humans.

The liquid refreshments of man are not as a rule so strange as their solid foods. If we were dining on roast monkey in an Indian camp in Guiana in South America, we undoubtedly would be served with paiwari, already described in Chapter III; or perhaps that other popular beverage of the Carib tribes, casiri, which is a fermented drink prepared from the cassava plant.

Knowing how the paiwari is prepared, we might prefer not to drink it with our meal; but the casiri, which looks like pink lemonade and tastes like slightly hard cider, is made by squeezing out the juice of the cassava and allowing the juice to ferment slightly.

If we chanced to be invited to a meal of iguana or sloth by an Indian of Central America, our beverage would be pineapple or banana chicha, which is really pleasant and refreshing, even if it is prepared by Indian girls who chew the fruit before allowing it to ferment.

On the other hand, we might find ourselves among the Quechuas in the Andes of Peru. The chances are that our meal would consist of frozen potatoes and parched or hulled corn, with perhaps some leather-like charki, or jerked meat; but there would assuredly be a goodly supply of cold corn-chicha. We would have no scruples about drinking that, for it is made "without human hand touching it," as some of our bakeries claim for their products.

If we dined in the heart of the Amazon jungles and were served alligator tail or fried caterpillars, we might tap a cow tree and secure a copious draught of a rich, creamy, nourishing milk.

In Africa or the South Seas our beverage would probably be palm wine; but we would have to drink sparingly, for it is heady, potent liquor, as are the rice toddy and banana toddy which we could be expected to drink in Japan, Sumatra, or New Guinea. Finally, if we had enjoyed a filet of rattlesnake in Florida or Mexico, we might find that tuna wine made from prickly pears was just the right beverage with which to wash down the unusual meal.

The Ravenala tree, or so-called "traveler's tree" of

STRANGE FOODS

the island of Madagascar, off the eastern coast of Africa, has thick, bananalike leaves in the petioles of which are quantities of clear, watery, refreshing sap. The natives collect it in gourds after puncturing the leaves.

The roots, vines, and enormously enlarged trunks of species of the bottle tree contain a juicy sap that is collected and drunk like water. It has, however, an odd taste to the newcomer. Bottle trees are plentiful in Queensland and northwestern Australia.

Certain tropical vines, too, contain drinking water much purer than that of the stagnant forest pools. Bamboo joints holding water were cut off and offered to soldiers fighting in the Philippine bush in the Second World War. In the Philippines, sweet sap from the coconut palm is gathered by the bucketful. Fermented, it constitutes a strong but delightful drink called "tuba."

Blood is a definite drink, or food, among many peoples. The Baila people of Central Africa cook the blood of animals with salt, let it coagulate, and then eat it. The blood of freshly killed cattle is drunk by men, women, and children in demon-exorcising ceremonies among the semi-civilized Antandroys, who are natives of the southern sections of the island of Madagascar.

Germans, Scandinavians, and other Europeans make various types of sausages and puddings in which an important ingredient is fresh blood from slaughtered animals. Certain Italian cakes which are seasonal at Easter time are frosted with a creamy chocolate that is mixed with fresh animal blood. Blood, of course, is a nourishing part of any flesh, and it is not strange that some races should have found it useable and palatable.

The Dinkas, an African tribe in the vicinity of Lake Albert, rarely kill their cattle, which are kept solely for their milk and blood. Blood is extracted judiciously, mixed with Sesamum oil, and then eaten as a delicacy.

The Nandi and Masai tribes of East Africa are also blood drinkers. There is very little salt in their section of the country and the drinking of animal blood is necessary to health. The blood of animals which they kill is carefully collected.

The Masai also have the custom of bleeding the cattle in the neck and healing the wounds again. The animal is bled by having a leather thong tied tightly around the throat. Below this bandage, the warrior shoots an arrow into the neck, only just far enough to tap the vein. The animal suffers small pain or inconvenience in being a blood donor. The arrow is drawn out and the blood flows into earthen pots.

When enough blood has been collected, the thong is removed and the wound sealed up with a mixture of cow dung and dust. The frothing blood is sometimes mixed with sour or sweet milk. This blood drink supplies the salt necessary for the system.

Strange to us are the chopsticks which the Chinese and the Japanese use in place of forks, knives, and spoons. Stranger still than the little sticks of wood or ivory is the amazing skill with which a Chinese or a Japanese can use them. Even rice is eaten by means of chopsticks. While many Americans and Europeans have learned how to use them after a fashion, few white men ever acquire the real technique of the Orientals.

Just as there are recognized rules of etiquette governing the correct handling of our table cutlery, so there are rules for the polite use of chopsticks. We would think it strange indeed if the person seated beside us at a table should select some choice morsel on his plate, and, lifting it with his fork, reach across and place it between our lips. Yet to do just that with chopsticks and food is a sign of good breeding and a knowledge of chopstick etiquette.

Why, you may have wondered, do the Chinese and Japanese use chopsticks? The Japanese merely copied them, as they did their written characters, from their Chinese neighbors. But the origin of Chinese chopsticks is shrouded in fantasy and old tales.

Many years ago, according to one story, there was an emperor of China who, fearing an uprising and an attempt upon his life, passed a law forbidding any inhabitant of the country to use or possess utensils or implements of metal. Since everyone had to eat, and as many Chinese disliked eating with their fingers, chopsticks were invented. Perhaps there is no truth in this account. It is far more probable that some clever Chinese created the story as an answer to a curious "foreign devil" who inquired about the origin of chopsticks. Persistent inquirers often are given fictitious answers, in any part of the world. Thus fact and fiction join to form legend.

Chapter XIV

TALKING DRUMS AND MUSIC

Drums are undoubtedly the oldest of all musical instruments, if we can properly consider them musical. No doubt the first drum was merely a hollow tree. Some early man, happening to strike it, perhaps while trying to drive some bird or four-footed creature from its hole, noticed and liked the deep resonant sound.

Probably the only drums that human beings possessed for many a long year were hollow trees. But some more inventive or intelligent savage undoubtedly bethought himself of cutting off sections of hollow trees and using them as noisemakers. They would be far more convenient and also less cumbersome. Furthermore, instead of being obliged to journey into the forest and bang upon a tree in order to satisfy his love of music or to send a message, a man could carry the drum right to his own cave or hut door and keep it near.

It was quite a step from a section of hollow tree to a drum with a tightly drawn head of skin, a far longer step in fact than that from the primitive tom-tom to a modern snare drum. Even when the skin-headed drum had been invented, it did not entirely or even largely supersede the hollowed-out tree trunk.

Many races and tribes still prefer the wooden type of

TALKING DRUMS AND MUSIC

drum to all others They are a vast improvement over the original section of a hollow tree. By carefully cutting away the interior until the shell was thin, the savages made their drums lighter and more resonant. They discovered that certain kinds of wood gave better results than others. They learned to cut holes or slits in the sides or top of the hollow log and thus "tone" the pitch of the drum's notes.

Primitive man acquired a knowledge of drums which no civilized white man has ever fully attained. By means of drums of wood, primitive man can transmit long messages for incredible distances. Very often he can receive the drumbeats and interpret their meanings when so far from the drum that its booming notes are inaudible to the ear. This is true savage wireless communication. It was in use ages before the invention of the telegraph and centuries before civilized men dreamed there was such a thing as electricity.

When I was on an expedition in the jungles in northern South America, one of my Indian guides stepped from the trail and began to pound upon a huge, hollow mora tree. Curious, I asked him why he did it. He replied that he was "talking to his village" and informing the chief that we were coming. As his village was more than twenty miles distant, his statement seemed ridiculous. But I found I had much to learn about Indian wireless messages.

When, several hours later, we arrived at the village, I found the Indians expecting us. There was a house vacated and cleaned for my accommodation, extra food was being prepared, and the inevitable paiwari or welcoming beverage was in readiness to be passed around as soon as we arrived.

I was puzzled; but it was not until some time later that I learned how the Indians knew we were coming. My Indian guide had actually "talked" to his fellows by means of the mora tree. When I asked him to explain the mystery, he grinned and showed me a dead tree near the village. Like most of the Indian villages, this one was on the summit of a small hill, well above the surrounding forest.

When anyone drummed upon the hollow mora tree, so he assured me, the sounds could plainly be heard in the dead tree at the village. By a regular code understood by the Indians almost any message could be transmitted in this way. It sounded incredible, and at first I could not believe his story. I wanted some means of proving its veracity.

It so happened that one of my camp boys was returning over the trail I had followed. I instructed him to pound upon the mora tree in a certain way and at a certain time. When I knew he should have reached the spot, I stood beside the dead tree, ears tensed, but not really expecting to hear a sound. I actually jumped when suddenly the dead tree commenced to emit sounds exactly as if someone were striking it with a stick. Just as clearly as though I had been standing beside Sam, I heard his blows as he hit the hollow mora tree many miles away.

There was no doubt about it, the dead tree was tuned or synchronized to pick up and amplify the vibrations from the hollow mora. Perhaps, for all I know, there may have been scores, even hundreds of other trees which also picked up and magnified the sounds, or there may have been any number of hollow trees which would have served just as well for sending a message to the village. But only one was used, and whether the Indians discovered the strange synchronization by accident or tried out various trees, I never knew.

At another time I started overland from a small settlement to visit a Carib Indian village nearly fifty miles distant. As far as I was aware, there was not a village or hut or an Indian between the two spots, yet when I reached the Carib village, I found they knew of my coming, the number of men in my party, and just how many guns we carried. The only detail they did not have straight was the reason for my visit to them.

According to the chief (who afterwards became my blood brother) the message they had received told them that I was coming to "catch Indians." As the Caribs could not imagine why an armed white man should wish to catch them, they were very nervous. They feared I was on a far from peaceful mission. I soon reassured them and won their confidence. But despite the fact that Chief Kumwarry and I were made blood brothers, and I was therefore an adopted member of that Carib tribe, I never understood just how they knew all the details of my party and the time of our arrival.

Not that Kumwarry did not try to explain. It was done with drums, he told me; but no drum could have been heard for nearly fifty miles through the jungles. The only way I can account for it is by assuming that there must have been Indian houses somewhere in the forest, and that the drumbeat message was relayed by the occupants.

Most amazing are the talking drums of some of the Indians of the upper Amazon. With these big drums the Indians communicate over distances of more than fifty miles. Moreover, they do not send their wireless drum messages through the air but through water.

Two drums are used for sending these long-distance messages. The sending drum consists of a hollowed-out wooden shell with peculiar slits near the lower end and with the other end fitted with a head of thick hide. The receiving drum is much larger and has longitudinal slits in the shell, with a double head of very thin monkey-skin, which in use is covered with a bowl-like calabash with a hole in it.

When these drums are in use, the open ends are submerged in a stream or lake. The message, delivered by code, is beaten upon the head of the sending drum. It is "picked up" by a man who places his ear to the hole in the amplifier calabash over the head of the receiver drum.

If the message is sent against the current of the stream, it cannot be picked up at a greater distance than ten or fifteen miles, depending upon the speed of the current. If there are rapids, falls, or broken water between the sending and receiving drums, it is impossible to transmit a message. If the message is sent downstream and the water is deep, with an even, gentle current, it may be received by an Indian listening in more than fifty miles from the transmitting station.

These strange and truly remarkable instruments are regarded by the Indians as sacred and magic; and no woman is ever permitted even to see them. They are kept, when not in use, in a special hut which is taboo to women. When the big drum is carried to or from the hut, the women are driven into the jungle. Any woman caught peeping or snooping about the hut is promptly put to death by drowning, so that her spirit may become a slave of the talking drums.

At certain times very sacred, elaborate ceremonies are held, in which the drums are presented with offerings, and their spirits are propitiated by dances, chants, and sacrifices. Similar ceremonies are held when new drums are made, and after the drums have been used. At such times no women or girls are permitted to approach within sight or sound of the spot where the ceremonies are taking place, the penalty for violation of the taboo being death by slow torture.

Although to a civilized white man the booming of an Indian drum may sound meaningless and merely so much noise, every beat conveys a meaning or a thought to the tribesmen. The cadence may bring up visions of past glories, battles, and victories. It may remind the Indians of the wrongs they have suffered at the hands of the white men. It may tell of brave deeds. It may be joyful, sad, boastful, or furious, according to the mood of the drummer.

When the drums are used to mark time during dances, each rhythm has its meaning. Even a white man can distinguish the characteristic drumbeats of a war dance, a harvest dance, a medicine dance, or some other dance. Drums play a very important part in the religion of primitive man. Sometimes primitive man will use a drum to talk with the spirits or his gods; in other words, pray (as we would call it) with his drum. In a way, they take the place of the bells and organs in our own churches and temples.

To savages, certain drums possess mystical or magical powers. They believe that a drum may possess a spirit of its own. They are certain that even if the sound it gives forth is not audible to others, it will reach those for whom the message is intended, through the medium of the drum's spirit.

In the West Indian island of Haiti, various groups of natives assign definite personalities to their huge Big-Mama tom-toms and Papa tom-toms and their smaller drums, which are believed to be the spiritual children of the larger drums and are named accordingly.

In the Peyote ceremonies of the Western Indians of North America specially decorated drums play a very important part (Plate VII, Fig. 91). When a member of the Peyote cult is far from the spot where a ceremony is being held, he will be present in spirit through the medium of his drum.

I have seen a Sioux Indian do this very thing when he was visiting me at my home in an eastern city of the United States. At the hour when the Peyote ceremony was being held in far-off Dakota, he took his drum and beat the cadence softly, a rapt expression on his face and his mind concentrated on the ceremonial.

Oblivious of all that was going on about him, he sent drum messages to his friends in the West and afterwards insisted that he himself actually had taken part in the ceremony. He explained that his spirit had been car-

TALKING DRUMS AND MUSIC

ried to Dakota by the vibrations of the drum. Moreover, he declared that not only had he received return messages from his friends in Dakota, but he related what his friends had said, what they had been doing, and whether they were well or ill. Incredible as it may seem, much of what he reported would prove true when letters arrived days later. I do not pretend to say how he knew. Perhaps the soft cadence of his drum induced a sort of hypnosis and the power of mental telepathy.

Kumwarry, my Carib blood brother in South America, would sit for hours beating a big drum with an old human leg bone—his last link with the good old cannibal days—and to all intents and purposes thinking by means of his drum. After I had dwelt in his village for some time, I could almost read his thoughts as expressed by the drumbeats. I could distinguish his moods. I could tell whether he was planning a hunt, for example, or a dance.

Anyone who has ever heard the measured booming of voodoo drums or *tamboolas* (Plate VII, Fig. 92) throbbing through the blackness of night, knows the strange, almost eerie sensations they produce. There is something indescribably savage and ominous in their monotonous reverberations as they issue from the depths of the jungles.

Even the most unimaginative person feels a strange tingling of the scalp as his mind visualizes the weird mysterious rites which the drums provoke. The gleaming fires, the madly posturing, half-naked devotees of strange African cults, and the bloody sacrifice of the "goat without horns" to the bestial serpent god hidden somewhere in the depths of the impenetrable, silent forest—these are the pictures conjured up by the sound of voodoo tom-toms.

To the traveler wandering in an unknown, unexplored jungle, the sound is infinitely more menacing. He feels his pulses quicken as he hears the pulsating rhythmic sound of an Indian or Negro drum, even if it be but a mere shadow of sound, thin and dim, and felt rather than heard. There is something indescribably wild, something that savours of savage dances and cannibal feasts, in the booming of a tom-tom quavering through the still, humid, air of a tropical jungle, even if one has been told that there are neither hostile savages nor cannibals anywhere around.

It is not strange that the sound of a drum should have a psychological effect upon us. It brings up subconscious instincts—vague, mysterious, inherited memories of the distant past when our ancestors were savages and the drums summoned the tribesmen to war or to a feast. Civilization, after all, is but a thin veneer. The sound of a drum penetrates it and reveals dormant primitive instincts that lie within all of us.

No wonder that the drums ever have remained such an important part of military bands. There is nothing that so fills a man with fighting spirit and martial zest as the drum. Who has not felt a strange thrill at the sound of a fife-and-drum corps or martial elation when almost deafened by the thunder of a drum beaten by a Highlander? Yet civilized man, as I have said, has never acquired the mastery or learned the intimate possibilities of drums which many savage races possess.

TALKING DRUMS AND MUSIC

It seems incredible, I know, yet drums actually can be made to talk. Not, as I have already explained, in code by means of certain beats, but by real words. Numerous experienced and reliable travelers have declared that the Kaffirs and other African tribes have talking drums, and that these, when beaten by their owners, emit clearly pronounced and recognizable words.

Of course only certain words are possible. The sentences or messages to be communicated are simple and made up of a limited number of syllables and sounds adapted to the possibilities of the drums. Also, we must remember that the words of many primitive races are very different from those of our own language and some of them are especially well suited for reproduction by a drumbeat.

The majority of primitive languages are even more complex than those of civilized races. They may not contain a greater number of words, but they often hold finer shades of sound and pronunciation. Yet savages, as a rule, can convey ideas or make themselves understood in a few very simple words. Their subtle inflections and their "words between words" carry shades of special meaning that are difficult for a stranger to comprehend or imitate. Any person who has lived with primitive people and has attempted to master their tongue knows this. It is quite easy to acquire a sufficient knowledge of a primitive language to make one's wants known, and even to carry on an ordinary conversation, but there are very few white men who really master a savage tongue.

One man whom I knew had dwelt with a South American Indian tribe for seventeen years, and, as far as an outsider could judge, knew the Indian language as well as any member of the tribe. Yet he told me that very often he failed to understand the greater part of a conversation among the Indians, and that not a day passed when he did not learn something new about the language. Hence it is not difficult to understand that by the selection of words having resonant, guttural sounds, and by constant practice and by endless experiments with drums of various types, a savage may be able to make his drum really talk.

Even North American Indians succeed in doing this to a certain extent. Several tribes, including the Sioux, have water drums (Plate VII, Fig. 93). These drums are made of wood, pottery, or metal, which are partly filled with water. They emit notes startlingly like the sounds of the human voice. The Sioux Indians use three-legged iron pots for their water drums, and by using several of different sizes and containing varying quantities of water, they imitate the calls of wild animals and produce words and sentences in their own tongue. During some of their most secret and sacred ceremonies, especially the Peyote ceremony, these talking drums play a very important part, the "spirit" of the Indian supposedly talking or chanting through the medium of his drum.

The variety of drums known to man, especially primitive man, is unlimited. Nearly every sort of material is used in making drums. They range in size from the tiny affairs of bamboo with snakeskin or lizard-skin heads that are made by many African, South Sea, or

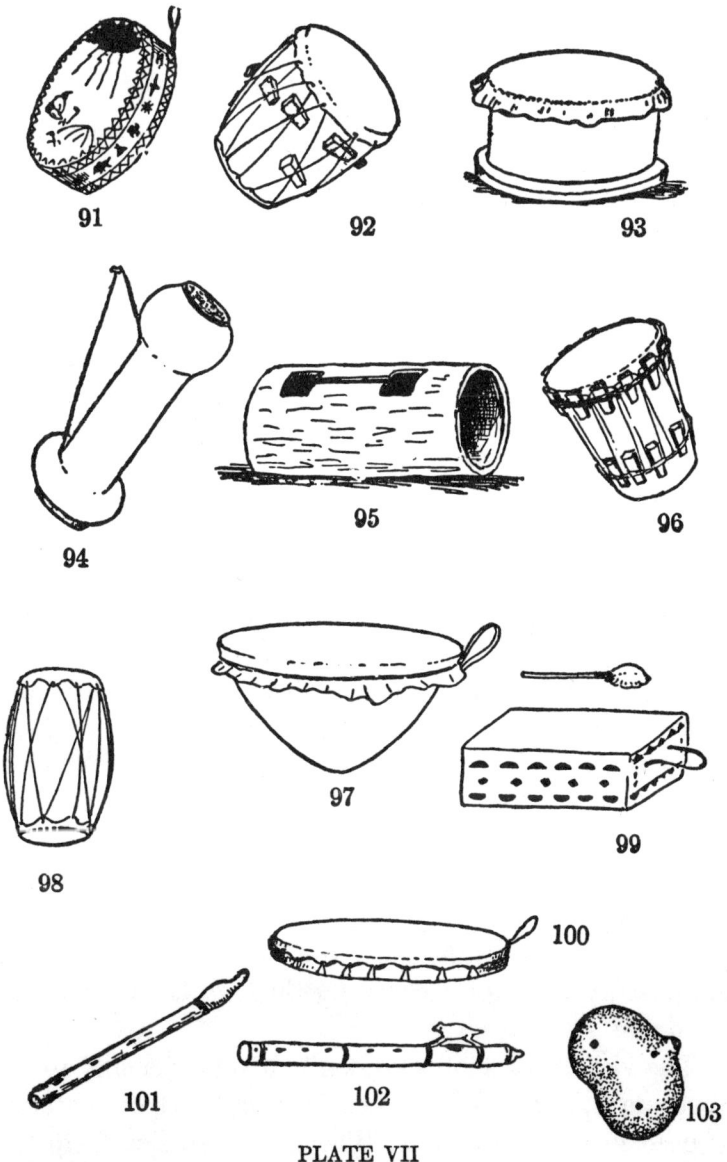

PLATE VII

91 decorated drum 92 voodoo tamboola 93 water drum 94 snakeskin drum 95 drum of hollowed-out wood 96 voodoo drum 97 drum with closed end 98 drum with skin heads 99 square drum 100 thin drum 101 nose flute 102 Indian love flute 103 ocarina

TALKING DRUMS AND MUSIC 239

Malay tribes (Plate VII, Fig. 94) to the giant drums of the Negro tribes of Africa. Some drums are of solid wood, such as the talking drums of the Angola Bantu tribes of the West African coast. Others are made of hollowed-out wood, basketwork smeared with pitch, baked clay, or bent wooden shells with rawhide heads (Plate VII, Fig. 95).

There are drums with a skin covering one end and open at the other, such as the voodoo drums of the West Indian Negroes and the drums of the Cocle Indians of Panama (Plate VII, Fig. 96). Still others may either have a skin head with the other end closed (Plate VII, Fig. 97) or may have tightly drawn skin heads at both ends of the barrel (Plate VII, Fig. 98).

Square drums are not uncommon. They are used by the Korok and other Indians of the American Northwest (Plate VII, Fig. 99). The Apaches and other tribes prefer very thin drums (Plate VII, Fig. 100). Finally there is the marimba or xylophone. This well-known, modernly used musical instrument is nothing but a number of drums, each emitting a certain note when struck.

No one knows what race first invented the marimba. It is a very ancient form of musical instrument and has been known to many widely separated races in various parts of the world for thousands of years. The Aztecs, Incas, Mayas, and other American Indian races all had the marimba when Europeans first reached the New World. It was in use in Africa, in the Pacific Islands, in the Orient, in Russia, in India, and in western Europe long before America was discovered. While the exact forms of the instruments varied, all were alike in general principle.

Like the drums, the marimbas or xylophones varied greatly in size and the material used in their construction. Some were designed for solo use. Others, such as the immense marimbas of the Guatemalan Indians, were so large that ten men were required to play them. Some marimbas had slabs of resonant wood for keys; others were made of bamboo, still others of metal; while some had keys of stone or even pottery. In America the marimbas usually had sounding boxes of wood, either square or cylindrical, while the African marimbas had gourds for the sound boxes beneath the keys.

All were nothing more than highly perfected and carefully tuned sets of drums. The instruments were made up of a number of units. Each had its sounding box, which corresponds to and serves the same purpose as the barrel or body of a drum. Each had a vibratory resonant key, which is the modified head of the drum.

The old saying that there is nothing new under the sun is particularly true of musical instruments. It is almost impossible to name a wind instrument that was not used by primitive man ages ago. There are few which were not known to races in nearly every part of the world. No American race ever hit upon the principle of a stringed instrument other than a sort of jew's-harp and the aeolian harp.

The latter is well-known to many primitive tribes. In South America it is very common. It consists ordinarily of a hollow reed or cane with fine strips of the bark raised by means of bridges. The instrument is sus-

TALKING DRUMS AND MUSIC

pended so that it will turn, swing in the wind, and give forth low-toned, birdlike music. Jew's-harps are made in much the same way, but with a single string. The sound produced by picking the string is almost inaudible. Yet by placing one end of the instrument between his lips so that his mouth acts as a sound box, the Indian produces quite loud and sweet music.

Flutes of one form or another are used by practically every race. While most of these cannot be considered strange, the nose flutes of the Chokoi Indians of Panama and those of the Amazon tribes are really strange instruments (Plate VII, Fig. 101). Just why these Indians prefer to play their flutes with their noses is a puzzle. Perhaps it is because it leaves their mouths free for tobacco chewing while they are playing their nose music!

Although most flutes used by primitive man are simple affairs, really more like fifes, the love flutes of some of the North American Western Indians are quite complicated. They are fitted with bits of wood, rawhide, or horn, which serve the same purpose as the reed in a flageolet (Plate VII, Fig. 102).

Ocarinas are another odd musical instrument used by many races. One of the strangest of this type of instrument is the kidney-shaped clay ocarina of the Wapisiana and neighboring Indian tribes of Guiana in South America (Plate VII, Fig. 103). How any human being can conjure music from such a simple affair is a mystery, yet the Indians play very sweet and haunting music upon it.

Six-foot-long brass trumpets furnish weird, raucous

music for Tibetan devil dancers when played at the same time with drums and cymbals at Tibetan religious ceremonials. The players of these super-long trumpets sit upon stools and hold the long brass instruments before them in such a manner that the farther ends rest upon the ground.

Even to mention a small proportion of the strange whistles and rattles in use by various races would require many pages, for there seems to be no limit to them. The ingenuity shown by many tribes in making whistles and rattles out of a multitude of materials and natural objects is amazing. Among the whistles I have collected are some made from horns, others from gourds and nuts, and others from clay or stone.

There are whistles formed from the skulls of birds, the skulls of anteaters and armadillos, and the teeth of various animals, as well as from the beaks, feet, the wing bones of birds, and the bones of many kinds of quadrupeds. There is a whistle made from the claw of a crayfish, and there are several made from fresh water, land shells, and seashells.

There is even greater variety in rattles; for rattles, to primitive people, are almost as important as drums. No dance is complete without the accompanying rattles, and there are certain kinds of rattles which are used only for some certain purpose or in some special dance.

Gourds, nuts, and shells are very commonly made into rattles. Turtle and tortoise shells are widely used (Plate VIII, Fig. 104), as are horns of buffalos, antelope, oxen, and other hollow-horned creatures (Plate VIII, Fig. 105). Toucan beaks are much used for rattles by

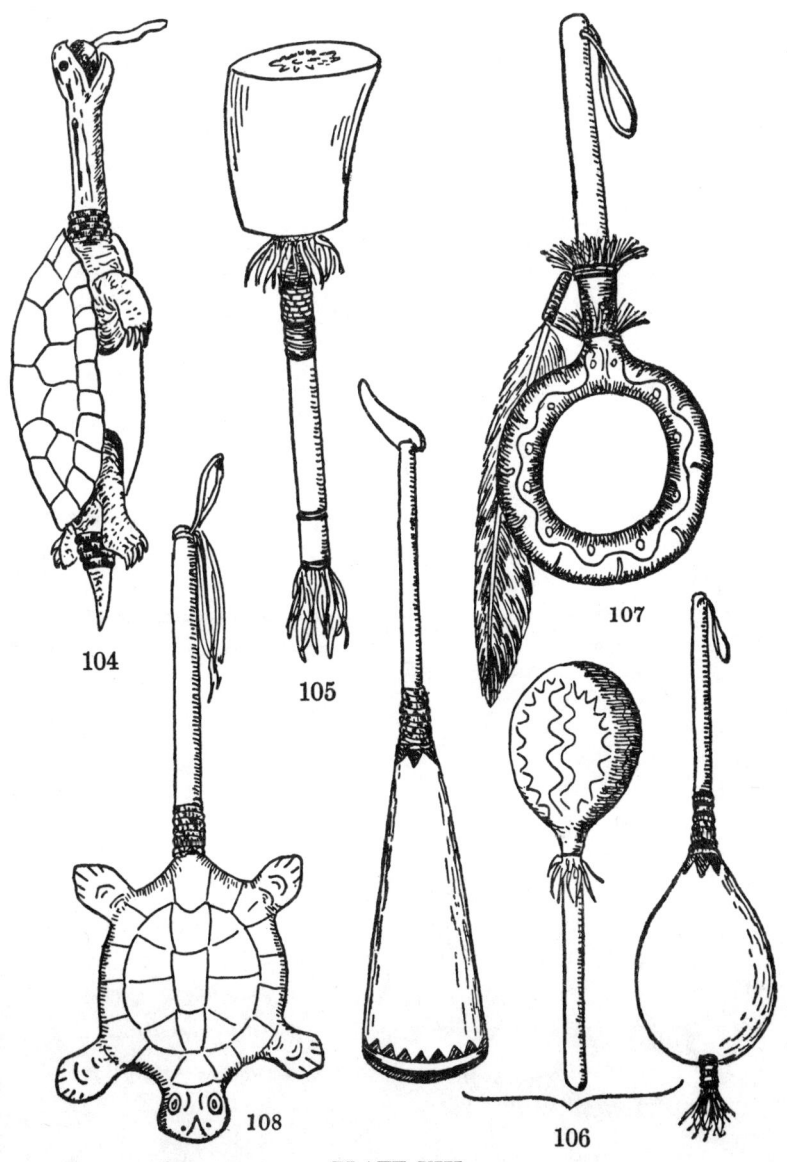

PLATE VIII
104 tortoise-shell rattle   105 horn rattle   106 round and oval rattles   107 hollow-ring rattle   108 rawhide rattle

TALKING DRUMS AND MUSIC 245

the Indians of tropical America, and many races use wooden rattles.

North American Indians employ rattles of birchbark and rawhide. Among the latter are many very inter-

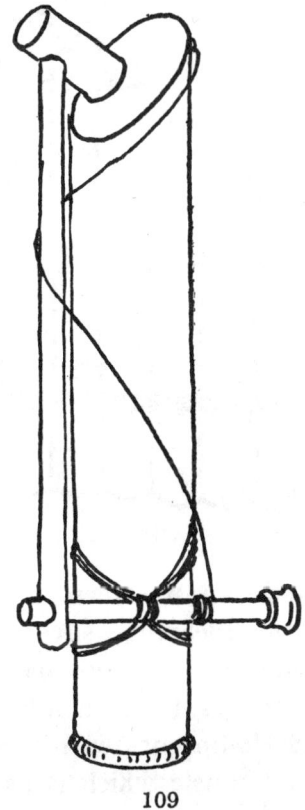

109

esting and strange forms. Some are round, others square; some are conical, others elliptical (Plate VIII, Fig. 106). One type used in very secret ceremonies by some North American Western Indians is in the form of a hollow ring (Plate VIII, Fig. 107), and many rawhide rattles are made in the forms of birds, quadrupeds, or turtles (Plate VIII, Fig. 108).

Even saxophones are used by some primitive people.

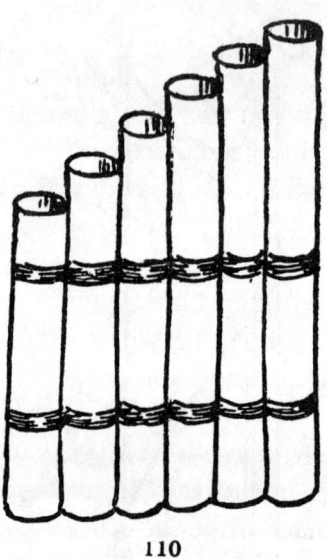

110

Perhaps the strange affair shown in Fig. 109 doesn't look much like the gleaming silver-and-gold instruments that are such an essential part of all modern orchestras. Nevertheless, the principle is the same; and the natives of the Philippines who invented and use it manage to produce music which is as mellow as any that issues from the mouth of a modern five-hundred-dollar saxophone.

Aside from drums, whistles, and rattles, the most widely used of all primitive musical instruments are the Panpipes (Fig. 110). They are found in the most ancient graves and tombs of many races in all parts of the world, and I do not think there is a savage race anywhere (unless it be in Australia) which does not make and use these pipes.

No race in the world at any time, however, has ever surpassed the Aymara Indians of Bolivia, in South America, when it comes to Panpipes. Only our church organs approach them, for the instruments used by these Indians at certain ceremonies and celebrations are gigantic affairs with the pipes a foot or more in diameter; and the longest of these tubes are twelve to fifteen feet in length.

Of course no one man would have wind enough to play a tune on these huge instruments, even if he could spring from one mouthpiece to another in time to produce the notes smoothly. When these enormous organ-like pipes are used, they are played by several men, two for each pipe. As soon as one of the blowers is out of breath, his mate takes his place while the other regains his wind.

Think of the skill and practice required to enable a dozen or more Indians to play a tune on such a device and never sound a false note, miss perfect time, or make a mistake! Our quartettes and sextettes are nothing by comparison, and, moreover, the Aymaras play wholly by ear—or perhaps I should say by mouth. They have no printed music to guide them or to let them know just when and how hard to blow.

CHAPTER XV

STRANGE SAILING CRAFT

It is certainly interesting that any race of primitive people should have designed a water craft which has never been improved upon insofar as the model and lines are concerned. We have become so familiar with the canvas-covered canoes made in our factories that we forget all about the origin of the canoe or what a strange craft it really is.

The canoe is the lightest, swiftest, most easily handled of all primitive boats. It was so perfect that the civilized man adopted it, copied it, and still uses it where no other type of craft would serve as well.

The birchbark canoes of the Eastern Indians of North America were the models for all modern canoes now in use, except for a few types of sailing canoes. These canoes were unique in the materials used and in the method of construction.

Birchbark is not a substance that is easy to handle. It would have been far easier to have built canoes out of hides instead of the bark of white birch trees, but the Indians knew what they were about. They developed a technique in working bark which no white man has ever equalled. Instead of setting up a frame and fitting the

STRANGE SAILING CRAFT

covering to it, the Indians reversed the process by placing the birchbark "skin" upon the ground and fitting the framework of wood inside it.

The only real improvement of civilized man has been to substitute canvas for birchbark; and in the opinion of many woodsmen, that really is no improvement at all. If a birchbark canoe leaks or is punctured or ripped when one is traveling through the wilderness, it is a simple matter to secure some bark from a near-by birch tree, with some pitch from a pine or spruce, and to repair the damage in a short while. If a canvas canoe is injured, however, and one is not provided with patching equipment, the interrupted trip ends then and there, temporarily at least.

The birchbark canoe is no more remarkable than the skill of the Indians in handling the frail craft. The average white person who uses a canoe for pleasure knows how easily it capsizes, and how much skill is required to manage it even in moderately rough water. Yet the Passamaquoddy Indians of Maine, members of the Algonquin tribe, paddle far out to sea in their tiny canoes to fish and to shoot porpoises.

It is a sight never to be forgotten to see two of these Indians hunting porpoises. Seated in the bobbing craft, the men paddle through the choppy, heavy waves of the tide rips of the Bay of Fundy until a school of the porpoises is sighted. Dropping his paddle, one of the men seizes his gun. Standing erect, he balances himself with remarkable skill as his companion urges the canoe within range of the porpoises.

When the porpoise has been killed, the paddler

hurries forward and the men reach over the side of the canoe and drag the heavy creature over the gunwale. How they balance themselves so well in the rough waves is a mystery; yet the Indians perform the amazing feat again and again and think nothing of it.

Often, too, I have seen a Passamaquoddy canoe far out at sea with its occupants, consisting of an Indian, his squaw, numerous children, and a few dogs for good measure, fishing for pollock in a half-gale when the fishing schooners were making heavy weather of it under reefed sails.

They fish until at last the sun sinks low and the canoe is so laden with silvery fish that its gunwales are but a few inches above the waves. Then the Indians tie a blanket or a bit of old canvas to a pole or paddle. Under this make-shift sail they go scudding toward land as unconcernedly as though they were paddling across some tranquil pond.

We must not assume, however, that North American Indians are the only people who used the bark of trees for their canoes. In Central and South America and the West Indies, the Carib Indians and other tribes use bark craft that in some respects are even more remarkable than the birchbark canoes of the North American Indians. When one of these Indians wants a boat in which to navigate a jungle stream, he searches about until he finds a suitable specimen of the purpleheart, a South American tree that has a strong, elastic wood of a purplish color.

Cutting two girdles about the tree and some distance apart, he connects these by a deep cut, whittles some

STRANGE SAILING CRAFT 251

wooden wedges from some convenient branch, and drives these under the edges of the perpendicular slit. Presently the bark separates from the trunk of the tree and comes free in the form of a long cylinder of smooth, tough bark.

Securing some bush rope, or lianas, the Indian binds the ends of the bark cylinder together, forces some strong sticks between the two sides, and presto—he has a trim little canoe! He has used no tools other than his machete and sheath knife, no materials other than those supplied by the forest, and it has not taken him over an hour to build his odd, light craft (Fig. 111).

These "woodskins," as they are called, are strong and buoyant and will carry a much larger load than might be expected. When traveling up or down the jungle rivers, it is often necessary to portage around rapids and cataracts. However, only the dunnage need be carried overland if the distance is considerable, for it is an easy matter to construct a new woodskin and abandon the old one at the portage.

Centuries before Indians or other savages learned to make canoes of bark, they had used dugout canoes. In all probability a floating log, perhaps with a squirrel or some other creature perched upon it, first gave man the idea of a boat. Later, someone probably discovered that a hollow or partly hollow log would support a greater weight than an ordinary log, and the invention of the dugout followed.

It was no easy matter, however, to hollow out a log when the only tools were crude stone axes or mauls. But savages are resourceful fellows. By burning the wood and patiently pecking and hewing away the charcoal, they accomplished the task at last.

Of course these earliest dugouts were crude affairs, lacking in lines and curves, and were no larger than the logs from which they were made. In time man learned how to shape the outside of the logs, how to steam and soften the wood by filling the hollow with water and

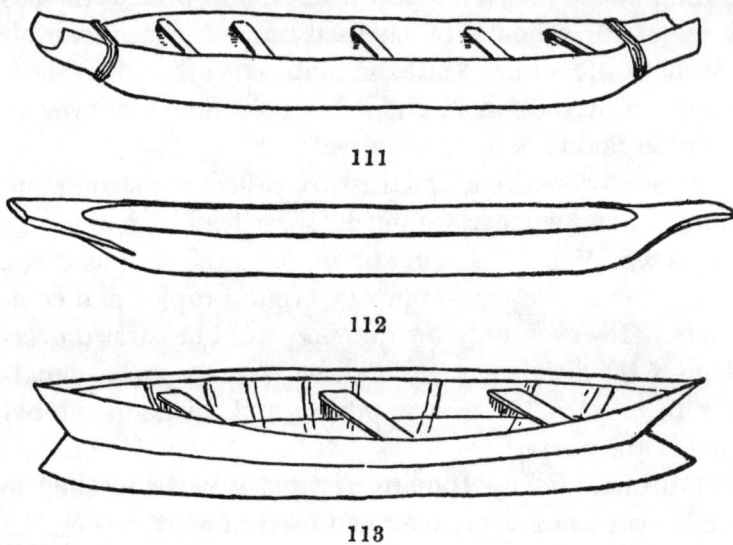

111

112

113

dropping hot stones into it, and how to spread the sides of the dugout to give greater beam.

Yet even today many of the dugout canoes in use by various races of people are scarcely more than hollowed logs with the exterior shaped and smoothed (Fig. 112). They may be hewn so thin that they are light in weight. They may be made graceful in outline, but they are half-cylinders in section and are as "cranky" and treach-

STRANGE SAILING CRAFT

erous as any log. Yet the owners are perfectly at home in them and pole or paddle them about, standing upright in them without the least difficulty.

There were peoples who required better, roomier, more seaworthy craft in which they could put to sea. Some solved the problem in one way and some in another. The Carib Indians of the West Indies added planks to their shell dugouts and produced canoes which for speed and seaworthy qualities cannot be beaten (Fig. 113). The Polynesians, or natives of the Pacific Islands of the South Seas, lashed a buoyant log, a section of

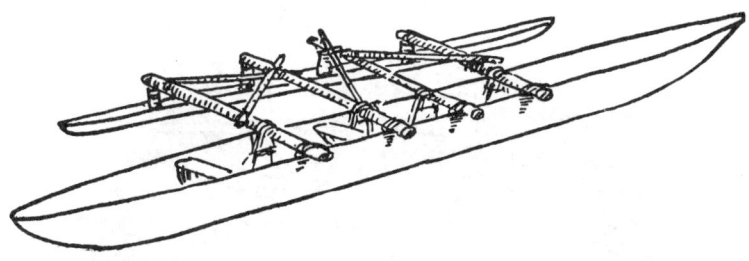

114

bamboo, or even a second smaller canoe to strong timbers or poles. These were attached to the larger craft, thus producing the outrigger, or catamaran. Non-capsizable and capable of carrying an enormous spread of matting sail, these outriggers of the Polynesians make voyages of thousands of miles in safety, and have ever remained the favorite and typical craft of the mariners of the South Seas (Fig. 114).

Unusual as they are, these outrigger boats are less strange than the circular gufas of the Arabs, the bullboats of the Western Indians of North America, and the coracles of ancient man in Great Britain, all of which were made of skins. Perhaps man traveled across water in a tublike contraption of skins before he fashioned a canoe, for in lands where there were no trees to be hollowed out and no bark for making a canoe, hides were about the only material which would serve the purpose.

115

Undoubtedly the idea of a skin boat was the result of seeing a dead beast floating in the water, just as the idea of a canoe probably came from seeing a floating log. If the swollen carcass of some beast floating in a stream happened to have vultures perched upon it—as it doubt-

STRANGE SAILING CRAFT   255

less would—it conveyed the idea of a craft even more quickly.

Perhaps the first man to try it out in the stream clung to some dead animal and floated along with it; but an inflated skin soon proved an excellent float. Clinging to it, a man could kick and paddle himself across a river too wide or swift for him to swim.

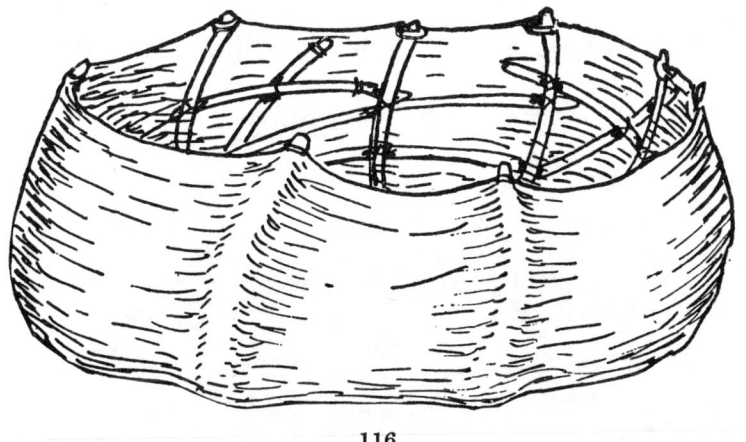
116

Strange as it may seem, the Arabs still cross streams in this identical manner. It is no unusual sight in Arabia to see a man supported by an inflated goatskin and kicking himself across a river.

However, inflated skins with human beings outside in the rain or getting soaking wet in the stream had their limitations. They had to be improved upon. It must have been a long step from such means of transportation to skins stretched over a framework of sticks, but the gufa was used by Mesopotamians of the Far East thousands of years ago, and still remains the most common, widely used craft in many parts of **Arabia and Palestine**. It is a round boat made of wickerwork (Fig. 115).

Great men think alike, the old axiom assures us, and certainly men must have thought alike in Asia and in America, for the bullboats of the Plains Indians of North America are almost exact counterparts of the gufas of the Old World (Fig. 116). Perhaps the first coracles of the ancient Britons were also made of skins,

117

but coracles of willow withes or closely woven rushes smeared with pitch were used by the natives of Great Britain long before the Norsemen raided the English villages. They are still in daily use in many places (Fig. 117).

In South America, also, the natives used craft made of inflated skins, but the Indian natives of **Peru** used the skins of sea lions. Instead of making them into tublike boats, such as the bullboats or gufas, they lashed two sea-lion skins together, constructed a rude deck upon them, and made a sea-lion-hide catamaran.

STRANGE SAILING CRAFT

They must have proved very satisfactory craft, for the fishermen of some parts of Peru still use them (Fig. 118). In the far North the Eskimos built their famous kyaks and other boats from skins of walrus and seals.

Neither boats made of hides nor hollowed-out logs nor canoes fashioned from bark are as strange as the reed boats, or balsas, of the Peruvian and Bolivian Indians. Stranger still is the fact that similar reed boats are used by several tribes of California Indians, though none of these can compare with the balsas of Incaland.

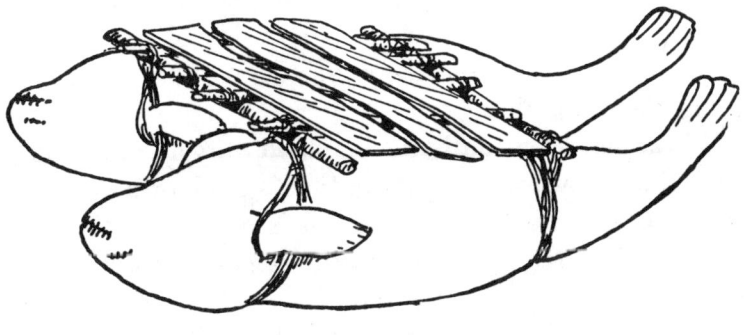

118

When the Spaniards first reached Peru, they found the natives using reed balsas everywhere along the western coast of South America. Many were good-sized craft, in which the Indians sailed far out to sea. Usually they were equipped with sails of woven reed matting or of coarse cotton cloth. This is unquestionably the strangest feature of all, for at the time the conquistadores arrived, no other race in the whole of America had learned to use sails. The Spaniards, however, thought nothing of this, though they marvelled that boats made

of bundles of rushes should be able to brave the open
sea and the heavy swells of the Pacific Ocean.

However, a reed balsa is about the safest and most
buoyant of all craft. As it is constructed entirely of
hollow reeds tied and lashed together, it cannot sink
until the reeds have become waterlogged through weeks
of immersion. Also, only a terrific sea and an awful
beating can tear the bundles of reeds apart and break
the lashings.

Finally, a balsa is the cheapest of boats as well as the
easiest to build. Wherever there are reeds in abundance
an Indian can construct a balsa in a day or two and at
no cost other than the labor of cutting the reeds and
tying them together.

If the balsa is small and intended only for paddling
or poling about, nothing more than a stick or a board is
required as an oar. But if a sail is needed the Indian
must find a tree to serve as a mast and must weave a
sail of the leaves of the rushes (Fig. 119). Very often
this is the hardest part of the job, for balsas today are
used only on Lake Titicaca, which lies between Peru
and Bolivia in South America; and trees of any kind
are few and far between in the bleak Andes around this
famous lake, which is nearly three miles above the sea.

On one occasion when I visited Lake Titicaca, I com-
missioned an Indian to build me a small twelve-foot
balsa for a museum in New York.

A few days later he announced that the craft was completed. When I asked him the price, he replied that it
would be ten soles, or about four dollars. He explained
that he and his wife and son had worked for three days

making the balsa. He added rather apologetically that it was so expensive because they had to go far to get the sticks for the mast and spars. Surely four dollars was very cheap for the pretty little reed craft he had made.

119

The Indian was honest. The next day he was back and insisted upon returning one sol, or forty cents, explaining that he had made a mistake in his figuring and had recalled that his son worked only one day.

Most persons visualize these reed boats of the world's

highest navigable lake as small craft—nothing more than canoes. It would surprise them were they to see some of the big cargo balsas which sail the icy blue waters of Titicaca. Quite often these craft are seventy-five feet in length and carry dozens of cattle or several tons of freight in addition to their owners and their families.

There is only one drawback to the balsa. It must be hauled out and dried at frequent intervals to prevent it from becoming waterlogged. This is not much of a drawback, for the boats are so easily and cheaply made that almost any Indian can own several of them.

To navigate Lake Titicaca from the city of Guaqui in Bolivia to Puno in Peru is a long voyage for a balsa. When engaged in carrying cargoes, the Indians move bag and baggage to their boats. The whole family lives upon the balsa until it becomes so water-soaked that it is necessary to haul it out of the water to dry.

In many lands the people spend their lives upon their boats, but the greatest of all boat dwellers are the Chinese. In China more than fifty thousand persons spend their entire lives on boats and never know any other homes.

Speaking of the Chinese and their boat dwellings reminds us of those famous boats of the Chinese called "junks." If we were not so familiar with the appearance of junks, we would think them very strange boats. It is odd, too, that the Chinese, who were among the first of all races to venture out to sea on boats, should still stick to these out-of-date craft, which seem as much out of place among present-day ships as would a small dinosaur browsing among cattle.

STRANGE SAILING CRAFT

A Chinese is one of the most conservative of mortals, and he worships his ancestors; so he probably feels that what was good enough for the Chinese a thousand years ago is good enough for him. With their lofty sides, their unusually high sterns, their squarish shape, and their great, clumsy-looking matting sails, the junks seem about the most awkward of all craft.

We marvel that they can sail at all, much less stand heavy weather or ever reach a given destination. But it is never safe to judge anything or anybody merely by appearances.

As a matter of fact, junks are really wonderful sea boats. All the clumsy, outlandish features of the junk are above water. The hull below the surface has good lines, and it is the structure under the water, not what is above it, that counts. Moreover, the sails, heavy and cumbersome as they appear, can be set much "flatter" than any canvas sails. They are constructed on the principle of Venetian blinds and can be reefed much more quickly and more easily than an ordinary sail of canvas.

One Englishman who has lived for many years in China owns a palatial junk-yacht. I happened to be in the city of Colon when he came through the Panama Canal on his way to England in his strange craft. One of my friends, who was a retired sea captain and had sailed clipper ships all over the seven seas, knew the owner of the junk. He ridiculed the strange boat.

"Why on earth did you ever pay good money for a junk?" he wanted to know.

"Because I happen to like to travel in one," said the Englishman.

"Why, man," continued the sea captain, "you'll die of old age before you get to England in that crazy thing— that is, if she ever gets there. You must want to spend the rest of your life drifting about the ocean. I'd as soon try to sail this hotel across the Atlantic as to try the trip in that junk of yours."

The Englishman smiled. "All right, Captain," he said. "But remember the old adage about the man who laughs last. Maybe if you take a squint at my junk when we sail out of the harbor tomorrow morning you'll change your mind."

Indeed, the old skipper of many a speedy windjammer did change his mind most decidedly. It happened that a trim three-masted American schooner was outward bound at the same time as the junk. To our amazement the ridiculous-looking, cumbersome Chinese craft, with her huge matting sails, slipped past the Yankee schooner almost as if the latter had been at anchor.

When the two ships had passed beyond the breakwaters and were in the open sea, the junk headed half a point nearer the wind than the schooner. Nor did her owner "die of old age" before she reached England. On the contrary, the junk made the Atlantic crossing in almost record time for sailing vessels.

Like all other junks, this luxury junk had two great eyes painted on the bows, for the ancient Chinese originated the custom that boats must be made able to see (Fig. 120).

We should not smile at the Chinese because he paints eyes on his boats, for our ancestors, as well as sailors of all races, did the very same thing. Moreover, although

STRANGE SAILING CRAFT

very few persons are aware of the fact, the custom still persists. In many parts of the world, especially in the Mediterranean Sea, fishermen's boats still have eyes painted upon the bows.

Men who go down to the sea in ships are the most conservative of all people. They are almost slaves to tradition and custom. Although they ceased long ago to

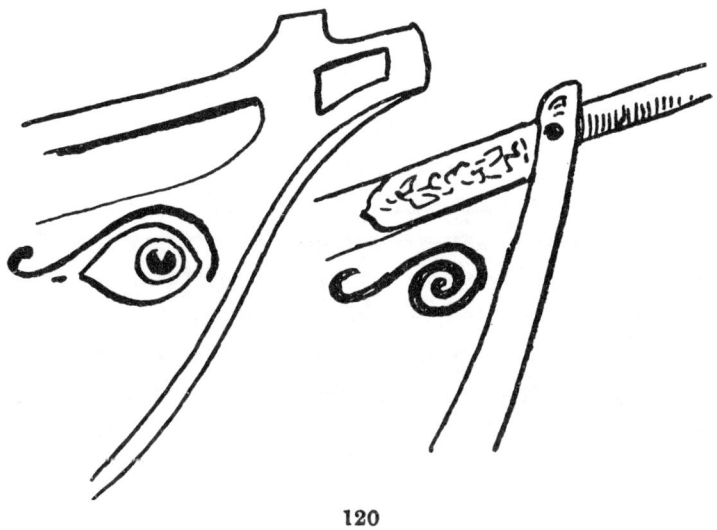

120

believe that boats must have eyes to see their way over the ocean, they still continue to paint eyes upon their craft. They are merely symbols today. Little by little they lost their eye-like appearance and became more and more decorative, until today few persons would recognize them as the boats' eyes.

Perhaps you may have wondered why many of these foreign craft have high stems extending above the bows of the boats. Some of these are plain timbers, others are elaborately carved or painted; and the gondolas of Venice have lofty stems unlike those of any other boats (Fig. 121).

Like the eyes, these are survivals of strange customs of ages ago which have no meaning or significance today, although once upon a time they were most important. They are all that remain of the sharp beaks or rams of ancient war vessels.

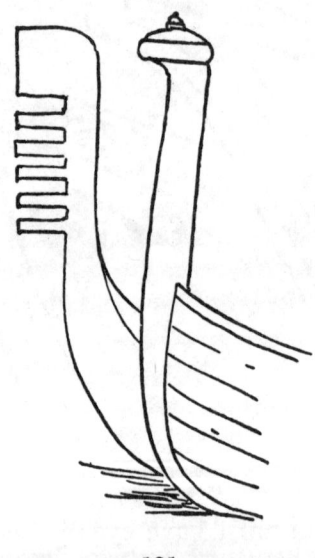

121

That brings up another strange fact in connection with boats. The word "ram" was given to the beak of a ship because originally the boats' bows were made in the shape of a ram's head with great curved horns. In the waters of Southern Europe and the Near East you may

STRANGE SAILING CRAFT 265

often see boats with rams' horns. They are either real or carved from wood or painted upon the bows.

If you examine our own sailing vessels, the fine old square-rigged ships and schooners that are almost things of the past, or any of the old frigates, such as the famous

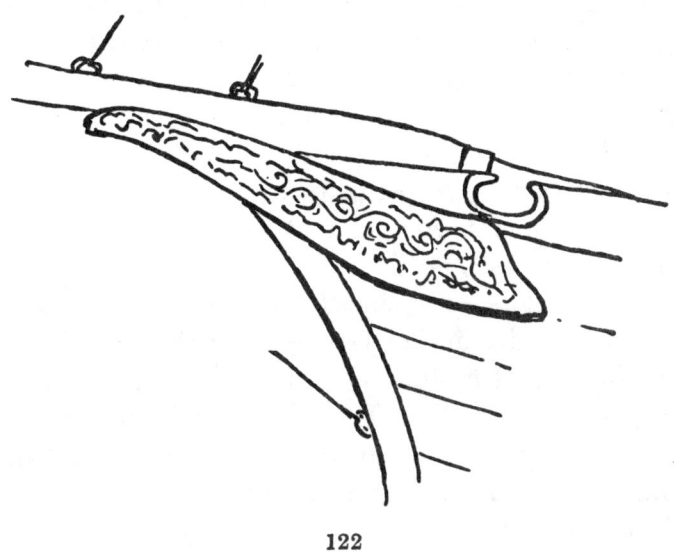

122

Constitution or the British *Victory,* you will find the rams' horns are there on the ships' bows, although they may be nothing more than curved, tapering planks at the heel of the bowsprit or even carved curlicues on either side of the bow (Fig. 122).

Eyes and rams' horns are not the only strange customs of sailor men which have survived. Every sailing ship used to have its figurehead, and even those which had no carved human figure, human head, or eagle beneath the bowsprit had an ornament of some sort to take its place. Very often the figurehead represented the man or woman, the nymph, the bird, or the beast for which the vessel was named. Quite frequently it was a carved Neptune, a mermaid, or some other fanciful figure.

Very few persons, whether seamen or landsmen, know why it was thought so necessary for a ship to have a figurehead. If you had lived two thousand years ago and had asked a Roman, a Grecian, a Phoenician, or a Viking sailor why the vessels had figures of deities, mythological characters, serpents, or dragons on their prows, you would have been told that they were to drive off evil spirits and sea devils.

Later, sailors of civilized races lost their faith in sirens, sea devils, and evil spirits; but they couldn't get over the ancient custom of having a guardian figure at the bow of every ship. Even today you will find that some of our gigantic superliners bear a small emblem of some sort on their mighty steel prows.

There is very little resemblance between these slight decorations and the ferocious-looking dragonheads of the Vikings' ships, the statues of deities on the bows of Grecian galleys, or the beautifully carved figureheads of our fine old clipper ships. But they all really are the same thing, and the modern emblems are proofs of the survival of an impressive old-time custom.

CHAPTER XVI

OTHER STRANGE CUSTOMS

THE lines of the old nursery jingle, "Barber, barber, shave a pig," may sound like nonsense, but if you visit a certain section of China you might see a man actually shaving a pig. If you should recover from your astonishment sufficiently to inquire why the pig was being shaved, you would be still more amazed at the unusual explanation.

The Chinese would calmly inform you that he was shaving the pig because he slept with the animal. He would add that a shaved pig is a much warmer and nicer bedfellow than a pig covered with bristles, especially if the bristles are caked with mud. These Chinese are not the only people who use live pigs as warming pans. I have known stray white men who have shared beds with animals (including pigs) on cold nights, although they did not trouble to shave the porkers.

Shaving a pig is a strange custom, but there are many other strange shaving customs in other lands. In India, in the West Indies, and in the Guianas of South America (where there are thousands of Hindu laborers) it is a common thing to see a man being shaved in the street. Seated upon the sidewalk, an empty packing-box, or some other convenient object, he holds a bowl of water under his chin while the turbaned barber lathers his face and plies the razor quite heedless of traffic and the passing throngs.

Very often one may see half a dozen or more men being shaved within the distance of a block and so surrounded by a motley crowd of men, women, and children —black, brown, white, and yellow—that the swarthy barbers have scarcely space enough in which to move.

When we stop to think of it, shaving in itself is a strange custom. How did man happen to shave in the first place? Why should he devote so much time and trouble to removing the hair from his face?

No one really knows the answers. But we do know that men of many races have been averse to wearing the hairs which Nature bestowed upon them, even though whiskers and full beards from time to time are very fashionable among civilized races.

Shaving must have been a most unpleasant, rather painful process before razors were invented. Even today, when we are possessed of safety razors and electric razors, shaving is a great nuisance. In the case of men with stiff, wiry beards it is far from pleasant. Yet merely for the sake of being whiskerless men must have endured tortures in the past. Think of being shaved with a bronze knife, a sliver of stone, or a bit of glass, and without shaving cream or soap to make it easier!

Some races, such as the American Indians, took a more painful means of doing away with their beards. They plucked out the hairs, one by one. Many North American Indians preferred to shave, despite the crude substitutes for razors. Sharp-edged flakes of flint did

OTHER STRANGE CUSTOMS 269

fairly well, and later, when white men introduced glass, a bit of a broken bottle took the place of the stone razor.

Even today many Indians prefer a piece of glass to a steel razor. One Sioux chief whom I know always carries a supply of broken glass with him, although he is a civilized Indian, wears conventional clothes, and is a college graduate.

It may seem strange to speak of Indians shaving, for most people have the impression that Indians do not have beards. This, however, is a great mistake, for almost all Indians have beards and moustaches. As a rule their beards are scanty; but some full-blooded Indians have quite heavy beards. It is not at all unusual to see an Indian with a luxuriant moustache. Among the Mapuche Indians of Chile, moustaches are the rule rather than the exception and many of the men wear beards as well.

In many places where sharks are plentiful the natives use the teeth of tiger sharks for razors. These are so hard and keen-edged that they serve very well indeed. On more than one occasion I have shaved myself with a shark's tooth.

Razors that grow in the jaws of fish are not so strange as razors that grow on plants. In northern Panama the Guaymi Indians shave with razors which grow on bushes. These vegetable razors are the seeds of a kind of grass which grows so high and rank that it appears more like a shrub or bush than grass.

The seeds, growing in bunches on the flower stalks, look very much like oats; but if we examine them closely, we will find that each seed has two slender spurs

STRANGE CUSTOMS

or blades projecting from the sheath or husk back of the "beard" (Fig. 123). One has to be careful in handling the seeds, for these spurs are the Indian razors, as keen as any razors of steel.

If one of the seeds is held firmly by its tough filaments or beard and is drawn across the skin, the tiny sharp-edged blades shave off the hairs as well as any razor. The only trouble with these seed razors is that they will not hold an edge, and a goodly number must be used in order to get a clean shave.

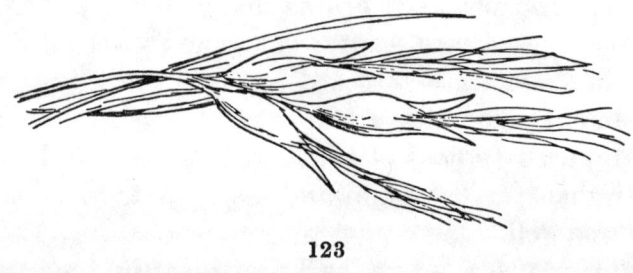

123

Not only do these strange seeds serve as razors for the Indians but they also trap birds and other creatures. Once a bird alights in a mass of the razor-bearing grass, it cannot easily escape. The countless blades hold it fast. If it struggles, the spines cut deeply into its flesh. Even good-sized quadrupeds are sometimes trapped by these sharp seeds. It is a regular custom of the Indians to visit the masses of grass near their homes every morning in order to secure any small game that has been caught in these strange natural traps.

Finally, the grass serves still another useful purpose. When the seeds are planted about a field, a village, or a house, the grass that grows from them forms a fence

OTHER STRANGE CUSTOMS 271

which no animal or man can pass. Even by hacking away with a machete it is almost impossible to get through a narrow barrier of the strange plant. The stems are tough and wiry and grow in tangled masses, and the razor-edged seeds are everywhere, ready to tear and lacerate the hands at a touch.

The question of whether to have hair or to get rid of it is a universal problem among the races of mankind. It seems never quite fully settled and varies with time and custom, but it is always a matter of particular importance with all human beings.

When I was a boy, two of my schoolmates were Chinese princes who had been sent to America to be educated. In those days all Chinese wore long pigtails and took great pride in the length of their braided hair. The two princes had the longest pigtails of any Chinese I had ever seen. They were so long that the boys had to loop them up and fasten the lower ends to the lapels of their coats.

The pigtails of the princes, however, did not interest me nearly so much as their fingernails. Each of the boys had one extremely long nail. It was a sign of belonging to the nobility or the leisure class to allow a nail to grow, thus showing that the owner did not condescend to do manual labor.

The two princes very soon discovered that fingernails several inches in length were most inconvenient things when it came to playing baseball and other American games, or for that matter, when using the schoolroom blackboards. Yat and Kan were very rapidly becoming Westernized, and they decided to sacrifice the symbols of nobility in favor of sport. Off came their long nails.

Perhaps the nails were not compulsory, and no penalty was provided for discarding them; but it was a different matter with the pigtails. Having abandoned the customs of their ancestors in the matter of fingernails, the princes decided to become thoroughly American in appearance. They did away with their long braids, which were a nuisance, anyway. This was a most unlucky decision for them. Word of what they had done in due time reached the Chinese Minister. The shock-

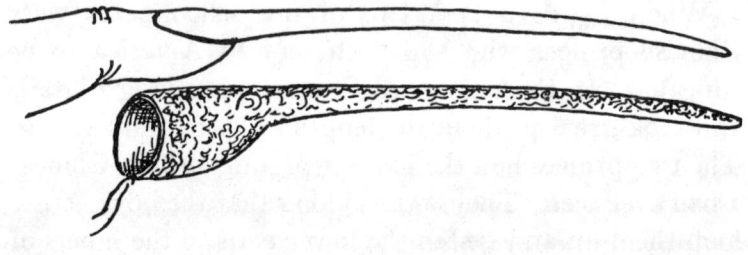

124

ing news was transmitted to China and the two boys were ordered back to their native land.

Although the Chinese pigtail is no longer compulsory and has gone almost entirely out of fashion, some old-fashioned aristocratic Chinese still take pride in their long fingernails. As gigantic, talon-like nails are very much in the way and are likely to be injured or broken, they are protected from harm by sheaths or cases of thin gold fitted with a thimble-like socket that closes snugly over the end of the finger (Fig. 124).

Nowadays it is the fashion for our women to have long, pointed fingernails, though I doubt whether any

OTHER STRANGE CUSTOMS 273

of them stop to think whether their long nails are supposed to be purely ornamental or whether, like the Chinese custom, long fingernails are supposed to indicate membership among the leisure class. Possibly our women merely slavishly follow a prevailing fashion.

Many women's fingers appear to be equipped with sharp claws rather than nails; but imagine what they would be if the nails were twenty times as long! Think what an added expense it would be to provide them with gold protectors.

Long fingernails, pigtails, and sleeping with swine are all strange customs, but equally strange is the custom of the Suka Negroes of Africa, who live on the Abyssinian border. They make their beds and sleep in the ashes of their fires. These people seem to be particularly fond of ashes. Not content with sleeping in ashes, they smear their bodies with grease and rub on ashes until they have the appearance of ghosts.

This strange custom has a good reason, however, for the land of the Sukas is infested by voracious mosquitoes, and the people have found a coating of grease and ashes a most effective protection from the insects.

There seems to be no reason, however, for the manner in which bracelets are worn by the leaders among the Suka men. These are purposely made so tight that they almost stop the circulation of the blood, and the hands of some of the men become atrophied, shrunken, and almost useless. Incredible as it may seem, these high-ranking fellows are very proud of their withered, useless hands, and the more useless they are, the greater the pride of the owner.

The custom of wearing very tight arm bands or leg bands is quite common in various parts of the world among numerous races, although no other race carries the practice to the same extreme as do the Suka tribes. When a man's hands become so useless that he cannot even feed himself, he feels that he really is somebody and lords it over his fellows who are only partially crippled. Naturally, with such hands it is impossible for the men to do any work, so that all labor falls upon the women, who do not wear tight bracelets and have normally capable hands.

We might reasonably suppose that lady Sukas would resent these consequences and would insist that their menfolk abandon such a foolish custom. One would imagine they might go on strike until their men did so. The women, however, are as proud of the useless hands of their men as are the men themselves.

The women of several South and Central American Indian tribes, such as the Kunas and Caribs in regions on both sides of the Isthmus of Panama, wear very tight ligatures about their legs. Those of the Caribs are made of woven cotton. They are placed about a girl's legs as soon as she is well able to walk and are never removed during her lifetime.

Very often the ligatures are so tight that the flesh bulges out above and below them and almost conceals the bands. Yet the women do not appear to suffer either pain or inconvenience. The ligatures certainly do not seem to affect the circulation or muscles. The women are wonderful walkers. They will carry a load weighing seventy or eighty pounds from morning until night

OTHER STRANGE CUSTOMS 275

and then spend the evening and most of the night in dancing.

The leg bands and arm bands worn by the Kuna women are very tight but are removed and replaced frequently. Although at first sight they appear to be solid bands covered with beadwork, in reality they are merely strings of beads wound around and around the limb. Great skill is shown in making the strings of beads and in winding them on. These strings are so arranged that when the windings are in place, the variously colored beads form beautiful geometrical patterns.

Many of the South Sea Island tribes and numerous African tribes wear leg bands or arm bands, or both. These fit so tightly that they sink deeply into the flesh, yet no injuries to the limbs result, which rather upsets the old idea that elastic garters are injurious and interfere with one's circulation. Probably the reason why these primitive persons can wear such tight ligatures without injury is that they use them from infancy and the veins and muscles gradually become accustomed to the strictures. Hence the natives are able to function properly in spite of the ligatures. At any rate, there is no evident discomfort because of them.

Why human beings should prefer to have their arms and legs bound with bands as tight as tourniquets is inexplicable. There are countless other customs of other peoples, but of all customs with which I am familiar I think one of the strangest is that of the Indian women of some of the Guiana tribes in South America. At the close of a long journey or at the end of a long day's toil, they deliberately slash their legs until the blood flows!

276 STRANGE CUSTOMS

Why do they do it? When I asked them that question, they replied that it was to let "the weariness out with the blood." Surely a very strange method of resting oneself! Yet this custom of bloodletting as a cure or relief was once widely used by civilized man. There

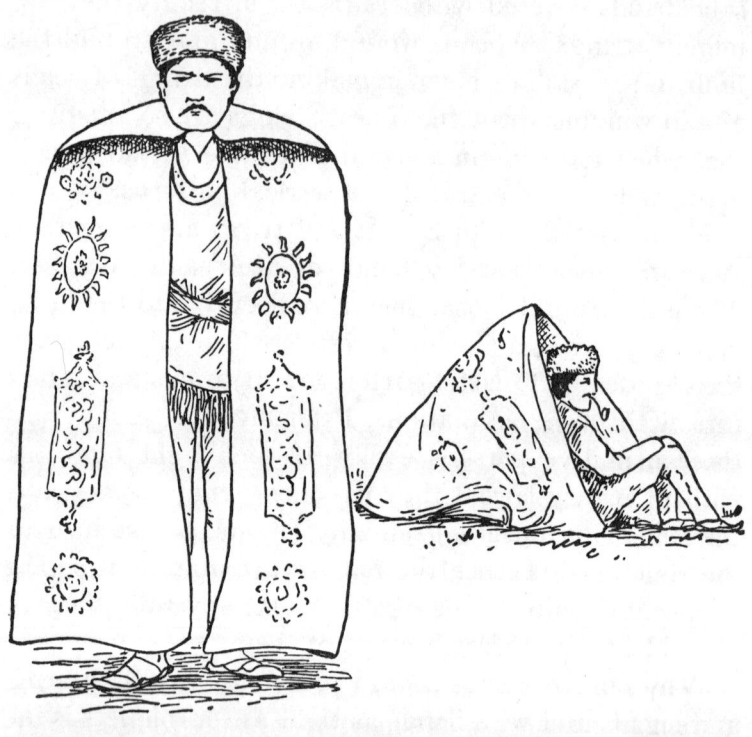

125

may well be something more to judicious bloodletting than the mere loss of blood.

An entire book might be written on the subject of odd garments alone, yet I doubt if there is a more useful strange garment than the huge felt capes used by the

OTHER STRANGE CUSTOMS

men of Anatolia in Greece. They may be worn as an overcoat by day; and when night comes, they may be quickly transformed into a snug little shelter tent (Fig. 125).

These capes of Anatolia are really sensible garments, but there seems to be little sense in the case of some other types of garments to be found in the world. However, we may find that some article of wearing apparel that seems to have no reason for its existence is merely a survival or leftover from some useful custom of the past. Veils, for example, as worn by our women today, are useless (except for purposes of beautification) and merely a passing style. But in many lands, especially in times gone by, veils which really obscured the wearer were highly important and custom decreed that they must be worn. In Oriental lands the women were not permitted to expose the faces below the eyes; and even in Peru in South America a similar custom was in vogue until quite recently. Less than fifty years ago no respectable Peruvian woman would have dreamed of appearing upon the public street without having her head and face wrapped in a somber black manta or cloak which left only her forehead and eyes visible.

Times as well as customs change; and today the Peruvian women dress as smartly—and as foolishly perhaps—as do any women of New York, London, or Paris. Turkish ladies have almost completely abandoned the age-old yashmak. This curious face covering was formerly a compulsory part of the costume of all women of Turkey, Arabia, Egypt, and other Eastern lands, and is still worn by many of these women.

In some cases the yashmak is merely a thin veil so transparent that it really does not conceal the wearer's features. It complies with the letter if not the spirit of the custom. Women of other Far Eastern tribes and

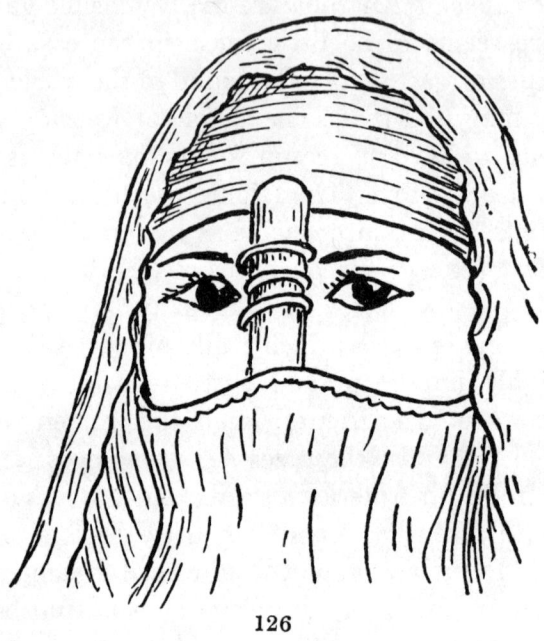

126

other districts wear heavy cloths covering their faces, and, as has been mentioned in an earlier chapter, Bedouin women of Palestine often wear their dowry coins strung upon cords to hide their faces.

In its truest form the yashmak consists of a closefitting opaque veil covering the lower half of the face and a loose mantilla-like head covering. In order to support the yashmak, keep it in place, and to prevent it from interfering with normal breathing, there is an ornamental gold or silver nosepiece, one end of which is fastened to a tight-fitting headband, and the other end of which is attached to a veil (Fig. 126).

Usually one or more rings are fastened to this nosepiece, one to show that the wearer is single, two that she is engaged to be married, and three that she is married. In North Africa the Berber women wear somewhat similar face coverings, as do the Bedouin women; while the Tuaregs, both men and women, often go to the extreme by wrapping their heads and faces in folds of cloth, leaving only the eyes visible.

One might suppose that a long burnoose, a cloaklike garment and hood woven in one piece, such as is worn by Arabian and Moorish men, would be quite enough clothing in a sun-scorched, desert land. But the Tuareg men seem to feel that something more is needed. They finish off their enveloping costumes by wearing heavy turbans as well.

Most of us have walked on stilts when we were youngsters. I remember that when I was a boy I often thought how fine it would be if I could use stilts all the time. To us, stilts are merely toys or playthings, but to the peoples of the Landes district near the Bay of Biscay in France they are just as important as shoes or any other wearing apparel. In fact, these people could not make a living without stilts although their principal industry is raising sheep.

There doesn't seem to be much connection between sheep and stilts, but if you should visit the Landes district you would quickly understand. This part of France is boggy. Much of it is partly covered with water,

280 STRANGE CUSTOMS

although there is rich pasturage for the roving flocks. It would be almost impossible for the shepherds to tend their sheep if they tried to wade and wallow across the bogs on foot, so they have solved the problem by using

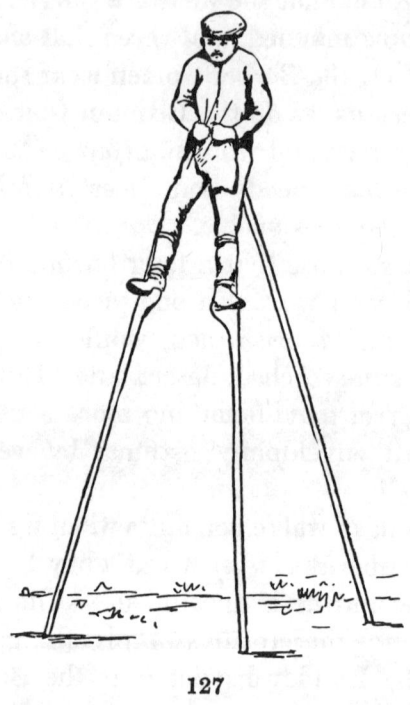

127

stilts. These are fitted with straps and braces and may be securely fastened to the wearer's legs, leaving his hands free.

In order to keep his balance in the soft, uneven ground, each man carries a long pole or staff with a crotch at the upper end. Then, when a stilt-walking shepherd wants to rest, or when he has to remain in one spot to watch his flock, he uses the long pole for a seat and transforms the contraption into a tripod (Fig. 127). As he sits there, high above the soggy ground and with his lofty perch enabling him to keep an eye on the sheep far and near, how do you suppose he passes the time? He spends hours in knitting. Imagine what a strange sight it is to see half a dozen men, each at the summit of a tripod and all busily knitting!

Shepherds on stilts, tending flocks of sheep cropping the herbage upon quaky bogs, are no stranger than farmers in boats cultivating crops that float upon the surface of the water. If you should visit Mexico or some parts of the East Indies, you would see this being done.

These floating gardens are sometimes natural and sometimes artificial. Near Mexico City there are large gardens and good-sized farms on floating masses of dead vegetation, although many of these have now become firmly anchored by roots and accumulations of trash.

In the Far East there are many floating farms cultivated on artificial islands of woven withes, bamboo, and other materials, which are covered with soil and produce luxuriant crops. Perhaps floating farms may have some disadvantages but they have one great advantage over all other farms—they are never likely to suffer from a drought.

It is a strange experience to visit one of these floating farms. As one steps to the garden from the canoe in which one has been ferried to the spot, it is hard to believe that the garden is resting upon the surface of the water like a raft. Here beneath waving palms and the broad leaves of the banana trees is the little thatched hut of the owner. Scarlet-flowered hibiscus shrubs form a hedge about it. Within an enclosure of bamboo, chickens scratch and roosters crow. Big black pigs root and grunt in a pen, and a cow grazes upon the rich Guinea grass.

Here and there are good-sized trees. There are also clumps of feathery bamboo and slender raffia palms. Flowers are in blossom everywhere. Gorgeous orchids blaze amid the foliage of trees. There are neat, well-tilled patches of maize, melons, sweet potatoes, pumpkins, beans, peppers, tomatoes, and other vegetables.

Tall papaya trees display large golden fruit. There are orange and lime trees, custard apples, soursops, and many other tropical fruits. Butterflies flit from blossom to blossom, hummingbirds with flashing, gemlike throats hover motionless as they probe the deep bells of trumpet flowers, finches twitter, and a flock of parroquets chatter above our heads.

It is a tiny, floating world, detached and apart, but inhabited by the same life that teems on the mainland. Even the insects, the grasshoppers, and the bees are there, and at night the crickets chirp and trill just as they do on farms that are part of the solid Mother Earth. Working a floating farm is certainly a strange occupation for any family.

Amusements, too, can be odd or unusual. I am reminded that a peculiar custom of some peoples is their cricket fights. No doubt, to the inhabitants of other lands, our own manly prizefights appear very strange. How, they wonder, can anyone find pleasure in seeing two men pound and batter each other? What sport can

OTHER STRANGE CUSTOMS

there be in seeing one man knock another down? They cannot understand it any more than some of us can understand why or how a Spaniard finds enjoyment and relaxation in a bullfight.

If a cricket fight seems strange to us, our sports probably seem just as strange to the Chinese, who think a battle between two champion crickets is one of the most exciting of contests.

The area in which the two insects fight savagely is a bowl six or seven inches in diameter. Each contestant is urged on and excited by his owner, who scratches the creature's back with a rat's whisker fastened to the end of a little stick. You may think that a cricket battle would be a very tame affair, but the Chinese become wildly excited and wager heavy bets on their favorites.

Cricket fights are no more odd than fish fights, which are the favorite contests of the Siamese. They sometimes wager all they possess on the outcome of a battle between two fighting fish (See *Strange Fish and Their Stories*).

So highly esteemed are these fighting fish and so famous are the victors of many battles that when a finny champion dies or is killed, it is given a real funeral! This event is accompanied with all the ceremonies which would be accorded a well-known man, even including the professional mourners. Probably you would never realize that they were mourners, for they are not garbed in black, nor do they weep or appear sad. They are clad in gaudy, picturesque costumes. They dance, sing, and play weird-looking musical instruments.

We must remember, however, that different groups of

people have different ideas as to the correct and most sincere method of expressing grief or mourning. Most Western people wear black as a sign of mourning, but the Chinese think white is the proper thing, while among some other races the color typical of mourning is purple, or yellow, or scarlet.

We grieve and lament at the loss of a dear friend or loved one; but many savage races rejoice and celebrate, feeling that the one who has passed away has gone onward to a better life. Instead of this attitude being strange, our own behavior is really the odd one. We profess to believe that existence in the hereafter is much better than the present life. Why, then, should we be sorry when a person dies, other than to miss him as we would if he had merely moved to another country to live?

Probably one of the strangest mourning customs is that of the Indians of the Parana River in South America, who have been known to cut off a finger as an expression of grief or bereavement. Perhaps the loss of their fingers helps to produce the requisite amount of mourning; but the self-mutilation is really symbolical. The pain symbolizes the pain they have suffered through the death of a dear one, the sacrifice being an offering to the deities, and the severed digits being "killed" so that their spirits may accompany that of the deceased and help it on its way to the spirit world.

Funeral customs are many and weird and often gruesome. To inherit or absorb some of the fine qualities of the deceased is the wish of many a primitive person when a tribal member of note has passed away. Among some tribes of the Uapes Indians (the Tarianos and the

OTHER STRANGE CUSTOMS

Tucanos of the upper Amazon) bodies of the dead are burned to a fine ash powder which is mixed into their local drink, casiri, and drunk rather ceremoniously. The Indians believe that the good qualities of those who have passed on are thus transmitted to the drinkers.

Accounts of all the strangeness of human groups would fill many volumes. Each race and tribe is in some ways unique, as, after all, is each human being who appears upon the earth. Modern speedy means of travel and education are causing men all over the world to drop old habits and to take on new ones; to forget old superstitions and prejudices in the light of clearer understanding; and to conquer the ghost of fear, which is the root and source of most peculiar beliefs and customs.

However, there will perhaps never come a time when people will cease to be a fascinating study in the wide diversity of their manners, customs, and beliefs. Education, travel, and imposed governing laws will probably never fully obliterate man's universal natural tendency to invent his own beliefs, fetishes, and taboos. They are the universal antidote to mortal fear and insecurity, and as such are undoubtedly destined to hold their places for untold ages yet to come.

INDEX

Abalone, 25
Abraham, 84
Abyssinians, 273
Aeolian harp, 240, 241
Africa, Central, 44, 187, 223
Africa, East, 40, 188, 192, 214, 215
Africa, Equatorial, 22, 30, 40
Africa, North, 202, 279
Africa, South, 14, 15, 17, 45, 46, 185
Africa, West, 53
Akawoian tribes, 136
Alaska, Alaskan tribes, 25, 159, 218
Algonquin tribes, 124, 249
Alligator tail, 205, 222
Alsatian headdress, 9, 18
Amazon tribes, 56, 64, 88, 112, 130, 132, 137, 154, 183, 211, 212, 230, 241, 284, 285
Amulets, 73
Amunsha tribes, 144
Anatolia, 277
Andes, 222
Andjra, 195
Angola, 239
Antandroy tribes, 187, 223

Ants, honey, 214, 215
Ants, leaf-eating, 211-215
Apache tribes, 239
Arabs, Arabia, 43, 61, 253, 256, 277, 279
Areca nut, 215
Arekuna tribes, 135
Arm bands, 37, 274, 275
Armenia, Armenians, 61, 197
Arnica, 107
Arowak tribes, 86
Artifacts, 117
Asafetida, 113
Asia Minor, 19
Ath Abahthi, 195
Atlatl, Aztec, 121, 129
Aurucanian tribes, 35, 184
Aural pockets, 26
Australian tribes, 110, 125-128, 138, 191
Autosuggestion, 82, 97-105
Axes, 116, 120
Aymara tribes, 11, 12, 165, 247
Aztec tribes, 38, 59, 120, 129, 159, 175, 209

Bahima tribes, 186
Baila tribes, 223
Bali, 18, 182

INDEX

Balsas, 258-260
Bamboo, 14, 223
Bamboo headdress, 14
Bantu tribes, 239
Banyankole tribes, 186
Banyoro tribes, 40
Barbados, 218
Basketball, 159
Basketwork headdress, 14
Basque, 197
Batoro tribes, 192
Batrachians, 205
Bay of Biscay, 279
Bay of Fundy, 249
Beads, 28
Beauty culturist, 21
Beauty parlor, 21
Beaver skins, 150
Beche-de-mer, 219
Bedouins, 20, 202, 278, 279
Beds, in ashes, 273
Beef, jerked, 219, 220
Beena, 62, 88, 89, 90, 98
Beetles, water, 217
Beggar's hat, 18
Belemites, 86, 87
Bengal, 195, 196
Berbers, 196, 279
Best man, 192
Betelnut, 215
Bimiti, 173
Birhors, 196
Blackfellow's grub, 211
Blood, as a food, 223, 224
Blood avengers, 97-105
Blood brother, 229, 233

Blood ceremonial, 196
Blood letting, 275, 276
Blood, potion, 101
Blowguns, 130, 131, 134
Blubber, 218
Bludgeons, 120
Boat, goatskin, 255
Boats, 248-266
Boats, Chinese, 260-262
Boat, sea-lion skins, 256, 257
Boats, skin, 254-256
Boats, toy, 179, 180
Boats, wickerwork, 256
Body shrinking, 147
Bolas, 137, 138
Bolivia, Bolivian tribes, 11, 13, 165, 167, 247, 257-259
Bolos, 119
Bombazen, 141
Boneset, 107
Bonnet, double-tailed, 6, 7
Boomerangs, 121, 125
Boone, Daniel, 142
Boorabee tribes, 131
Botocudo tribes, 30-32
Borneo, 12, 36, 130, 143, 196
Boston, 141
Bougainville, 215
Bouncing game, 159
Bouncing mat, 159
Bows and arrows, 117, 118, 124, 125
Bracelets, tight, 273
Brahmans, 199
Brazil, Brazilians, 30, 31, 107, 144, 184, 197

INDEX 289

Bride's ale, 193
Buffalo stones, 87
Bulgaria, Bulgarians, 44
Bullboats, 253
Burma, Burmese, 1, 29, 130
Burnoose, 279
Burdock, 107
Bushman tribes, 185
Bustad, Jeremiah, 141

Cakes, blood, 228
Caladium, 88
California, California tribes, 152, 257
Calmores, 217
Camot cumara, 58
Candles, 84
Candy, bee, 214
Candy, white-ant, 214
Cannibalism, 221
Canoes, 248-260
Canoes, birchbark, 248-251
Canoes, canvas, 249
Canoes, dugout, 251-253
Canoes, outrigger, 253
Canoes, skin, 254
Canoe, toy, 179, 180
Capes, 12
Capes, Anatolian, 276, 277
Capes, "invisible," 88, 102
Card games, 176
Carib tribes, 30, 32, 33, 91, 131, 135, 177, 179, 222, 229, 250, 253, 274
Caroline Islands, 168, 189
Cartoons, 83

Casiri, 221, 285
Cassava, 221, 222
Cassava bread, 61
Catamaran, 256, 257
Caterpillars, sphinx, 212
Caterpillars, fried, 212, 222
Cats, 208, 209
Cats' cradle, 177
Ceiba tree, 134
Celebes, 201
Celts, 86, 87
Central America, Central Americans, 39, 44, 69, 130, 131, 205, 250, 251
Cereals, ceremonial, 198
Chains, 28
Charivari, 200
Charki, 219, 222
Charm-bags, 90
Charms, luck, 85-96
Chatham Islands, 195
Cheek decorations, 38
Cheeks, rouged, 21-24
Chicha, banana, 222
Chicha, corn, 222
Chickasaw tribes, 142
Chile, Chileans, 35, 80, 184, 269
China, Chinese, 24, 41, 44, 108, 109, 200, 208-210, 217, 219, 225, 260, 262, 267, 271, 273, 283, 284
Choctaw tribes, 142
Chokoi tribes, 10, 241
Chopsticks, 224
Chota Nagpur, 202

Cicatrization, 51-58
Civil War, 208
Clay figures, 78-79
Clay, red, 27
Club, gunstock form, 121, 123
Club, paddle-like, 120, 121
Clubs, 116-124
Club, skull-cracker, 121, 123
Club, square, 120, 121
Club, stone-bladed, 121
Coati, 133
Coca plant, 107
Cocaine, 107
Cocle tribes, 164, 239
Coiffure, Mangebetou, 41
Coin dowry, 20
Colombia, Colombian tribes, 10, 125, 155, 156
Colon, 261
Colorado, 118
Coloring tints, 21
Colors, for mourning, 284
Comb, silver filigree, 37
Compact, 21
Congo, 30, 53
Congo, Belgian, 119, 121
Connecticut, 150, 154
Constitution, 265
Cook Islands, 194
Coracles, 253, 256
Corn, 222
Cortez, 9
Costume, palm-leaf, 169, 170
Cotton headdress, 7, 9
Coup bonnet, 4
Crapaud, 206

Creek tribes, 142
Crickets, dried, 212
Crockett, Dave, 142
Crossbows, 118
Cumara, 58
Customs, funeral, 283-285
Customs, marriage, 181-203
Customs, miscellaneous, 267-285
Cuttlefish, 217
Cyprus, 192

Daggers, 116, 120
Dakota, 232, 233
Dampier, 10
Dance, devil, 164-171, 242
Dance, flying, 175
Dance, self-torturing, 173-175
Dances, ceremonial, 175, 176, 194
Dances, mystical, 171, 172
Dance, snake, 174, 175
Dance, snow-snake, 177
Dance, tribal, 11, 175, 176
Dance, war, 176
Darts, poisoned, 130-136
Dentalium, 25
Devil dancers, 164-171, 242
Devil dancers, Bolivian, 165
Devil dancers, Cocle, 164
Devil dancers, Guaymi, 164
Devil dancers, Iroquois, 166
Devil dancers, New Britain Island, 169
Devil dancers, New Guinea, 167

INDEX

Devil dancers, New Ireland, 167
Devil dancers, North American Indian, 167
Devil dancers, South Seas, 167
Devil dancers, Tibetan, 167
Devil dancers, Tuscaroran, 166
Devils, 106
Devil-stick, 78
Dice, 176
Dinka tribes, 224
Dishes, breaking of, 197
Djukas, 53, 54, 91
Dog, Aztec hairless, 209
Dog, roast, 204
Dogs, 208, 209
Dogs, chow, 208
Dragons, 108
Drink-charm marks, 62, 63
Druse headdress, 19
Drum, bamboo, 236, 237
Drum, decorated, 237
Drum, receiving, 230
Drums, baked-clay, 239
Drums, basketwork, 239
Drums, Big-Mama tom-tom, 232
Drums, giant, 239
Drums, hollow-tree, 226-231, 237
Drum, mora-tree, 227-229
Drums, Papa tom-tom, 232
Drums, sacred, 230-232, 236, 237
Drum, sending, 227-231
Drum, skin-head, 236-238
Drum, snakeskin, 236, 237
Drums, square, 237, 239
Drums, talking, 226-247
Drums, thin, 237, 239
Drums, voodoo, 233, 237, 239
Drums, water, 230, 236, 237
Drums, wood, 227-239
Duckbill people, 31, 32
Dulse, 209
Durban, 17
Dyak tribes, 12, 36, 37, 130, 143

Earlobes, distended, 27
Ear ornaments, 25-27, 35, 36, 65
Earplugs, 25-27, 30
Earrings, 25, 27
Earthworms, 213
East Africa, 175
Eastern tribes, 5, 123, 248
East Indies, 12, 36, 130, 143, 182, 196, 201
Ecuador, Ecuadoreans, 107, 144
Edo-speaking peoples, 201
Effigies, 72-75, 77, 100
Eggs, ancient, 209
Eggs, breaking of, 197
Eggs, smoked-turtle, 211
Eggs, water-beetle, 217
Egypt, Egyptians, 72, 277
Elephant feet, 215
Elephant meat, 215

INDEX

Eskimos, 25, 26, 124, 159, 181, 218, 257
Evil eye, 66, 100, 202
Eyebrows, plucked, 21-23
Eyelashes, artificial, 22
Eyes, boat, 262-265

Face cream, hippopotamus-fat, 22
Face powder, charcoal, 22
Faldetta, 19
Fanti tribes, 41, 44, 75, 92
Far East, 255, 278, 281, 282
Farms, floating, 281, 282
Feather head adornments, 7, 9, 10, 11, 13, 14, 17, 37
Feet, elephant, 215
Fence, grass, 271
Fetish, 92, 106
Fez, 196, 201
Fights, cricket, 282, 283
Fights, fish, 283
Figureheads, 265, 266
Fiji Islands, 213
Filet, rattlesnake, 222
Filipinos, 119, 130
Fingernails, tinted, 21
Fingers, cut off, 284
Fishing, pollock, 250
Fish, raw, 218
Flathead tribes, 1, 48
Flesh, human, 221
Flies, 216
Florida, Florida tribes, 63, 130, 204, 222
Flute, Indian love, 237

Folsom points, 118
Flute, nose, 237, 241
Flutes, 241
Foochow, 201
Foods, strange, 204-225
Fossils, 86, 87
Fox, flying, 208
France, 197, 279-281
French Alsace, 9, 18
Frogs, 205-206
Frogs' legs, 205
Fruit bat, 208
Fulah tribes, 44
Fungus, 216
Fuzzy-Wuzzy tribes, 43

Game, cup-and-ball, 177
Games, card, 176
Games, primitive, 158-180
Game, stick-and-hoop, 177
Gardens, floating, 281, 282
Gauchos, 138
Gazelle Peninsula, 197
Gentian, 107
Georgia, 158
Germans, Germany, 197, 223
Ghurkas, 119
Ginseng, 107
Goajira tribes, 125, 155, 156
"Goat without horns," 83, 233
Gold Coast, 44
Gold thread, 107
Gondolas, 264
Gonds, 183
Good-luck bundles, 90
Gran Chaco tribes, 99, 131

INDEX

Grasshoppers, dried, 212
Grease, 27
Great Britain, 254
Greece, Grecians, 192, 200, 266, 277
Greenland, 181
Grubs, palm, 211
Grubs, tree, 211, 213
Guadalcanal, 213, 215
Guanaco, 138
Guatemala, Guatemalans, 240
Guaqui, 260
Guaymi tribes, 60, 61, 75, 77, 79, 129, 130, 164, 269
Gufas, 253, 255, 256
Guiana, Guiana tribes, 53, 54, 57, 58, 91, 93, 94, 102-105, 136, 154, 171-173, 221, 241, 267, 268, 275, 276
Guide plume, 6, 7
Gypsies, 82, 197

Hair, bleached, 23
Hair, bobbed, 21
Hair, Chinese-style, 271, 272
Hair coiffure, Fulah, 41
Hairdress, Fanti, 41
Hair gum, 44
Hair, marcelled, 22
Hair, Nusu style, 41
Hair, shaved, 27
Hair wad, Uganda, 41, 43
Haiti, Haitians, 69, 83, 214, 232
Halberds, 118
Hamitic tribes, 43

Hammers, 116-121
Haris, 196
Harlem, 95
Hat, metal-covered, 18
Headdress, Alsatian, 9
Headdress, Aymaran, 12
Headdress, Bali, 18
Headdress, beggar's, 17, 18
Headdress, Bolivian, 11, 12
Headdress, Darien, 10
Headdress, hoop, 12
Headdress, Indian, 4-14
Headdress, Javanese, 18
Headdress, Kaffir, 17
Headdress, Kenyan, 14
Headdress, Mexican, 9
Headdress, Mindayan, 17
Headdress, Papuan, 17
Headdress, Peruvian, 11, 12
Headdress, rattan, 14
Headdress, Samoan, 16, 17
Headdress, Siamese, 18
Headdress, Sioux, 5, 6
Headdress, strange, 1-20
Headdress, Tehuanan, 7, 9, 18
Headdress, war-bonnet, 4-9
Headdress, Zulu, 14, 15
Head hunters, 12, 139-148
Head-selling, 143-147
Heads, preserved, 139-148
Hexing, 81
High heels, 24
Hindus, 32, 61, 198, 200, 267
Hobby, 140
Hockey, 159-161
Holland, 154

Honeymoon, 193
Hoop-corset, 37
Howling monkey, 133
Huichol tribes, 79
"Hunt the thimble," 177
Hypnotism, 93, 94

Igorot tribes, 209
Iguana, 205
Images, 72, 73, 75, 77, 78
Incan pre- tribes, 1, 38, 73, 75, 111
Incantations, 106, 107, 112
Incan tribes, 38, 73, 111, 126, 129, 156, 157, 239, 257
India, Indians, 32, 119, 183, 184, 195, 196, 198, 199, 200, 202, 239, 267
Indo-China, 198
Indo-European, 198
Inti, 73, 75
Ipecacuanha, 107
Ipurina tribes, 184
Irish, 83, 209
Iroquois tribes, 64, 130, 166
Islands, artificial, 281, 282
Isthmus of Darien, 10
Isthmus of Tehuantepec, 9
Italy, Italians, 83, 198, 223

Jackstones, 176
Jaluo tribes, 40
Japan, Japanese, 17, 217, 219, 222, 224
Java, Javanese, 18, 197, 201
Jelly, calves'-foot, 209

Jew's-harp, 240, 241
Jivaro tribes, 144
Junks, Chinese, 260-262

Kaffir tribes, 17, 155, 170, 171, 235
Kanakas, 27
Kavirondo tribes, 14, 15, 22, 48
Kayans, 196
Kenaima, 102-105
Kenaima*pu*, 105
Kenya, 14, 22, 27
Kewats, 196
Kipling, 43
Kirtles, palm-leaf, 170
Kite flying, 178, 179
Knitting, on stilts, 281
Knives, 118-120
Knob kerries, 124
"kop-kop," 152
Korok tribes, 239
Kris, 119
Kukwah dances, 164, 165
Kumwarry, Chief, 229, 233
Kuna tribes, 32-34, 74, 75, 111, 131, 154, 274, 275

Labrets, 27, 30
Lacrosse, 158
Lahore, 195
Lake Albert, 192, 224
Lake Edward, 192
Lake Titicaca, 258-260
Lake Victoria Nyanza, 48
Lances, 118

INDEX

Landes, 279-281
Lasso, 137, 138
Lebanon, 19
Leg bands, 274, 275
Leopard men, 97-105
Liberia, 100
Lip disc, 30
Lip ornaments, 26, 27, 29, 30, 35
Lips, reddened, 21, 22
Lisu tribes, 183
Little Russians, 202
Liverwort, 107
Lizard, 205
Lamas, 164
Lockjaw, 40
London, 21, 277
Love charm, 93
Luzon, 208

Maces, 118
Machetes, 118, 119
Macusi tribes, 135
Madagascar, 110, 187, 191, 197, 223
Magic seeds, 110
Maine, 138, 150, 249
Malay Archipelago, 197
Malays, 51, 119, 130, 164, 239
Malta, 19
Mana tali, 154
Manchu, 200
Mandrake, 107
Mangebetou tribes, 41
Manicures, 22

Mantle, "invisible," 88, 102
Maori tribes, 56-58, 144
Mapuche tribes, 35, 80, 160, 269
Maquahuitl, 120, 121
Marbles, 177
Marimba, 239, 240
Marriage by capture, 181-186
Marriage by purchase, 181, 186-190
Marriage by selection, 181, 190-203
Marriage, Auracanian, 184
Marriage, Bali, 182
Marriage, Burma-China, 183
Marriage, Bushmen, 185
Marriage, East Indian, 182
Marriage, Eskimo, 181
Marriage, Gond, 183
Marriage, Greenland, 181
Marriage, India, 183
Marriage, Ipurina, 184
Marriage, Lisu tribes, 183
Marriage, Matabele, 185
Marriage, Purang, Tibet, 182
Marriage, Uacarra, 183, 184
Marriage, Uapes, 183
Marriage customs, 181-203
Masai tribes, 27-29, 188, 189, 224
Mascara, 22, 23
Masks, 11, 166-171
Masks, animal, 1
Massachusetts, 141
Matabele tribes, 185, 198
Mayan tribes, 59, 159, 239

INDEX

Meat, elephant, 215
Meat, jerked, 219, 220, 222
Meat, raw, 218
Meat, snake, 204
Medals, 73
Medicine baskets, 112
Medicine bonnet, 6, 7
Medicine bundle, 88
Medicine men, 106-114, 131
Medicine shields, 88, 99
Medicine weapons, 99
Mediterranean Sea, 19, 192, 263
Medusa, 45
Melanesian tribes, 189
Mental suggestion, 97-105
Mesopotamia, 255
Mexico, Mexicans, 9, 79, 159, 175, 209, 214, 216, 217, 222, 281
Micronesians, 27, 152
Middle Ages, 118
Middle West, 200
Milk tree, 222
Mindanao, 197
Mindaya, 15, 17, 197
Mindaya hat, 15
Mississippi, 208
Mobira, 30, 32
Money, bead, 149, 150
Money, beaver-skin, 150-151
Money, *betellin*, 154
Money, buckskin, 151
Money, cattle, 155, 156
Money, coin, 151
Money, country, 151
Money, cowry shell, 152
Money, curare poison, 153
Money, dentalium shells, 151
Money, farm products, 155
Money, feather, 153
Money, gold standard, 157
Money, iron, 151
Money, iron pyrite, 152
Money, *mana tali*, 154
Money, metal-disc, 150
Money, obsidian, 152
Money, onion, 154
Money, ox, 151
Money, Panamanian centavo, 154
Money, pig, 155
Money, pony, 155
Money, primitive, 149
Money, shell, 151, 152
Money, stone-disc, 152-153
Money, tobacco, 154
Money, tusk-shell, 151
Money, wampum, 149, 150
Money, wheat, 151
Money, wire, 153
Money, wives as, 155
Money, wooden, 149
Monkey, roast, 220, 221
Moors, Moorish, 279
Moqui tribes, 174, 175
Moriori tribes, 195
Morocco, Moroccans, 195, 197, 199, 201, 202
Moslem, 20
Moss, Irish, 209
Moth, ghost, 211

INDEX

Mourning, 283-285
Mourning, Chinese, 284
Mourning, Western, 284
Mullein, 107
Mummy, 21, 73
Mundas, 198, 202
Mundrucu tribes, 65
Museum of The American Indian, 147
Mushrooms, 216
Music, 226-247
Muskohegan tribes, 142
Mussels, 216
Mutilation, self-, 284
Myagong tribes, 136

Nail socket, 272
Nails, talon-like, 272, 273
Nalukatuck, 159
Nandi tribes, 40, 137, 224
Natal, 45
Navajo tribes, 160, 196
Near East, 264, 265
Neck wire, 29
Negrito tribes, 195
Neli, 74, 77, 112
New Britain Island, 169
New Caledonia, 137
New England, New England tribes, 64, 141, 149-151
New Guinea, 1, 17, 36, 37, 167, 190, 191, 208, 222
New Ireland, 167
New York, 19, 204, 277
New Zealand, 56-58, 144
Nigeria, 48, 201

Nile, 217
Norsemen, 256
North Hope, 159
Northwest tribes, 10, 48
Nose ornaments, 26, 32-36
Nose pieces, 278, 279
Nusu women, 41, 44

Obeah magic, 94-96
Obsidian, 120
Ocarina, 237, 241
Oceania, 195
Octopus, 213, 217
Oglala tribes, 5
Oil, Sesamum, 224
Orangewood stick, 21
Orient, 239
Orinoco, 45, 217
Ostrich, South American, 138
Otterskin hat, 6, 7

Pacific, North, 25
Pacific, South, 27, 51, 56, 69, 110, 119, 137, 168, 189, 190, 193, 195, 197, 213, 239, 253
Painting, body, 59
Painting, facial, 60, 61
Painting, medicine, 65, 66
Paiwari, 61, 221, 227
Palestine, 20, 256, 278
Palm, coconut, 223
Palm oil, 23
Palms, groo-groo, 211
Palm wine, 222
Panama Canal, 261

Panama, Panamanians, 10, 32, 60, 74-77, 111, 154, 167, 239, 241, 269, 274, 275
Panpipes, 246, 247
Papuan tribes, 17
Papyrus, 48
Parakan tribes, 48
Parana River, 284
Parasara tribes, 171
Paris, 19, 277
Passamaquoddy tribes, 249, 250
Patamonan tribes, 136
Pawnee tribes, 196
Peai, 69, 93, 102, 131
Pecunia, 155
Pecus, 155
Pemmican, 220
Perai, 134
Periwinkles, 216
Permanent wave, 22
Persia, Persians, 197
Peru, Peruvians, 11, 21, 48, 56, 58, 73, 75, 107, 129, 144, 156, 157, 219, 222, 257-259, 277
Peyote tribes, 232, 236, 237
Pharaohs, 72
Philippines, Filipinos, 17, 119, 130, 197, 208, 209, 211, 223, 246
Phoenicians, 266
Pie, white-ant, 214
Pig, as bedfellow, 267
Pigtails, Chinese, 271, 272
Plains tribes, 5, 9, 44, 87, 99, 124, 142, 155, 160, 256 (*see also* Western tribes)
Plants, medicinal, 107-109
Play, primitive, 158-180
Point Hope, 218
Poisons, curare, 125, 131-136
Poison, strychnine, 132
Poland, 202
Polynesian tribes, 51, 57, 144, 253
Pomades, 21
Ponape, 168, 189
Ponca tribes, 173
Potatoes, frozen, 222
Powder puff, 21
Printing cylinders, 59, 60
Proxies, 72-84, 112
Pudding, blood, 223
Pueblo tribes, 5, 126, 160
Punjab, 200
Puno, 260
Purang, 182
Purpleheart, 250

Quassia, 107
Quechua tribes, 222
Queensland, 223

Rabbit sticks, 126
Racquet-and-ball game, 159
Rams' horns, 264, 265
Rapier, 119
Rasle, Friar, 141
Rats, 208, 209
Rattles, 242-245
Rattles, ceremonial, 245

INDEX

Rattles, gourd, 242
Rattles, hollow-ring, 243, 245, 246
Rattles, horn, 242, 243
Rattlesnake, canned, 204
Rattlesnake, filet of, 204
Rattles, nut, 242
Rattles, rawhide, 243, 245
Rattles, round and oval, 243, 245
Rattles, shell, 242
Rattles, tortoise-shell, 242, 243
Rattles, toucan-beak, 242
Razors, 27, 269
Razors, fish-jaw, 269
Razors, flint, 268, 269
Razors, glass, 268, 269
Razors, sharks'-tooth, 269
Razors, stone, 268
Razors, vegetable, 269-270
Revolutionary War, 141
Rhea, 138
Rheumatism cure, 113, 114
Rib collecting, 147
Rice toddy, 222
Rio Negro tribes, 88, 213
Rome, Romans, 21, 155, 201, 266
Running game, 173
Russia, Russians, 198, 239

Sabre, 119
Sacrifice, bloody, 233, 234
Sago-palm cap, 46
Sailing craft, 248-266
Sakalava tribes, 191
Samoa, Samoans, 15, 17, 51, 213
Samoan headdress, 15, 17
San Blas tribes, 32, 34, 74, 77
Santa Cruz, 153
Sarsaparilla, 107
Sassafras, 107
Sausage, blood, 223
Saxophones, 245, 246
Scalp lock, 44, 142, 143
Scalps, 140-142
Scalp-selling, 141-143
Scalps, New England, 141-143
Scandinavians, 223
Scimitar, 119
Sea caterpillar, 219
Sea eggs, 218
Sea urchins, 218
Seaworm, 213
Self-mutilation, 284
Self-torture, 50, 66, 67, 284
Seminole tribes, 5
Seneca tribes, 166, 167
Senegalese tribes, 190
Sepik warriors, 37
Serpent god, 233
Sesamum oil, 224
Shan tribe, 29
Sharp, Captain, 10
Shaving, 267-271
Shaving, by plucking, 268
Shaving, on street, 267, 268
Shayshan tribes, 131
Shell patterns, 53

Shivaree, 200
Shuttlecock, 177
Siam, Siamese, 18, 19, 130, 164, 198, 283
Siberia, Siberians, 198, 199, 200
Sinhalese, 195
Sioux tribes, 5, 110, 159, 236, 269
Skin bleaches, 21
Skulls, flattened, 1, 48
Slavs, 198
Snake, black, 204
Snake, bull, 204
Snake, chicken, 204
Snake, coach-whip, 204
Snake dance, 174, 175
Snakes, food, 204
Snakes, gopher, 204
Snow-snake dance, 177
Solomon Islands, 46
Somali tribes, 43, 175
Soudan, French, 44, 119
Soup, birds'-nest, 209
Soup, green turtle, 205
Soup, shark-fin, 204, 209
South Sea tribes, 13, 38, 46, 92, 120, 143, 151, 152, 155, 164, 215, 236, 275
Souvenirs, gruesome, 139-148
Souvenirs, heads, 139-148
Souvenirs, horns, 140
Souvenirs, scalps, 140-142
Souvenirs, teeth, 140, 148
Spain, Spanish, 83, 119, 217, 257

Spears, 116
Spear-throwing stick, 121, 128, 130
Squirrels, forest, 208
Stamps, painting, 60, 61
Stamps, wooden, 60, 61
Stick dance, 161-163
Stilts, 279-281
Stomacher, 47
Substitutes, 72-84
Sudanese tribes, 45
Suka Negroes, 273, 274
Sumatra, 222
Sun dance, 173, 174
Swifts, 209
Sword, cross-hilted, 119
Swords, 118-121, 124
Sword, tiger-shark, 120
Syrians, 61

Taboos, 50-71
Talking drums, 226-247
Tamboolas, 233, 237
Tariana tribes, 212, 284, 285
Tartars, 202
Tattooing, medicine, 65, 66
Tattoos, 50-71, 144
Tchanku Tanka (Big Road) 5, 6
Teeth decorations, 38-40
Tehuana tribes, 7, 9, 18
Terrapin, 205
Teso tribes, 43
Tetanus, 40
Throwing stick, Incan, 121, 129

INDEX

Throwing stones, 116
Thunder stones, 86, 87
Tibet, 164, 167, 182, 242
Timbo, 137
Toddy, rice, 222
Toenails, tinted, 21
Tomahawk, 116, 118, 123, 124
Tops, 177, 178
Torres Strait, 191
Transylvania, 197
Trap, bird, 270
Traveler's Tree, 222, 223
Tree, bottle, 223
Tree, cow, 222
Tree, Ravenala, 222, 223
Tribal mark, 60, 61
Trophies, human, 139-148
Trumpets, 241, 242
Tuaregs, 279
Tuba, 223
Tucano tribes, 65, 284, 285
Tuelche tribes, 138
Tupi tribes, 132
Turbans, 279
Turkana tribes, 43
Turkey, 197, 277
Turks, 119
Tuscarora tribes, 166, 167
Tweezers, 21, 27

Uacarra tribes, 183
Uapes tribes, 65, 112, 183, 284, 285
Ubangi, lip stretching, 1, 30-32

Uganda tribes, 40, 41, 43, 186
Upas tree, 130
Urary, 132

Vanity bag, 21
Veils, 20, 277-279
Veils, Arabian, 277
Veils, Bedouin, 20
Veils, Egyptian, 277
Veils, oriental, 277-279
Veils, Peruvian, 277
Veils, Turkish, 277
Venice, 264
Viburnam, 107
Vicksburg, 208
Victoria Nyanza tribes, 176
Victory, 265
Vikings, 266
Vines, water, 223
Virginia, Virginian tribes, 63, 149, 154
Voodoo, 69, 83, 94, 95

Wabenaki tribes, 138, 220
Wadders, 196
Wampum, 149
Wampum peag, 149
Wapasiana tribes, 241
War bonnet, 4
War dance, 176
War medicine, 99
War paint, 64
Warali, 132
Warts, 113
Wataveta tribes, 187, 215
Waurrau tribes, 45

Weapons, 115-138
Western tribes, 9, 11, 41, 86, 92, 123, 152, 159, 167, 173-175, 220, 232, 241, 253 (*see also* Plains tribes)
West Indies, French, 107, 218, 267, 268
West Indies, West Indians, 22, 69, 83, 86, 94-96, 131, 153, 154, 205, 211, 214, 217, 232, 250, 253
Western Islands, 191
Whale, 218
Whipping game, 163, 164
Whistles, 242, 243
Wind instruments, 240
Wine, palm, 222
Wine, tuna, 222
Wire, brass ornamental, 28, 29

Woodskins, 251
World War, First, 190
World War, Second, 3, 53, 70, 190, 216, 223
Worms, groo-groo, 211

Xylophone, 239, 240

Yap Island, 27, 152
Yashmak, 278, 279
Yataghan, 119
Yokuts, 198
Yucatan tribes, 159
Yukaghirs, 199

Zanzibar, 214
Zulu tribes, 14, 15, 45, 99, 198

Ugr
GN
400
V4
1969